T0141904

Lecture Notes in Information Systems and Organisation

Volume 31

Lecture Notes in Information Systems and Organization—LNISO—is a series of scientific books that explore the current scenario of information systems, in particular IS and organization. The focus on the relationship between IT, IS and organization is the common thread of this collection, which aspires to provide scholars across the world with a point of reference and comparison in the study and research of information systems and organization. LNISO is the publication forum for the community of scholars investigating behavioral and design aspects of IS and organization. The series offers an integrated publication platform for high-quality conferences, symposia and workshops in this field. Materials are published upon a strictly controlled double blind peer review evaluation made by selected reviewers. LNISO is abstracted/indexed in Scopus

More information about this series at http://www.springer.com/series/11237

Isabel Ramos · Rui Quaresma ·
Paulo Silva · Tiago Oliveira
Editors

Information Systems for Industry 4.0

Proceedings of the 18th Conference
of the Portuguese Association
for Information Systems

 Springer

Editors
Isabel Ramos (ID)
Department of Information Systems
University of Minho
Guimarães, Portugal

Rui Quaresma (ID)
Department of Management
University of Évora
Évora, Portugal

Paulo Silva (ID)
Department of Management
University of Évora
Évora, Portugal

Tiago Oliveira (ID)
NOVA Information Management School
Lisbon, Portugal

ISSN 2195-4968 ISSN 2195-4976 (electronic)
Lecture Notes in Information Systems and Organisation
ISBN 978-3-030-14849-2 ISBN 978-3-030-14850-8 (eBook)
https://doi.org/10.1007/978-3-030-14850-8

Library of Congress Control Number: 2019933703

This Springer imprint is published by the registered company Springer Nature Switzerland AG.
The registered company address is: Gewerbestrasse 11, 6330 Cham, Switzerland

Program Commission

Coordinators

Paulo Resende da Silva, Management Department, Social Science School/University of Évora
Rui Quaresma, Management Department, Social Science School/University of Évora
Tiago Oliveira, NOVA *Information Management School*/New Lisbon University

Members

Agostinho Sousa Pinto, ISCAP/Instituto Politécnico do Porto
Alberto Freitas, Universidade do Porto
Alberto Silva, INESC-ID/Instituto Superior Técnico
Alexandre Valente Conceição Pereira Sousa, Instituto Universitário da Maia
Álvaro Rocha, Universidade de Coimbra
Ana Azevedo, ISCAP/Instituto Politécnico do Porto
Ana Camarinha, ISCAP/Instituto Politécnico do Porto
Ana Cristina dos Santos Amaro, Instituto Superior de Contabilidade e Administração de Coimbra
Ana Mendes, Escola Superior de Ciências Empresariais/Instituto Politécnico de Setúbal
Ana Paula Afonso, Faculdade de Ciências/Universidade de Lisboa
Ana Rosa Pereira Borges, Instituto Superior de Engenharia de Coimbra
Anabela Mesquita, ISCAP/Instituto Politécnico do Porto
Ângelo Jesus, Escola Superior de Tecnologia da Saúde do Porto
Antonio Carlos Maçada, Universidade Federal do Rio Grande do Sul, Brasil
António Guerreiro, Escola de Ciências Sociais/Universidade de Évora

António Jorge Gonçalves de Gouveia, Universidade de Trás-os-Montes e Alto Douro
Artur Marques, Escola Superior de Gestão e Tecnologia/Instituto Politécnico de Santarém
Bráulio Alturas, ISCTE-IUL—Instituto Universitário de Lisboa
Carla Alexandra da Silva Azevedo Lobo, Universidade Portucalense
Carla Sofia Pereira, Escola Superior de Tecnologia e Gestão de Felgueiras/Instituto Politécnico do Porto/INESC Porto
Carlos Costa, Instituto Superior de Economia e Gestão/Universidade de Lisboa
Carlos Coutinho, Universidade NOVA de Lisboa
Carlos Ferreira, Universidade de Aveiro
Carlos Filipe Campos Rompante da Cunha, Instituto Politécnico de Bragança
Carlos Morais, Instituto Politécnico de Bragança
Carlos Pampulim Caldeira, Escola de Ciências e Tecnologia/Universidade de Évora
Carlos Serrão, ISCTE-IUL—Instituto Universitário de Lisboa
Célio Gonçalves Marques, Escola Superior de Gestão/Instituto Politécnico de Tomar
Ciro Alexandre Domingues Martins, Universidade de Aveiro
Christophe Soares, Universidade Fernando Pessoa
Constantino Martins, Instituto Superior de Engenharia do Porto
Cristiane Drebes Pedron, Universidade Nove de Julho, São Paulo, Brasil
Cristina Wanzeller, Escola Superior de Tecnologia de Viseu, Instituto Politécnico de Viseu
Elsa Cardoso, ISCTE-IUL Instituto Universitário de Lisboa
Elsa da Piedade Chinita Soares Rodrigues, Instituto Politécnico de Beja
Fernando Brito e Abreu, ISCTE-IUL—Instituto Universitário de Lisboa
Fernando José Ferreira Lucas Bação, NOVA *Information Management School*/ Universidade NOVA de Lisboa
Fernando Moreira, Universidade Portucalense
Fernando Paulo dos Santos Rodrigues Belfo, Instituto Superior de Contabilidade e Administração de Coimbra
Filipe Madeira, Escola Superior de Gestão e Tecnologia/Instituto Politécnico de Santarém
Filipe Manuel Simões Caldeira, Instituto Politécnico de Viseu
Francisco Antunes, INESC Coimbra/Universidade da Beira Interior
Francisco José García Peñalvo, Universidade de Salamanca, Espanha
Frederico Cruz Jesus, NOVA *Information Management School*/Universidade NOVA de Lisboa
Gabriel David, Faculdade de Engenharia/Universidade do Porto
Gonçalo Dias, Universidade de Aveiro
Hélder Quintela, Escola Superior de Tecnologia, Instituto Politécnico do Cávado e do Ave
Henrique O'Neill, ISCTE-IUL—Instituto Universitário de Lisboa
Henrique S. Mamede, Universidade Aberta
Henrique Santos, Escola de Engenharia/Universidade do Minho

Inês Pereira, ISCAP/Instituto Politécnico do Porto
Irapuan Noce, Universidade Federal de Mato Grosso, Brasil
Isabel Ferreira, Instituto Politécnico do Cávado e do Ave
Isabel Pedrosa, Instituto Superior de Contabilidade e Administração de Coimbra
Isabel Ramos, Escola de Engenharia/Universidade do Minho
Isabel Seruca, Universidade Portucalense
João Álvaro Carvalho, Escola de Engenharia/Universidade do Minho
João C. Martins, Escola Superior de Tecnologia e Gestão/Instituto Politécnico de Beja/INESC-ID
João Carlos Costa Faria da Cunha, Instituto Superior de Engenharia de Coimbra
João Carlos Silva, Instituto Politécnico do Cávado e do Ave
João Paulo Costa, Faculdade de Economia/Universidade de Coimbra
João Paulo Magalhães, Escola Superior de Tecnologia e Gestão de Felgueiras/Instituto Politécnico do Porto
João Paulo Mestre Pinheiro Ramos e Barros, Instituto Politécnico de Beja
João Paulo Ribeiro Pereira, Instituto Politécnico de Bragança
João Samartinho, Escola Superior de Gestão e Tecnologia/Instituto Politécnico de Santarém
João Varajão, Universidade do Minho
Joaquim Arnaldo Martins, Universidade de Aveiro
Joaquim Gonçalves, Instituto Politécnico do Cávado e do Ave
Joaquim Silva, Instituto Politécnico do Cávado e do Ave
Joaquim Sousa Pinto, Universidade de Aveiro
Jorge Augusto Castro Neves Barbosa, Instituto Superior de Engenharia de Coimbra
Jorge Coelho, Sisconsult/Universidade do Minho
Jorge Miguel Sousa Barreiros, Instituto Superior de Engenharia de Coimbra
Jorge Oliveira e Sá, Escola de Engenharia/Universidade do Minho
Jorge Remondes, Instituto Superior de entre Douro e Vouga
Jorge Simões, Instituto Superior Politécnico de Gaya
José Alberto Lencastre, Universidade do Minho
José Luís Pereira, Universidade do Minho
José Manuel Matos Moreira, Universidade de Aveiro
José Miranda, Devise Futures—IT Solutions, Lda
José Saias, Escola de Ciências e Tecnologia/Universidade de Évora
José Tribolet, Instituto Superior Técnico/Universidade de Lisboa
Leonel Morgado, INESC TEC/Universidade Aberta
Leonilde Reis, Escola Superior de Ciências Empresariais/Instituto Politécnico de Setúbal
Lino Oliveira, Escola Superior de Estudos Industriais e de Gestão/Politécnico do Porto
Luís Amaral, Escola de Engenharia/Universidade do Minho
Luís Borges Gouveia, Universidade Fernando Pessoa
Luís Cláudio Barradas, Instituto Politécnico de Santarém
Luís Ferreira, Instituto Politécnico do Cávado e do Ave
Luís Seabra Lopes, Universidade de Aveiro

Luís Silva Rodrigues, ISCAP/Instituto Politécnico do Porto
Luísa Domingues, ISCTE-IUL—Instituto Universitário de Lisboa
Luísa Miranda, Instituto Politécnico de Bragança
Manuel da Costa Leite, Universidade Lusófona do Porto
Manuela Aparício, ISCTE-IUL—Instituto Universitário de Lisboa
Marco Painho, NOVA *Information Management School*/Universidade NOVA de Lisboa
Maria Antónia Rodrigues, ISCAP/Instituto Politécnico do Porto
Maria Bernardo, Universidade Aberta
Maria Helena Monteiro, Instituto Superior Ciências Sociais e Políticas/Universidade de Lisboa
Maria João Tinoco Varanda Pereira, Instituto Politécnico de Bragança
Maria José Angélico Gonçalves, ISCAP/Instituto Politécnico do Porto
Mariana Curado Malta, CEOS.PP—Instituto Politécnico do Porto
Maribel Yasmina Santos, Escola de Engenharia/Universidade do Minho
Mário Caldeira, Instituto Superior de Economia e Gestão/Universidade de Lisboa
Mário Silva, Universidade Autónoma de Lisboa
Mateus Daniel Almeida Mendes, Escola Superior de Tecnologia e Gestão de Oliveira do Hospital
Miguel Neto, NOVA *Information Management School*/Universidade NOVA de Lisboa
Mírian Oliveira, Pontifícia Universidade Católica do Rio Grande do Sul, Brasil
Nelson Duarte, Escola Superior de Tecnologia e Gestão de Felgueiras
Nuno Guimarães, ISCTE-IUL—Instituto Universitário de Lisboa
Nuno Melão, Instituto Politécnico de Viseu
Orlando Belo, Escola de Engenharia/Universidade do Minho
Óscar Rafael da Silva Ferreira Ribeiro, Universidade Lusófona do Porto
Paula Peres, ISCAP/Instituto Politécnico do Porto
Paula Prata, Universidade da Beira Interior
Paula Ruivo, Instituto Politécnico de Santarém
Paulo Cortez, Universidade do Minho
Paulo Gonçalves, ISCAP/Instituto Politécnico do Porto
Paulo Quaresma, Escola de Ciências e Tecnologia/Universidade de Évora
Paulo Teixeira, Instituto Politécnico do Cávado e do Ave
Pedro Campos, INESC Porto
Pedro Coutinho, Instituto Politécnico de Viana do Castelo
Pedro Isaías, The University of Queensland
Pedro Rangel Henriques, Escola de Engenharia/Universidade do Minho
Rita Espanha, ISCTE-IUL—Instituto Universitário de Lisboa
Roberto Henriques, NOVA *Information Management School*/Universidade NOVA de Lisboa
Rui Dinis Sousa, Escola de Engenharia/Universidade do Minho
Rui Gomes, Instituto Politécnico de Viana do Castelo
Rui Lopes, Instituto Politécnico de Bragança
Rui Pedro Lourenço, INESC/Universidade de Coimbra

Sandra Cunha, Instituto Politécnico do Cávado e do Ave
Vítor Carvalho, Instituto Politécnico do Cávado e do Ave
Vítor Santos, NOVA *Information Management School*/Universidade NOVA de Lisboa

Organizing Committee

João Samartinho, President, Management and Technology School/Polytechnic Institute of Santarém

Cristina Rodrigues, Management and Technology School/Polytechnic Institute of Santarém

Danielson Alves, University of Santiago, Cape Verde

Filipe Madeira, Management and Technology School/Polytechnic Institute of Santarém

Indira Brito, University of Santiago, Cape Verde

Isabel Ramos, University of Minho/President of the Portuguese Association for Information Systems

João Nascimento, Management and Technology School/Polytechnic Institute of Santarém

Luís Cláudio Barradas, Management and Technology School/Polytechnic Institute of Santarém

Luís Rodrigues, University of Santiago, Cape Verde

Maria Potes Barbas, Research Center/Polytechnic Institute of Santarém

Paulo Resende da Silva, Management Department, Social Science School/University of Évora

Rui Quaresma, Management Department, Social Science School/University of Évora

Tiago Oliveira, NOVA *Information Management School*/New Lisbon University

Afonso Carvalho, Student at Management and Technology School/Polytechnic Institute of Santarém

Carina Aurélio, Student at Management and Technology School/Polytechnic Institute of Santarém

David Morais, Student at Management and Technology School/Polytechnic Institute of Santarém

Diogo Ramos, Student at Management and Technology School/Polytechnic Institute of Santarém

Duarte Santos, Student at Management and Technology School/Polytechnic Institute of Santarém

João Cardoso, Student at Management and Technology School/Polytechnic Institute of Santarém
João Pereira, Student at Management and Technology School/Polytechnic Institute of Santarém
Leonardo Carvalho, Student at Management and Technology School/Polytechnic Institute of Santarém
Miguel Caetano, Student at Management and Technology School/Polytechnic Institute of Santarém
Rafael Soares, Student at Management and Technology School/Polytechnic Institute of Santarém
Rafaela Duarte, Student at Management and Technology School/Polytechnic Institute of Santarém
Ricardo Silva, Student at Management and Technology School/Polytechnic Institute of Santarém
Simão Godinho, Student at Management and Technology School/Polytechnic Institute of Santarém
Tiago Jesus, Student at Management and Technology School/Polytechnic Institute of Santarém
Tiago Romão, Student at Management and Technology School/Polytechnic Institute of Santarém
Vânia Besouro, Student at Management and Technology School/Polytechnic Institute of Santarém
Vitor Mira, Student at Management and Technology School/Polytechnic Institute of Santarém

Organizing Institutions

Polytechnic Institute of Santarém
University of Évora
University of Santiago, Cape Verde

Support and Sponsors

Santarém Municipality
Microsoft Portugal
NERSANT—Santarém Entrepreneurship Association
NOVA *Information Management School*/Universidade NOVA de Lisboa

Preface

The Portuguese Association for Information Systems organizes, since 2000, a national conference—Conferência da Associação Portuguesa de Sistemas de Informação (CAPSI).

In 2018, the conference took place in Santarém, in the School of Management and Technology, a structure of the Polytechnic Institute of Santarém. The conference was co-organized by this School and the Management Department of Social Science School of the University of Évora and the University of Santiago, Cape Verde.

The main goal of the conference is to connect the Portuguese IS community integrating researchers hosted in departments of business and management, computer and informatics, and information systems and information technology.

The main theme of the conference was the Industry 4.0 and the information systems. The papers and presentations were organized around specific sessions, such as

- Parallel sessions where full papers were presented;
- Poster sessions that allowed for the presentation of research in progress;
- Project sessions where two research projects in the area of the digitalization of work and the innovation for the Industry 4.0 set the stage for the interaction with participants from the academy and industry; and
- Workshop session where the future of work was discussed with participants from organizations of the labor market.

Axel Uhl, Professor at ZHAW School of Management and Law, Zurich; Manuel Dias, Artificial Intelligence Ambassador at Microsoft; and Ana Neves, Information System Society at Portuguese Foundation for Science and Technology were the conference's invited speakers. They discussed the positive and negative effects on our lives of key digital trends (Axel Uhl), the society's transformation promoted by artificial intelligence (Manuel Dias), and the Internet's governance in 2018 (Ana Neves).

The Lectures Notes integrate the papers that achieved greater consensus on the depth and rigor of the research described in them. They cover the topics such as business architecture, information system auditing, business process management, research and learning on information systems, information systems management, governance on information systems, innovation and digital government in public sector, innovation and open models, information systems and data modelling, security in information systems, decision support systems, shared services, database management systems, information systems for specific industry, organization and society information systems.

Guimarães, Portugal	Isabel Ramos
Évora, Portugal	Rui Quaresma
Évora, Portugal	Paulo Silva
Lisbon, Portugal	Tiago Oliveira

Contents

Data Warehouse for the Monitoring and Analysis of Water Supply and Consumption

José Soares, Patrícia Leite�ⓘ, Paulo Teixeiraⓘ, Nuno Lopesⓘ and Joaquim P. Silvaⓘ

Abstract Water is an essential resource that is increasingly scarce. Existing water supply networks are highly stressed due the increasing water consumption and the high quantity of water losses. In order to reduce water losses and improve water consumption management, EAmb—Esposende Ambiente, E.M. is implementing a data warehouse for storing water supply and consumption data. The available data will be used to monitor and analyze water supply and consumption in Esposende county.

Keywords Water supply system · Data warehouse · ETL process

1 Introduction

Water is essential to the existence of life on Earth and access to safe water is a legal right that all human beings should enjoy. However, currently around 2.1 billion people lack drinking water distribution services (United Nations, s.d.).

The organization where this project is being implemented, EAmb—Esposende Ambiente, E.M., is responsible for the drinking water distribution system in the municipality of Esposende. This service translates into the acquisition of water from the Águas do Norte entity, with a subsequent distribution by the households and

J. Soares · P. Leite · P. Teixeira · N. Lopes · J. P. Silva (✉)
Instituto Politécnico Do Cávado E Do Ave, Barcelos, Portugal
e-mail: jpsilva@ipca.pt

J. Soares
e-mail: a9639@alunos.ipca.pt

P. Leite
e-mail: patricialeite@ipca.pt

P. Teixeira
e-mail: pteixeira@ipca.pt

N. Lopes
e-mail: nlopes@ipca.pt

© Springer Nature Switzerland AG 2019
I. Ramos et al. (eds.), *Information Systems for Industry 4.0*,
Lecture Notes in Information Systems and Organisation 31,
https://doi.org/10.1007/978-3-030-14850-8_1

industrial services. There is a discrepancy of about 25% between the water volume purchased to the supplier and the total water volume invoiced to the households. This value is below the country average, which is about 29.8% (ERSAR 2017, p. 19). However, this means that for every 100 L, about 25 L are considered losses, potentially caused by leaks, breaches of supply, breakage, etc. These factors are commonly identified and classified as real losses and apparent losses.

The real losses reflect the efficiency of the distribution system and are present in all systems, being virtually impossible to eradicate altogether. These losses generally occur due to the use of weak materials, sloppy installations, excessive pressure, corrosion of materials, lack of maintenance, etc. The apparent losses, as the name implies, do not result from physical leakage of water, but from incorrect measurements or unauthorized use. Regularly, incorrect measurement can result from improper installation, inadequate sizes, wear over time, etc. The information on apparent losses is crucial for the distributor and reach a high level of importance since they represent a higher negative effect (Thornton et al. 2008, p. 5).

With a long-term vision and following a constant service improvement approach, the EAmb—Esposende Ambiente, E.M. intends to develop an analytical system that, integrating the data available in several systems, will acquire the knowledge about the factors that influence or may influence the efficiency of this service. This article describes the first step for the development of the analytical system, which consists of the implementation of a data warehouse that supports the gathering of service performance indicators and the extraction patterns. As such, the implementation of an Extract-Transform-Load (ETL) process is essential, combining different data sources in order to fill the data warehouse with value-added data.

In the following section, several studies relevant for the context of this project are presented on the monitoring and detection of water losses in the drinking water distribution systems. The third and fourth sections describe the information requirements and the modeling of the data warehouse. In the fifth section, we present the implementation of the Extract-Transform-Load (ETL) process and the constraints that were found. Finally, the conclusions of this stage of the project and the future work are presented.

2 Related Work

Despite the economic impact and increased management difficulties of the water distribution systems (González-Gómez et al. 2011), no strong measures have been taken to reduce water losses (Kanakoudis et al. 2013). This may be the reason why it is so difficult to find related work on the implementation of data warehouses and the use of performance indicators in the area of consumer water distribution systems. In the several moments of research that were carried out throughout this work, no data warehouse implementations were found in the drinking water sector.

The development of data warehouses and analytical systems is not one of the top priorities for dealing with the challenges related to the management of drinking water (OECD 2016).

There are many studies related to leak detection, specifically on the analysis of pressure values and network maintenance, the so-called real losses. A study by Puust et al. (2010) presents the main methods used in the evaluation, detection and control of water leaks. The use of artificial neural networks was found in a few references for short-term consumption forecasts (Bougadis et al. 2005) and the detection of flow peaks and leakages (S. R. Mounce et al. 2010; Mounce and Machell 2006). In another study, data mining techniques were used to determine peak flows and support the asset management of network infrastructure (Babovic et al. 2002). This study evaluates the deterioration and the level of risk in the distribution network based on factors such as the age, the diameter, the material, the ground where the pipeline is, etc., identifying the pipes to be replaced and the need for new piping.

There are many studies that focus on unbilled water consumption. Güngör-Demirci et al. (2018) identify the main factors influencing unbilled water losses. Vilanova et al. (2014) present a review of the literature on performance indicators of water distribution services. However, despite the exhaustive research made, only a study has been found that proposes the implementation of a data warehouse to monitor the quality of drinking water in a region of Taiwan, integrating information from various sources (Wang and Guo 2013).

3 Business Requirements

This section presents a brief description of the water distribution network and the identification of the main business requirements.

3.1 Water Distribution Network Description

The water distribution network of EAmb—Esposende Ambiente, E.M., since its foundation, has been subject to constant maintenance and improvement operations, through the integration of new components, replacement of deteriorated material and reorganization of pipes. The current composition of the network includes reservoirs, pipelines, distribution lines and branches, zone water meters and customer water meters. The relationship of these components can be represented in several inverted tree structures, one for each reservoir. Although the reservoirs do not belong to EAmb—Esposende Ambiente, E.M., they are the main source of water supply. Immediately after the reservoirs output, there are water meters that identify the volume and flow rate of water consumed. Subsequently, the water is conducted by pipelines and distribution lines, among which there are strategically placed zone meters. At the network endpoints there are branches and consumer meters.

The network management service defined control areas that aggregate all consumers served by certain pipelines in a given geographical area. The control areas usually are represented by a zone meter which records the volume of water consumed. This identification allows greater accuracy in detecting leakage by being able to isolate areas where the meter has experienced a sudden increase in consumption or a substantial decrease in pressure. In Fig. 1, which depicts this information visually and succinctly, counters stands for the different kinds of water meters.

There are also other components present in the network, not so important to this study, which help to maintain the stability of the network: pressure reducing valves that reduce water flow; water pumps that increase the pressure at more distant points; discharge mechanisms that are used to empty pipelines; and the shut-off valves which are operated jointly with the discharge mechanisms in case there is a need to repair a pipeline.

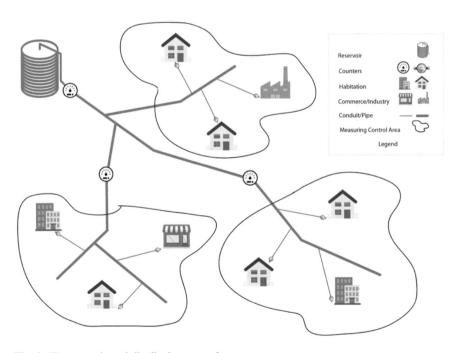

Fig. 1 Water supply and distribution network

3.2 Business Requirements

The development of the data warehouse was guided by the following business requirements that illustrate analytical needs in terms of measures, dimensions and types of analyzes:

- **Flow rate**: flow volume is one of the most relevant measures when detecting leakage of a water distribution system, although it is expected that it will be influenced be several factors, the flow rate tend to be similar for analogous periods.
- **Consumption**: corresponds to the measures of the distributed water volume and its consequent billing, representing the overall efficiency of the water distribution system.
- **Meter**: the various readings will always be assigned to a water meter, which may correspond to one or more control and measurement zones.
- **Consumer profile**: information about consumers and their consumption profile allows the detection of fraudulent behavior through sudden changes in consumption and the identification of irregular values that are not compatible with the consumer profile.
- **Climate influence**: climatic variations justify consumption changes depending on the type of activity, especially in agricultural areas, which represents a significant consumer segment.
- **Yearly homologous periods**: The comparison between yearly homologous periods represents a good source of operational performance indicators (KPI) and can be used to evaluate the investments made in the adoption of new materials and solutions.
- **Overnight minimum**: the analysis of the minimum values of flow and volume during overnight can serve as a basis for the adjustment of pressures as well as the detection of leaks when related to average values of analogous periods.
- **Seasonal influence**: being Esposende a geographic region characterized by coastal zones and higher affluence during the beach season, the consumption increases sharply in this high season, which makes its analysis of high interest.

The identification of the data warehouse deployment profiles and the validation of key performance indicators is still under study. Due to the need to accumulate historical data in the data warehouse, it was decided to proceed immediately with the implementation of the database and ETL process, incorporating all available data related to the water flow and consumption in the distribution network.

4 Dimensional Model

To prepare the data warehouse modeling and the ETL processes specification, it was performed a was performed, which is presented below. This section also includes the implemented data warehouse data model and the overall solution architecture.

4.1 Data Study

The data used for the development of this project includes topics such as instantaneous flow, flow volume in reservoirs, intermediate and endpoint meters, affectation areas, meteorological conditions and geographic location. Consumer areas are referred to as measurement and control zones (MCZs), although some of them currently do not have their own meter.

The data on the volume and flow of the reservoirs and the intermediate meters come from management applications databases. The remaining data, related to meter readings, are obtained in Excel files, through FTP access to the water supplier system. In addition to having several sources of provenance, the data collected presents a great discrepancy in the frequency at which new data are generated: irregular intervals between 1 and 2 min and update with the same periodicity for the databases; regular intervals of 15 min and daily update at a predefined time for the data obtained by FTP. These sources include data such as cumulative consumption volume, date and time of measurement, equipment identification and, in some of the equipments, instantaneous flow.

Regarding the final consumer, the data comes from the company's ERP system, based on Informix technology, and contains information on volume consumed, measurement date, type of consumer, branch of distribution and area of affectation. From this source, the temporary irregularity of volume measurements stands, with a period of approximately one month, can be highlighted, and may be delayed for some days, depending on the schedule of working days or availability of the reading staff.

In addition to those previously mentioned, and as attachment point, the geographic data includes information on the assigned area (MCZ), on equipment from the source to the end consumer branch, geographic location on cardinal coordinates and year of installation. The source is assured by an Oracle technology relational database, on the other hand, it stands out by the negative, the absence of a history of operation regarding changes in the network.

Lastly, weather information is also available on a database that has been filled daily at regular intervals of one hour. From this source, the various fields include temperature, precipitation and time stamp, data that are being collected by the possible influence on water consumption.

4.2 Data Model

Considering the previously stated requirements, a dimensional data mode, shown in Fig. 2, was developed, which contains several tables of dimensions and facts. In the ETL process, techniques of treatment of slowly change dimensions were applied to preserve the history of changes in the consumers and the MCZ. Despite the diversity of data, the model holds the information in a reduced number of tables, because several dimensions are shared between the tables of facts.

The model requires a greater effort in the ETL process to enhance the processes of analysis. The dimension tables are then identified except for the already known date and time dimensions:

- **DimCounter**: Supports the information of the water meters, the assigned control areas. The particularity of this dimension rests on the hierarchical relationship between meters (counters).
- **DimConsumer**: consumer is represented in this dimension, with activity history and interest attributes, whether these are the type of customer, geographical location, etc.

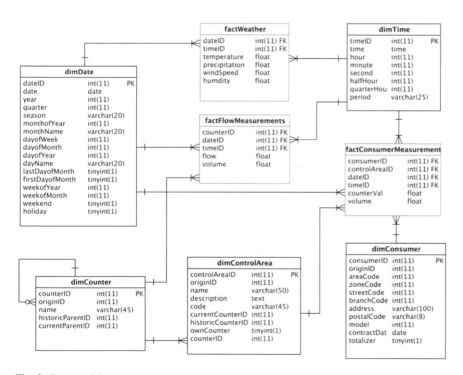

Fig. 2 Data model

- **DimControlArea**: this dimension identifies the MCZ inherent to consumers and meters. This dimension will be the main connection between consumers and MCZ meters.

The model includes the following fact tables:

- **FactFlowMeasurementes**: this table shows all measurements of meters, instantaneous flow (m^3/h) and volume (m^3), and their timing identification. It should be noted that the time intervals were adjusted to the longer period, 15 min, in order to maintain data uniformity.
- **FactConsumerMeasurements**: Given the irregular time period and the absence of pressure values in the consumer measurements, this table was created jut to store the facts related to the volume consumed expressed in m^3.
- **FactWeather**: this table stores the climatic facts, temperature (°C) and precipitation (mm^3/h), directly related to the date and time dimensions.

4.3 Solution Architecture

The main source of information for an analytical system is its database, which must be adequately filled with easily accessible and accessible data to simplify analysis (Jarke et al. 2000). Most of cases, the data are dispersed by several sources and formats, so it was necessary to implement all the required transformations using the Pentaho Data Integration ETL tool, as shown in Fig. 3.

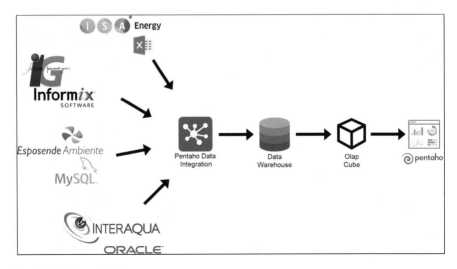

Fig. 3 Solution architecture

The architecture includes, in addition to the ETL process, the components of the subsequent processes of analytical processing and data visualization. The ETL process is responsible for this set of actions, from the extraction of data from various sources, through the treatment that can include cleaning actions, format revision, filtering, integration, etc. until reaching the loading phase of data warehouse (Kimball and Caserta 2004). OLAP technology, an acronym for Online Analytical Processing, is an approach to perform multidimensional analysis that allows to improve the performance of relational databases in data query by providing faster analysis and support for roll-up, drill-down and pivot operations (Kimball and Ross 2013). The Pentaho BI server supports the implementation of dashboards, which graphically display the data processed in the OLAP cube and allows users to manage their access to them. The choice of integration and analytical processing software was carried out according to company policies, which prioritize the use of open source tools.

5 Implementation and Constraints

The extraction of data, although diversified by various types of sources, such as FTP, Excel, Oracle, Informix and MySQL, proved to be a simple process since the information was in similar formats, except for the formats of date and time attributes that differ between sources.

5.1 Process Execution

As previously identified, the meters values have different origins, periods and fields, which requires an adaptation among them. The difference in periods is notorious, 15 min in one case and 1–2 min in another. We chose to filter the smallest intervals to obtain the closest possible result of the upper interval. The volume of consumption is given in a value of cumulative nature, being necessary to transform this value into a relation of consumption by time interval, which required a transformation. Despite the absence of instantaneous flow in some equipments, this value can be calculated by the relation between time intervals and volume using the following formula $\frac{Vf - Vi}{\Delta T}$. The identification of MCZ was made through the water supplier's own identifier, which is indicated in the geographic data source.

The consumer data comes all from the same data source and, like the meters, the volume is supplied as an accumulated value, so it is necessary to apply the same method, referred in the previous paragraph, to obtain the consumption value relative to the interval. In this case, the instantaneous flow values are ignored, since the measurement interval is lengthy and does not justify its calculation.

Table 1 Periodicity execution

Data sources	Start	End	Interval
DimConsumer	08:30 h	16:30 h	01:00 h
DimCounter, DimControlArea	08:30 h	18:30 h	01:00 h
FactConsumerMeasurements…	16:30 h	16:30 h	–
FactWeather	–	–	01:00 h
FactFlowMeasurements	–	–	00:15 h

An important point when loading consumer values is the existence of "parent" consumers, more specifically in cases such as residential buildings and condominiums, where, in addition to each consumer meter, a general meter is installed. The measurement of these includes, in addition to the consumption of common area, all the consumption generated by the residents. For reasons of analysis, it was decided to subtract from the general value the sum of the consumers of the building to enable cumulative operations and avoid double counting.

On the integration the spatial data with the MCZ in the treatment of consumer data, a discrepancy was detected between the consumer MCZ in the ERP system and the MCZ related to the consumer extension in the geographic database. In order to eliminate this discrepancy, it was decided to extract a listing of these inconsistencies with each execution of the ETL process and, later, send this to the staff responsible for identifying and correcting the problem.

Regarding the geographic data source, we found the need to transform geographic values from the *Datum 73* format to the *WGS84* global format. This operation was performed using the PROJ.4 library. Considering that the meteorological data the transformation was null, it only required to match the date and time dimensions and to filter the fields of interest.

The daily execution period of the ETL processes, already implemented, is not homogeneous, both in the periodicity and in the execution time window, depending on each of the data sources, as can be seen in Table 1.

The "DimConsumer" dimension is updated at regular intervals during the operation period of the company to the public domain, to insert new records and update existing ones. The "DimCounter" dimension and the "DimControloArea" dimension are updated according to the technical staff schedule.

The fact table "FactConsumerMeasusements" is only updated once a day, after the downloading by the staff of the water meter readings. The "FactFlowMeasurements" fact table is continuously updated without disruption with meter readings, at 15-minute intervals to ensure low data latency, although some of these records only are available at times determined by the data source manager. Finally, the "FactWeather" table is refreshed at one-hour intervals, corresponding to the meter readings data source time interval, thus reducing execution effort and the need for record storage.

In the first execution of the ETL process, about 1.5 million records were loaded into the "FactConsumerMeasurements" table, 10 thousand records for the "FactWeather" table and 3 million records in the "FactFlowMeasurements" table.

5.2 Constraints

On the execution of the ETL process, it was performed a detailed data analysis and validation, comparing the loaded data to the data warehouse with business applications data. This approach allowed to detect that some MCZ, which include in its name the "remaining" word, correspond to geographical areas without water meter. This means that, to obtain the consumption of this area, it is required to get the readings from the upper level meter and subtract the sum of meters from the MCZs assigned to that upper level geographical area. Following the detection of this error, we identified some MCZs in which the consumption value will not be possible to specify since the same upper level meter includes several MCZs without its own meter.

Although the integration process went quite well, it has been found that the history of meter readings is very small. While on the consumer side data are available from the beginning of 2010, first records of water meters are scattered by dates between June and September 2017. This limitation may be overcome if the water supplier company will be able to provide data for previous periods.

6 Conclusions and Future Work

Despite of all the problems mentioned above, the implementation of the ETL process for loading the data warehouse was fully achieved. At this point, the data warehouse is being continuously fed with quality data that will support the next stage of the project.

The data loaded into the data warehouse is accurate and structured. The only case that will make it difficult to analyze the data is that some high level meters integrate several MCZs without their own meter. This problem will certainly be solved in the future through the installation of meters of each MCZ. To mitigate this problem, an estimate of the consumption of these MCZs can be performed using historical user consumption values to determine a allocation percentage of the remaining consumption value to each MCZ.

The next stage in this project will be the implementation of the analytical processes to allow the calculation of indicators and the graphical visualization of the data collected, through the use of OLAP technology and dashboarding tools. A third stage of this project will consist in the implementation of machine learning processes to detect water losses, forecast consumption, detect irregularities, forecast supply interruptions, among others.

References

Babovic, V., Drécourt, J.-P., Keijzer, M., & Friss Hansen, P. (2002). A data mining approach to modelling of water supply assets. *Urban Water, 4*(4), 401–414. https://doi.org/10.1016/S1462-0758(02)00034-1.

Bougadis, J., Adamowski, K., & Diduch, R. (2005). Short-term municipal water demand forecasting. *Hydrological Processes, 19*(1), 137–148. https://doi.org/10.1002/hyp.5763.

ERSAR. (2017). *Caraterização do setor de águas e resíduos (volume 1). Relatório Anual dos Serviços de Águas e Resíduos em Portugal.* Retrieved from http://www.ersar.pt/pt/publicacoes/relatorio-anual-do-setor.

González-Gómez, F., García-Rubio, M. A., & Guardiola, J. (2011). Why is non-revenue water so high in so many cities? *International Journal of Water Resources Development, 27*(2), 345–360. https://doi.org/10.1080/07900627.2010.548317.

Güngör-Demirci, G., Lee, J., Keck, J., Guzzetta, R., & Yang, P. (2018). Determinants of non-revenue water for a water utility in California. *Journal of Water Supply: Research and Technology - Aqua, 67*(3), 270–278. https://doi.org/10.2166/aqua.2018.152.

Jarke, M., Lenzerini, M., Vassiliou, Y., & Vassiliadis, P. (2000). *Fundamentals of Data Warehouses.* Heidelberg: Springer. https://doi.org/10.1007/978-3-662-04138-3.

Kanakoudis, V., Tsitsifli, S., Samaras, P., & Zouboulis, A. (2013). Assessing the performance of urban water networks across the EU Mediterranean area: The paradox of high NRW levels and absence of respective reduction measures. *Water Science and Technology: Water Supply, 13*(4), 939–950. https://doi.org/10.2166/ws.2013.044.

Kimball, R., & Caserta, J. (2004). *The Data Warehouse ETL toolkit: Practical techniques for extracting, cleaning conforming, and delivering data.* Hoboken: Wiley. ISBN: 978-0764567575.

Kimball, R., & Ross, M. (2013). *The data warehouse toolkit: The complete guide to dimensional modeling* (3rd ed.), Wiley. ISBN: 978-1118530801.

Mounce, S. R., Boxall, J. B., & Machell, J. (2010). Development and verification of an online artificial intelligence system for detection of bursts and other abnormal flows. *Journal of Water Resources Planning and Management, 136*(3), 309–318. https://doi.org/10.1061/(ASCE)WR.1943-5452.0000030.

Mounce, S. R., & Machell, J. (2006). Burst detection using hydraulic data from water distribution systems with artificial neural networks. *Urban Water Journal, 3*(1), 21–31. https://doi.org/10.1080/15730620600578538.

Vilanova, M. R. N, Filho, P. M., & Balestieri, J. A. P. (2014, March 1). Performance measurement and indicators for water supply management: Review and international cases. *Renewable and Sustainable Energy Reviews.* Pergamon. http://doi.org/10.1016/j.rser.2014.11.043.

OECD. (2016). *Water governance in cities.* OECD Publishing. http://doi.org/10.1787/9789264251090-en.

Puust, R., Kapelan, Z., Savic, D. A., & Koppel, T. (2010). A review of methods for leakage management in pipe networks. *Urban Water Journal, 7*(1), 25–45. https://doi.org/10.1080/15730621003610878.

Thornton, J., Sturm, R., & Kunkel, G. A. (2008). *Water loss control.* New York: McGraw-Hill. ISBN: 978-0071499187.

Wang, H. C., & Guo, J. L. (2013). Constructing a water quality 2.0 OLAP system in Taiwan. *Journal of Cleaner Production, 40,* 40–45. https://doi.org/10.1016/j.jclepro.2011.04.019.

Performance Evaluation in IST Projects: A Case Study

José Luís Pereira(iD), João Varajão(iD), Jorge Oliveira e Sá(iD)
and António Silva

Abstract In order to be successful in an increasingly competitive business environment, organizations have to manage their human resources effectively and efficiently. To this end, the use of performance assessment approaches, not only at the individual level but also at the team level, is of utmost importance. In the particular case of information systems and technologies (IST) projects, there is not much research focused on the evaluation of human resources performance. Contributing to fill this gap, this article presents a case study, which took place in an academic setting, more specifically in the context of a postgraduate curricular unit, with the purpose of evaluating the feasibility of using various methods and techniques for performance assessment in the specific case of IST projects. Relevant results have emerged from this case study. For instance, this study allowed to conclude that a systematic multi-source performance evaluation, including continuous constructive feedback to project team members, results in improved attitudes and behaviours towards work, as well as enhanced trust in the assessment results. Additionally, there is strong evidence that the evaluation practices had a substantial impact on the success level of the IST projects under study.

Keywords Performance evaluation · Project management · Methods ·
Human resources · Information systems

J. L. Pereira (✉) · J. Varajão · J. O. e Sá
Department of Information Systems & ALGORITMI Center,
University of Minho, Campus de Azurém, Guimarães 4804-533, Portugal
e-mail: jlmp@dsi.uminho.pt

J. Varajão
e-mail: varajao@dsi.uminho.pt

J. O. e Sá
e-mail: jos@dsi.uminho.pt

A. Silva
Master's Degree in Engineering and Management of Information Systems,
University of Minho, Campus de Azurém, Guimarães 4804-533, Portugal
e-mail: a58889@alumni.uminho.pt

© Springer Nature Switzerland AG 2019   13
I. Ramos et al. (eds.), *Information Systems for Industry 4.0*,
Lecture Notes in Information Systems and Organisation 31,
https://doi.org/10.1007/978-3-030-14850-8_2

1 Introduction

It is widely recognized that Information Systems and Technologies (IST) projects, in particular, software development projects, do not have a good reputation concerning success, as many end up presenting problems regarding scope, time or cost (Paiva et al. 2011; Varajão et al. 2008, 2014). The success of IST projects depends on professional project management processes, being decisive the involvement of the top management as well as the clients, a clear definition of objectives and requirements, an effective management of human resources, among other aspects (Varajão et al. 2009, 2014, 2017; Uahi et al. 2018).

Performance evaluation emerges as an important component of human resources management, bringing together various approaches and techniques capable of creating the conditions for an improvement of the human performance in organizations. Even though the area of performance evaluation is acknowledged as essential in human resources management and fundamental to the success of organizations and projects, there is not much research focused on the particular case of IST projects (Silva et al. 2017a, b; Moura et al. 2018). In order to contribute to fill this gap, this article presents the results of a research project, carried out in an academic setting, whose purpose was to evaluate the feasibility and utility of the use of various methods and techniques of performance evaluation in the particular case of IST projects.

Regarding the structure of the article, in the following section the importance of performance evaluation is discussed. In the third section, the different kinds of IST projects are described. In the fourth section, the research method is presented. In the fifth section, the intervention model is described. In the sixth section, the main results are presented and discussed. Finally, in the last section, some final considerations and ideas for future work are presented.

2 The Importance of Performance Evaluation

Performance evaluation comprises an assessment, measurement and systematic comparison of individual, group and organizational variables, supported in a formally established set of competences and/or predefined objectives (Chiavenato 2003). The performance of an individual originates from her/his competences (knowledge, experience, and attitudes), her/his personality, her/his motivation, her/his interpersonal relations, the working atmosphere and the characteristics of the project and the organization (Sarmento et al. 2015).

In organizations performance evaluation processes are implemented with several objectives. At the organizational level, to assist administrative decisions (such as establishing remunerations, promotions, transfers, and layoffs); at the individual level, not only to allow personnel to know their performance assessment (positive or negative) but also to allow the appraiser to advise each person regarding her/his improvement. This evaluation process may be used to confirm the quality of the recruitment and selection of employees, to verify the effectiveness of the training processes, and to improve the team and organizational atmosphere (Sotomayor et al. 2014).

The successful implementation of the evaluation processes requires the commitment, involvement and active participation of all stakeholders, implying a process of communication, openness, and orientation for improvement, requiring that all stakeholders receive continuous feedback about their performance (Sarmento et al. 2014, 2015).

Performance evaluation is largely associated with measuring instruments and with the adopted process for evaluation (Varajão 2016, 2018; Varajão et al. 2018; Varajão and Trigo 2016). To implement a process for performance evaluation, it is necessary to reason about the objectives to be achieved, as well as the procedures to be followed, defining when, who and how they intervene in the evaluation (Caetano 2008).

3 IST Projects

Over the last few years, there have been growing investments in IST by organizations, often translated into significant changes in the way business is done (Pereira and Sá 2017; Trigo et al. 2007; Varajão et al. 2009).

There are several classes of IST projects, which can meet the different needs of organizations (Trigo et al. 2011; Varajão et al. 2008). Cadle and Yeates (2007) organize IST projects in several categories. In the present work, we focus mainly on software development, systems and/or business processes consulting, systems improvement and/or maintenance, and systems implementation.

Regarding software development, skills to analyse, specify, build, test, and deploy new computer applications, are typically required. On the one hand, projects may be carried out to develop software products based on an idea or on a new requirement identified in the market, destined to future customers that are unknown until the product is commercialized (development of *commercial off-the-shelf* software). On the other hand, software products might be developed to respond to the specific needs of each client (*custom development*), in which case an understanding of the application domain is essential and rigorous analysis is necessary to prioritize, analyse, validate and specify the requirements, together with the client. The software can be developed internally (*in-house*), or externally (*outsourcing*) by a contracted entity (Gonçalves et al. 2008).

The systems and/or business process consulting originates from the need to investigate a business problem or to propose solutions using IST. This kind of projects generally includes activities such as the analysis of the technological and/or organizational system (as the object of intervention), and the identification of the *As-Is* situation, to later identify possible improvements, taking into account the best practices of the business—*Ought-To-Be* situation. Finally, the processes are

validated with the top management in order to define their later implementation—
To-Be situation (Cadle and Yeates 2007).

The systems improvement and/or maintenance arises from the need to repair,
improve or add functionalities to existing systems, as a result, for example, of new
market requirements, or new laws and regulations, among many others. One of the
difficulties that often arises is to keep the existing systems operational while making
the repairs or adding the improvements/functionalities. The entire lifecycle of this
kind of project is similar to the life cycle of a software development project (Cadle
and Yeates 2007).

The implementation of systems (or software packages) arises from the need to
implement commercially available configurable software packages. Nowadays, it is
common for organizations to acquire integrated management systems (also known
as *Enterprise Resource Planning* or ERP) in the form of business packages, to
support most of their processes, to manage their resources (materials, people or
equipment) and to integrate the existing information systems into a single system.
The evolution of technologies has led the process of development of new systems to
evolve from tailor-made to component-based development by using *off-the-shelf*
components, significantly reducing development costs and times (Gonçalves et al.
2008). It is also necessary to define the implementation and data conversion
strategies to be adopted (if needed), to train the end users and to deploy the software
package (Cadle and Yeates 2007).

4 Research Method

In order to evaluate the feasibility of using various methods and techniques for
performance evaluation in the particular case of IST projects, a study was carried
out in the context of a post-graduate curricular unit[1]—"Projeto de Tecnologias e
Sistemas de Informação"—of the Master's degree in Engineering and Management
of Information Systems, of the University of Minho, which is structured according
to a *Project-Based Learning*[2] approach. In this curricular unit, students are organized into teams that are responsible for the management and execution of an IST
project in a context as similar to the real-life as possible (in all projects there is the
portfolio manager (role played by the faculty member responsible for the curricular
unit) and the proponent/client (role played by an entity external to the curricular
unit)). It should be noted that the objective of the study was also the evaluation of
individual and team performances, as well as the optimization of work and

---

[1]A curricular unit is a teaching and learning unit of a cycle of studies, which has its own training
objectives and is subject to formal evaluation (which translates into a final classification).

[2]Project-Based Learning is a teaching approach in which students acquire skills by working over a
period of time in a specific problem or challenge, investigating and developing activities to solve it.

Fig. 1 Cycle of the
action-research methodology
Adapted from Baskerville
(1999)

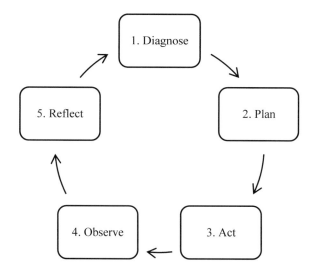

maximization of success. Thirteen teams constituted the target population of the study, each consisting of five students (except for three teams, which consisted of four students, due to the withdrawal of three elements). To this end, an action-research process was adopted, following the five phases presented in Fig. 1.

The process began by diagnosing and identifying the main reasons that led to the need for improvement in the curricular unit. Then, the activities to be implemented to intervene in the reality under study were planned. After, the actions were executed to produce the expected changes. Subsequently, the results obtained were evaluated and, finally, a reflection on their pertinence and usefulness was made.

To note that this process is systematic and cyclical. In this case, there were several iterations in order to correct and improve actions that did not adequately produce the expected changes and to investigate other pertinent and complementary aspects. According to Baskerville (1999), the collaborative participation of the various actors, via action-research, increases their competences and, consequently, their performance. It was possible to observe this in the study.

5   Intervention Model

Regarding performance evaluation in the context of IST projects, and taking into account the various existing approaches and methods (for detailed information see (Silva et al. 2017a)), as well as the different information sources (for detailed information see (Silva et al. 2017b)), several assessment and feedback moments were defined, which are identified in Fig. 2 and described in Table 1. The techniques and the main references used for data collection, as well as the relevant instruments, are also identified.

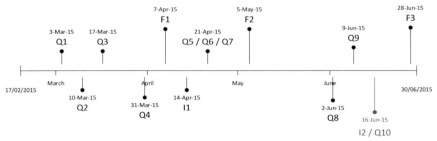

Subtitle: Q – Questionnaire | F – Feedback | I – Interview

Fig. 2 Major milestones of performance evaluation and feedback to people

Table 1 Description of the major milestones of performance evaluation and feedback to people

Milestone	Purpose	Used Instruments
Q1	It aimed to identify the level of individual knowledge and experience of team members concerning project management skills. For this purpose, a paper-based questionnaire was used to characterize each participant regarding her/his technical, behavioural and contextual competences (relevant to the project manager role). It was also intended to raise awareness among the participants about the specific competences that the project manager of their team should possess. Therefore, this questionnaire was not intended to evaluate performance, but rather to help support the selection of the team member with the best profile to perform the project manager competences	The key competences and the *Phrase Completion* scales (Hodge and Gillespie 2003), from 0 to 10, used in this questionnaire, followed the ICB recommendation (IPMA 2006)
Q2	The purpose was to analyse the personality characteristics of the participants (both the traits determined by their character and the acquired traits) in order to recognize their typical and predictable behavioural patterns, in order to select the team member with the best profile to perform the position of project manager	The key features, obtained through personal statements, were based on the *Five-Factor Model* (Cunha et al. 2007), using the graph scale method (from 1 to 5) based on the *Likert* model (Likert 1932)
Q3	It aimed to characterize the resilience of the team members, identifying complementary characteristics such as morale, satisfaction, depression, somatic health, among others. Sociodemographic information was also collected. Therefore, it was not intended	Metric scales were used and, predominantly, the method of graphical scales (from 1 to 7) based on the *Resilience Scales* model (Wagnild and Young 1993, p. 169, Amaral et al. 2015)

(continued)

Table 1 (continued)

Milestone	Purpose	Used Instruments
	to evaluate, but to provide relevant information to the portfolio manager (role played by the faculty member responsible by the curricular unit) to detect if the teams' members had abilities to deal with problems, overcome obstacles, or resist the pressure of adverse situations.	
Q4	Aimed to evaluate the performance of team members, using peer evaluation and self-assessment. The objective of this evaluation was not to generate a classification, but to detect behaviours that were not appropriate to the objectives of the curricular unit and to act upon them	The evaluation methods used were the graphical scales, from 0 to 5, based on the *Likert* model (Likert 1932), the forced choice method and the checklists method
F1	At this point, feedback was provided to each team member regarding the individual and collective performance results obtained from the previous survey (Q4). On the questions in which the result was less than the self-assessment performance, each team member should indicate whether or not she/he agreed with the (average) evaluation received by peers and stated the reasons that would justify such evaluation. Participants were also asked to indicate actions for improvement	The performance reports contained the self-assessment of the element, the average of the evaluations performed by her/his teammates, the difference between his self-assessment and the average evaluation by peers, and the average of the class evaluations (all the teams in the curricular unit)
I1	Each team was interviewed by the faculty member responsible for the curricular unit, which assumed a mentor role, by remembering the aspects to improve in the team. As such, the objective was not to judge and confront the elements of underperforming teams, but to reflect on what could be improved and to plan actions to improve team performance, involving counselling, the adaptation of functions, current job training, among other corrective actions	*Team performance reports* were used, in particular, the aspects indicated by the team as being interfering with the performance of their elements
Q5/Q6/ Q7	Q5 was designed to evaluate the performance of the key stakeholders (portfolio manager and project client) using the ascending hierarchical	The evaluation method used was the graphic scales, from 1 to 5, based on key competences recommended by the

(continued)

Table 1 (continued)

Milestone	Purpose	Used Instruments
	evaluation source. With Q6 and Q7, it was intended to evaluate, respectively, the performance of the teams from the perspective of the clients and project sponsors, as well as their performance, using the self-assessment of these stakeholders and the descending hierarchical evaluation	*IPMA Competences Baseline* (IPMA 2006)
F2	Performance feedback was provided to each element regarding the (intermediate) performance of her/his team, from the perspectives of the client and the project sponsor	The generated performance reports contained the level of stakeholder satisfaction and other considerations that the teams should take into account
Q8 e Q9	In order to compare the most recent performance of team members with their past performance, the eighth and ninth questionnaires allowed to verify whether or not there were improvements in comparison to previous evaluations	These questionnaires had the same structure and content as the Q4 and Q1 questionnaires, respectively
I2/Q10	Interviews were carried out, and performance evaluation questionnaires were used to identify the factors that harmed the most, or contributed the most, to the individual and collective performance. It also aimed to support the distribution of grades (merit) by team members	Open questions and closed questions were used using the *Likert Scale* method, from 1 to 7, and metrics based on several studies (Amaral et al. 2015; Burlea 2009; Moura et al. 2014; Woodcock and Francis 2008). The peer comparison method was also used
F3	To provide feedback to students regarding the final grades (from 0 to 20) obtained in the curricular unit	Report generated by the faculty member responsible for the curricular unit

In summary, the data were collected through questionnaire surveys (the list of questionnaires carried out is shown in Table 2) and by interviews. Only the initial questionnaire (Q1) was made available on paper; all others were implemented in the *Google Forms* platform. At each moment of data collection, response periods were defined, and a link to the form was sent via institutional electronic mail. In addition to the evaluation/feedback milestones identified, there was also a continuous monitoring of the projects. All the teams participated actively in the study.

In order to guarantee a measurement with a relevant impact and to mitigate some possible evaluation errors, it was necessary for the coordinator of the curricular unit to act as a facilitator of the process, clarifying the evaluated (if they needed) on any aspect of the applied evaluation instrument. In addition to assisting the evaluation, the coordinator of the curricular unit also managed the evaluation process to detect possible improvements in the evaluation, keeping in mind any ambiguities in the

Table 2 Carried out questionnaires

Questionnaire	Total Items
Q1. Characterization of skills in project management	94
Q2. Characterization of complementary competences of team members	20
Q3. Characterization of individual resilience	30
Q4. Evaluation of teams performance	63
Q5. Evaluation of key project stakeholders	45
Q6. Interim team evaluation and self-assessment of the project client	15
Q7. Interim team evaluation and self-assessment of the project sponsor	15
Q8. Evaluation of teams performance	63
Q9. Characterization of skills in project management	94
Q10. Evaluation of individual and team performance	91

metrics described, influences of responses among teammates, accusations of irrelevance, frustrations, and discomfort that could result from the required issues.

6 Presentation and Discussion of Results

Table 3 shows the demographic characterization of the study participants. The mean age was 24.97 years (SD = 4.718), ranging from the minimum age of 21 years to the maximum age of 45 years (Mo = 21). Regarding gender, the majority of respondents were male (54 men, corresponding to 87.1% of the participants). Regarding the student status, from the frequency analysis we can see that, in this sample, there were two types of status—Ordinary and Student-Worker—with a majority of students with Ordinary status (45 respondents, corresponding to 72.6% of the participants).

Table 3 Demographic characterization of the study participants

Characteristics	Value	Percentage (%)
Gender		
Male	54	87.1
Female	8	12.9
Age		
Under 25 years	44	71.0
From 26 to 30 years	13	20.9
From 31 to 35 years	3	4.9
From 36 to 45 years	2	3.2
Status		
Ordinary	45	72.6
Student-Worker	17	27.4

In order to verify if the evaluation instruments were considered useful by the teams, the opinion of the respondents was collected in the fourth and eighth questionnaires (Q4 and Q8) by answering two questions: "Was this questionnaire helpful in raising the awareness of the team about aspects relevant to an effective project management?"; and "This questionnaire was useful for giving feedback on the performance of team members so that they can maintain, improve or eliminate certain behaviours?"

Regarding the first question "Was this questionnaire helpful in raising the awareness of the team about aspects relevant to effective project management?", it is possible to observe on the graphs in Fig. 3 that the majority of the participants, in both evaluation moments, had a favourable opinion and did not give their time as lost (63% and 65% respectively). It is worth noting that the difference is minimal between both evaluation moments.

Concerning the second question "This questionnaire was useful for giving feedback on the performance of team members so that they can maintain, improve or eliminate certain behaviours?", it is also possible to observe a very favourable opinion, which in both moments was above 70% (see Fig. 4). In this case, from one

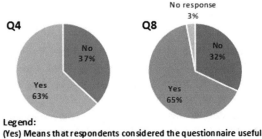

Legend:
(Yes) Means that respondents considered the questionnaire useful
(No) Means that respondents considered the questionnaire not useful
(No response) Means that the respondents did not answer the question

Fig. 3 Perceived utility regarding the awareness of the aspects relevant to an effective project management

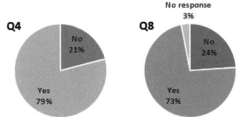

Legend:
(Yes) Means that respondents considered the questionnaire useful to improve certain behaviours
(No) Means that respondents considered the questionnaire not useful to improve behaviours
(No response) Means that the respondents did not answer the question

Fig. 4 Perceived utility from a continuous performance improvement perspective

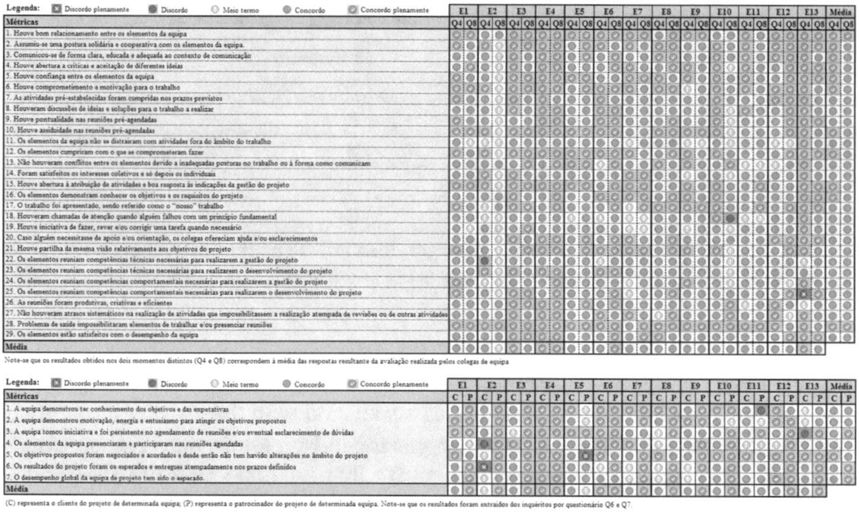

Fig. 5 Results obtained in the team performance evaluation questionnaires

moment (Q4) to the following (Q8), it is possible to notice that there was a slight decrease in the perception of utility (from 79% to 73%). This can be explained by the fact that the first questionnaire had a pedagogical effect, allowing the awareness of several aspects relevant to teamwork. In the second questionnaire, some respondents, having already the notion of these aspects, did not consider it useful to improve behaviour (this is expected and considered positive).

To follow the evolution of the teams' behaviour during the project execution were created two tables as shown in Fig. 5 (in the original tables in Portuguese, "E < team number>" identifies each team, "C" represents the client of the project, and "P" represents the sponsor of the project). The top table presents the team's behaviour change (from Q4 to Q8) and the bottom table the clients' and sponsors' opinion about the team (the best result is represented by a green circle with a white arrow, and the worst is represented by a red circle with a white "x").

It should be noted that the fourth (Q4), sixth (Q6) and seventh (Q7) questionnaire surveys were applied during the same period (from the end of March to the beginning of April) and that the eighth (Q8) questionnaire survey was applied in a moment of project pre-closure (beginning of June) in order to evaluate the evolution of skills in the teams. It should also be noted that it was intended to reapply the sixth (Q6) and seventh (Q7) questionnaire surveys in the same period as the eighth (Q8) questionnaire survey so that it would have been possible to provide the viewpoint and satisfaction level of the clients and the project sponsor to the teams but, unfortunately, this was operationally impracticable.

In determining the final individual grades (distribution of merit), several techniques were used in addition to the information gathered during the projects. Particularly noteworthy was the peer comparison method applied in the tenth (Q10)

Table 4 Results obtained from a given team in the tenth (Q10) questionnaire survey

Evaluator	High performance	Good performance	Moderate performance	Low performance
A	D	C	A	B
B	D	C	B	A
C	C	D	B	A
D[a]	D	C	B	A

[a]Element that held the position of project manager. It should be noted that each evaluator (in this case A, B, C and D) grades her/his colleagues according to her/his own perspective

questionnaire survey. This method, besides providing a hierarchical distribution of merit, also allowed to identify individuals unsatisfied with the distribution of merit. Table 4 presents an example of a report generated by performance comparison by peers. In this example, it is possible to verify that there are students classified by their peers in a position that does not coincide with their perspective, and may lead to dissatisfaction and complaint regarding the assignment of final grades. For example, according to student A's perspective (first line), she/he classifies herself/himself as having had a "Moderate Performance," while all other classmates rated her/him as "performing poorly."

Through the interpretation of the results obtained in Table 4, it is observed that: Element A was the one that demonstrated low performance (with 75% of the votes, being this classification in disagreement with her/his perspective); The element B was the one that showed a moderate performance (with 75% of the votes, being this classification in agreement with her/his perspective); The element C was the one that demonstrated good performance (with 75% of the votes, being this classification in disagreement with her/his perspective—she/he classifies herself/himself with high performance); The D element was the one that demonstrated high performance (with 75% of the votes, being this classification in agreement with her/his perspective).

The evaluator should recognize that the classification of collaborators with equivalent global performance may not correspond to the truth. As such, one should consider not only the peer perspective but also take into account the performance resulting from previous evaluations. Moreover, if possible, one should check the recording of past positive and/or negative aspects, in order to justify the distribution of merit. In practice, the combined use of various performance evaluation instruments proved to be extremely useful because, being complementary, they have allowed obtaining more rigorous and complete information to ensure a fair distribution of merit.

7 Conclusions and Future Work

In this case study, it was possible to confirm the pertinence of several approaches, methods, and techniques of performance assessment. The evaluation process implemented was bidirectional and proved to be an effective way to assess performance. The evaluation tools attested to be useful for evaluating team performance, providing justifications for performance, as well as showing positive and less positive aspects of each's behaviour. The evaluation process also contributed to equity and collective satisfaction, being a source of motivation for team members to improve their performance and to work effectively together. It was also possible to provide feedback to people, to identify training needs, and to recognize and reward individual performance. Also worth mentioning, the increase in the overall average grades of projects, as compared to the previous school year, reflecting the improvement in performance that was achieved.

Due to project differences, the key competences assessed in this study focused more on project management than on the technical development of information systems. For this reason, and because the sample studied was constituted exclusively by university students, the results should be considered in light of this context. In other words, although these students have carried out real projects with effective clients, some organizational variables that might affect an individual's performance, such as authority and incentives, are different in the academic context.

We should emphasize that, during the case study, it was intended to minimize the time and effort involved in completing the questionnaires. Unfortunately, this may not have always been achieved (notably in the first (Q1), ninth (Q9) and tenth (Q10) questionnaires) due to the high number of items in the evaluation, which may lead to a reduction in the commitment to respond.

The limited theoretical information available regarding performance evaluation practices in specific contexts, such as IST projects, has proved to be the main difficulty in carrying out the study. Another limitation was the identification of key competences or competency profiles appropriate to each profile in this study context. This problem has been investigated in some studies (Mcmurtrey et al. 2008; Trigo et al. 2012), which have presented competences recommended for the various areas and types of IST projects.

Concerning future work proposals, the limitations pointed out in this study that, for reasons of lack of time and resources were not considered, could be opportunities to continue this work. It is suggested that other evaluation tools, techniques, and approaches may be applied in a similar context (e.g., evaluation approaches centered on outcomes). The development of a Web platform or the use of an integrated management system that streamlines evaluation processes in the context of IST projects is another relevant work for the future.

Acknowledgements A word of appreciation to the students of the curricular unit "Projeto de Tecnologias e Sistemas de Informação" of the Master's degree in Engineering and Management of Information Systems, of the University of Minho, for having participated actively in this study.

References

Amaral, A., Fernandes, G., & Varajão, J. (2015). Identifying useful actions to improve team resilience in information systems projects. *Procedia Computer Science, 64,* 1182–1189.

Baskerville, R. L. (1999). Investigating information systems with action research. Communications of AIS, *2*(3), 4. http://www.cis.gsu.edu/~rbaskerv/CAIS_2_19/CAIS_2_19.html.

Burlea, A. S. (2009). Success factors for an information systems projects team creating new context. In *Innovation and Knowledge Management in Twin Track Economies Challenges Solutions.* (Vol. 13, pp. 936–941).

Cadle, J., & Yeates, D. (2007). *Project management for information systems (5.a Ed).* Harlow: Prentice Hall.

Caetano, A. (2008). Avaliação de Desempenho: metáforas, conceitos e práticas (1.a Ed). Lisboa: Editora RH, Lda.

Chiavenato, I. (2003). Recursos Humanos: o capital humano das organizações (8.a Ed). São Paulo: Editora Atlas.

Cunha, M., Rego, A., Cunha, R., & Cardoso, C. (2007). Manual de Comportamento Organizacional e Gestão (5.a Ed). Lisboa: Editora RH, Lda.

Gonçalves, D., Cruz, J., & Varajão, J. (2008). Particularidades dos diferentes tipos de projetos de desenvolvimento de software. In 21o Congresso Internacional de Administração - Gestão estratégica na era do conhecimento (ADM). Brasil.

Hodge, D. R., & Gillespie, D. (2003). Phrase completions: an alternative to Likert scales. *Social Work Research, 27*(1), 45–55.

IPMA. (2006). ICB - IPMA Competence Baseline. In G. Caupin, H. Knoepfel, G. Koch, K. Pannenbäcker, F. Pérez-Polo, & C. Seabury (Eds.) (3.a Ed). Nijkerk: International Project Management Association.

Likert, R. (1932). A technique for the measurement of attitudes. *Archives in Psychology, 22*(140), 1–55.

Mcmurtrey, M. E., Downey, J. P., Zeltmann, S. M., & Friedman, W. H. (2008). Critical skill sets of entry-level IT professionals: an empirical examination of perceptions from field personnel. *Journal of Information Technology Education, 7,* 101–120.

Moura, I., Dominguez, C., & Varajão, J. (2018). Information systems project teams: factors for high performance. Team Performance Management: An International Journal. https://doi.org/10.1108/TPM-03-2018-0022.

Moura, I. C., Dias, P. M., Dominguez, C. E., & Varajão, J. E. (2014). What team members perceive as important to achieve high performance: an exploratory case study. In *Procedia Technology: Proceedings of the ProjMAN'14* (Vol. 16, pp. 1010–1016). Elsevier Ltd. http://doi.org/10.1016/j.protcy.2014.10.055.

Paiva, A., Varajão, J., Domínguez, C., & Ribeiro, P. (2011). Principais aspectos na avaliação do sucesso de projectos de desenvolvimento de software. Há alguma relação com o que é considerado noutras indústrias ? Interciencia, *36*(3), 200–204.

Pereira, J. L., & Sá, J. O., (2017). Process-based information systems development: taking advantage of a component-based infrastructure. Business Systems Research Journal. *8*(2).

Sarmento, M., Rosinha, A., & Silva, J. (2015). *Avaliação do Desempenho.* Lisboa: Escolar Editora.

Silva, A., Varajão, J., Pereira, J. L., & Sousa Pinto, C. (2017a). Performance appraisal approaches and methods for IT/IS projects: a review. *International Journal of Human Capital and Information Technology Professionals, 8*(3).

Silva, A., Varajão, J., Sousa Pinto, C., & Oliveira e Sá, J. (2017b). Who can access HR performance in IT/IS projects: a review. In *Recent Advances in Information Systems and Technologies*, Advances in Intelligent Systems and Computing, Springer, 569.

Sotomayor, A., Rodrigues, J., & Duarte, M. (2014). Princípios de Gestão das Organizações (2.a Ed). Lisboa: Rei dos Livros.

Trigo, A., Varajão, J., Barroso, J., Soto-Acosta, P., & Molina-Castillo, F. J. Gonzalvez-Gallego, N. (2011). Enterprise information systems adoption in iberian large companies: motivations and trends. In *Managing Adaptability, Intervention, and People in Enterprise Information Systems* (pp. 204–228). http://doi.org/10.4018/978-1-60960-529-2.ch010.

Trigo, A., Varajão, J., Figueiredo, N., & Barroso, J. (2007). Information systems and technology adoption by the Portuguese large companies. In *EMCIS 2007—European and Mediterranean Conference on Information Systems* (Vol. 2007). València.

Trigo, A., Varajão, J., Soto-Acosta, P., Barroso, J., Molina-Castillo, F., & Gonzalvez-Gallego, N. (2012). IT professionals: an Iberian snapshot. In *Professional Advancements and Management Trends in the IT Sector* (pp. 32–45). IGI Global.

Uahi, R., Pereira, J. L., & Varajão, J. (2018). Improving work allocation practices in business processes supported by BPMS. *Advances in Intelligent Systems and Computing., 745,* 989–995.

Varajão, J. (2016). Success Management as a PM knowledge area—work-in-progress. *Procedia Computer Science, 100,* 1095–1102.

Varajão, J. (2018). A new process for success management—bringing order to a typically ad-hoc area. *Journal of Modern Project Management, 5*(3), 94–99.

Varajão, J., Cardoso, J., Gonçalves, D., & Cruz, J. (2008). Análise à gestão de projectos de desenvolvimento de software em grandes empresas portuguesas. Semana Informática (904), 10–12.

Varajão, J., Cardoso, J., Gonçalves, D., & Cruz, J. (2009). Sucesso de um projecto na gestão de projectos. Semana Informática (919), 10.

Varajão, J., Colomo-Palacios, R., & Silva, H. (2017). ISO 21500:2012 and PMBoK 5 processes in information systems project management. *Computer Standards & Interfaces, 50,* 216–222.

Varajão, J., Dominguez, C., Ribeiro, P., & Paiva, A. (2014). Critical success aspects in project management: similarities and differences between the construction and the software industry. *Tehnicki Vjesnik-Technical Gazette, 21*(2), 583–589.

Varajão, J., Magalhães, L., Freitas, L., Ribeiro, P., & Ramos, J. (2018). Implementing success management in an IT project. In *ProjMAN—International Conference on Project MANagement*, Elsevier: Procedia Computer Science.

Varajão, J., & Trigo, A. (2016). Evaluation of IS project success in InfSysMakers: an exploratory case study. In: *International Conference on Information Systems (ICIS)*. Dublin, Ireland.

Wagnild, G. M., & Young, H. M. (1993). Development and psychometric evaluation of the Resilience Scale. *Journal of Nursing Measurement, 1*(2), 165–178.

Woodcock, M., & Francis, D. (2008). *Team metrics: resources for measuring and improving team performance (1.a Ed)*. Amherst: HRD Press, Inc.

Learning Scorecard Gamification: Application of the MDA Framework

Tiago Pedroso, Elsa Cardoso⊙, Francisco Rações, Artur Baptista and José Barateiro⊙

Abstract The application of gamification techniques in higher education can be challenging. At times it is easy to lose focus and we can no longer explain the connections between players' motivation and the several elements of the game. This study focused on the application of the MDA framework (Mechanics, Dynamics and Aesthetics) to the platform Learning Scorecard (LS), currently used by several students at ISCTE—Instituto Universitário de Lisboa. The LS is a platform for Learning Analytics that has been used since 2016, on courses of Data Warehouse and Business Intelligence. LS has two views: the student and teacher views. In this work we will report on the application of the MDA framework to the student view of LS. This view aims to improve the learning experience of students increasing their engagement and motivation through the use of gamification.

Keywords Gamification · Learning scorecard · MDA framework

T. Pedroso
ISCTE- Instituto Universitário de Lisboa (ISCTE-IUL), Lisbon, Portugal
e-mail: Tiago_Pedroso@iscte-iul.pt

E. Cardoso (✉)
ISCTE-IUL and INESC-ID, Lisbon, Portugal
e-mail: Elsa.Cardoso@iscte-iul.pt

F. Rações · A. Baptista
ISCTE-IUL, Lisbon, Portugal
e-mail: Francisco_Barao@iscte-iul.pt

A. Baptista
e-mail: Artur_Teixeira@iscte-iul.pt

J. Barateiro
LNEC and INESC-ID, Lisbon, Portugal
e-mail: jose.barateiro@lnec.pt

I. Ramos et al. (eds.), *Information Systems for Industry 4.0*,
Lecture Notes in Information Systems and Organisation 31,
https://doi.org/10.1007/978-3-030-14850-8_3

1   Introduction

The gamification is the use of game design elements applied in different contexts other than games (Deterding et al. 2011). Gamification in teaching has been growing as evidenced by the number of papers published in this area (Dicheva et al. 2015), due to the need to change teaching to improve results. According to Hanus and Fox (2015) students can be motivated to learn in new ways or by reformulating the boring forms of teaching. The gamification is a new way of teaching that can change the most traditional teaching practices into a more innovative perspective (Regina et al. 2015). Even before the term gamification was talked about, Marc Prensky, a writer in the area of education, argued that schools should evolve and adapt to technological means, because the characteristics of the students changed radically. He affirms that today's students are no longer the people for whom the educational system was designed (Prensky 2001). Lee and Hammer (2011) also propose the application of gamification to change the more traditional methods of education.

The main challenges of gamification in education are the skepticism of the real benefits of this technique. The major change that implementation of gamification mechanisms entails is another big issue. The change implies costs (time and money) and an open mind to accept the changes. On the other hand, the positive factors demonstrate being able to improve the traditional educational processes that have not been able to meet the demands of today's students (Furdu et al. 2017; Sánchez-Mena and Martí- Parreño 2017).

The objective of this study is to critically present the steps needed to build a system with gamification, within the Learning Scorecard, a platform of Learning Analytics developed in a university context, whose focus is to improve the commitment and motivation of students with the intention to increase their learning experience in a curricular unit.

This paper is organized as follows. Section 2 describes the concepts and techniques to be applied in the design of the system with gamification elements. Section 3 demonstrates the application of the concepts and the MDA framework in a real case, that is, in the Learning Scorecard platform. Section 4 conducts the analysis of the results of the experiment. Finally, Sect. 5 presents the conclusions, the difficulties found in the study and the proposed improvements for future work.

2   Game Design

Game design is the process of creating a game through elements and techniques (Németh 2015). Game design elements and techniques are used to motivate and encourage players to perform their tasks with pleasure and commitment. But in certain circumstances, only the joy of playing and/or the possibility of winning

Fig. 1 MDA perspectives
(Hunicke et al. 2004)

create by themselves a competitive stimulus between the players (Dicheva et al. 2015). Thus, it is possible to demonstrate the motivational capacity of these elements and gamification techniques.

A term widely used in gamification is the gamification elements or game design elements, but the term is quite vast. The awareness of the term game design elements is a barrier. The authors generally do not differentiate the functions of each element and neither distinguish them (Monterrat et al. 2017). Yet when they do, *"there is no common classification of game design elements, the classification is unclear for these elements"* (Dicheva et al. 2015). Faced with a lack of concordance problem some taxonomies arise, among them stands out the MDA framework (Mechanics, Dynamics and Aesthetics) which is seen as a popular taxonomy among professionals of the gamification industry.

The MDA framework proposed by Hunicke et al. (2004) is a post-mortem analysis of game elements that allows us to use thought systems to describe the interaction of these elements and to apply them outside the concept of the game (see Fig. 1). Its name is due to be composed of three categories called Mechanics, Dynamics and Aesthetics. The mechanics form the functional components of the game with the ability to guide the actions of the players. Dynamics are the interactions of the player with the mechanics incorporated into the systems determining what each player does. Finally, aesthetics are the emotions that the game transmits to the player during their use. Aesthetics can be understood as a presentation of mechanics and dynamics as players interact (Zichermann and Cunningham 2011).

3   MDA in Learning Scorecard

The Learning Scorecard (LS) platform allows higher education students to monitor their learning evolution (Cardoso et al. 2016, 2017). This platform allows to generate data that, throughout the academic semester, support teachers to continuously monitor their classes. The LS uses gamification techniques to seek to increase student engagement/involvement with curricular units. It also seeks to use best practices of Business Intelligence to offer students and teachers an analytical environment so that they can monitor their performance.

The LS is underway for four consecutive semesters, from the 2016–17 academic year, at the ISCTE-Instituto Universitário de Lisboa (ISCTE-IUL) in the curricular units of Decision Support Systems I and II (in Portuguese, SIAD I and II), where the topics of Data Warehouse and Business Intelligence are taught. In each of the interactions there were modifications to the platform already with four versions, two of which were developed within the scope of this research.

The platform has two views, the student and the teacher. The Student view focuses on time management, monitoring, and gamification techniques to improve students' individual learning experience. The view of the teacher aims to increase the communication of the teachers with the students and to personalize the students' learning experience.

The gamification in versions 3 and 4 of the LS platform followed the six steps presented in the book "For the win" for the construction of game design (Werbach and Hunter 2012). The steps are to define the objectives (step 1) whose main purpose of the use of gamification techniques in LS goes through enhance the learning experience of students by improving the commitment and/or motivation.

Outlining desired behaviour (step 2); in this step the expected behaviour is that students follow the subjects taught during the semester so that they can carry out a balanced study in a fun way and, therefore, an improvement of the grade's averages in the curricular unit.

Describe the players (step 3), as previously mentioned platform users are young adults who attend the SIAD I and II curricular units. The fact that students are young can help with motivation and acceptance of the LS.

Drawing activity loops (step 4), at this point it was defined that students will have to complete tasks and missions and consequently gained experience points for having performed them as a feedback mechanism. This feedback will have to be given as soon as possible and cannot be in real time due to the reason of many of these challenges have to be corrected or approved by a teacher.

With the points scored (feedback) and the possible rises of ranks we are motivating the players to act again, thus completing the cycle of engagement proposed by Werbach and Hunter (2012), which will make the players committed and motivated.

Do not forget the fun (step 5) is a very important point when you want to build a gamified system that is often overlooked. To not forget the fun, the MDA framework will be used.

Use appropriate tools (step 6) is the last point and in this case, we follow the main rule of gamification which says that the system must be "iterated, improved, tested, iterated, improved, tested, …". We must continually seek to improve our systems using the tools available.

In another sense, the MDA framework was used as a taxonomy of game design elements to facilitate the understanding of the perspectives of the creators of the game and of the players. Thus, with the application of the MDA it becomes possible to distinguish the different elements of the games as the rules, the system and the fun. Next, the different steps in the application of MDA to the learning Scorecard platform will be described.

3.1 Mechanics in the LS

The mechanics chosen to guide the players throughout the game were the XPs (experience points) that allow to numerically represent the progression of the players in the game. The points are won on the platform with the completion of different objectives such as Quests, Trophies and Badges. The use of the Ranks or levels in the LS platform allowed to define the different stages in the progression of the players.

Ranks follow the rating scale from A to F, but with a motivating name for each scale (A—*Legendary*, B—*Master*, C—*Expert*, D—*Skilled*, E—*Rookie* and F—*Newbie*).

Quests are pre-defined challenges with goals and rewards. In the LS platform Quests are the main mechanism for players to win XPs. The types of Quests available in the Learning Scorecard are: Quizzes (multiple choice tests), Practical Assignments (tutorials), Exercises (written exercises), Class Attendance (attendance in class) and Forum (participation in the forum). Students will have to validate and classify the difficulty of certain quests (Quiz, Exercise and Practical Assignment) defined by the teachers in order to win the associated XPs. Associated with this mechanic came the need to create the Last Chances; this mechanism allows giving a bonus to the players so that they can validate and re-classify the quests they had performed but not validated. The Last Chances may imply a penalty, defined by the teacher, in the XPs earned for not having validated at the due time.

Also associated with the quests are events that are game guides that do not reward players with XPs when they are completed. Players that fail a mandatory UC event are moved to a Game Over status in the game.

The Guilds are the name called to the curricular unit work groups. Another mechanism also created was the concept of Alliance that represents the shift in which the student attends classes.

In the LS platform was used one of the most used mechanics Leaderboards, but with a particularity of being multi-dimensional leaderboards with the following five dimensions:

- Leaderboard All, players are sorted by descending order of all XPs accumulated in the curricular unit (see Fig. 2);
- Leaderboard Quizzes, players are sorted by descending order of XPs won on quizzes type quests in the curricular unit;
- Leaderboard Exercises, the players are sorted by descending order of XPs earned in quests of the type exercises in the curricular unit;
- Leaderboard Guilds, the student groups or Guilds are sorted in descending order of the average of XPs accumulated by the group members in the curricular unit; and
- Leaderboard Combined, players are sorted in ascending order by the sum of the positions obtained from leaderboads all, quizzes and exercises.

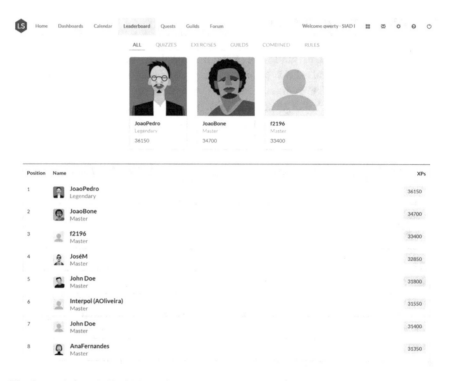

Fig. 2 Leaderboard all of LS version 3

Interconnected with leaderboards comes a new mechanic, trophies, which rewards players who are in the first position of the Leaderboards All (trophy Best Score Player), Guild (Best Guild trophy) and Combined (trophy Best Triathlon Player) with 1000 XPs. The trophy corresponds to a large number of XPs.

Players have the possibility to customize their profile with Avatars. A system was created where players as they ascend from ranks will unlock new Avatars, always with male and female Avatars (see Fig. 3).

It was also provided to the players a gaming dashboard so that students could see their progress and make decisions throughout their in-game experience (see Fig. 4).

Another mechanic provided in the LS platform are badges (medals). This is another mechanism that allows to guide students through the game and is also another system for obtaining XPs. There are 39 badges on the platform that are divided into four modalities: individual, guild, forum and final questionnaire. These badges are further divided into different materials like bronze, silver, gold and platinum as the challenges are more difficult to achieve.

Fig. 3 Avatars available in LS version 3

Fig. 4 Student dashboard in LS version 3

3.2 Dynamics in the LS

The LS platform sought to explore different dynamics with greater focus on cooperation and competitiveness. The LS players are young students, allowing the dynamics of competitiveness and cooperation to be well explored.

The cooperation was stimulated with the use of the mechanics of Guilds and Alliances where a focus on the mutual aid is sought. To further enhance team spirit, Badges and Trophies oriented to the Guilds were added to Leaderboards. Another point that allowed the help among all the students was the forum, which facilitated the sharing of knowledge among the students, as well as the communication with the teachers and the clarification of doubts.

The construction of a narrative to guide the players throughout the game experience inserts in the LS platform the dynamics of continuity and completion of the game. These two dynamics were explored using essentially the events and quests. These two techniques, intertwined with the ranks and the XPs, provide a constant feedback promoting the students' commitment to the platform.

The number of quests and badges available during the execution of the curricular unit has also made it possible to improve the dynamics of choice and consequence in LS, so students can make decisions like choosing their path through the course of the game. In these gamification systems it is very important to guarantee the possibility of failure for not lead to loss of motivation and commitment of the students. The enormous amount of challenges available and the introduction of Last Chances allowed to give players the ability to fail or make mistakes.

Lastly, we seek to encourage healthy competition among players. For this, it was important to use most of the mechanics inserted in the platform. The leaderboards are the main comparison mechanism between the players. Therefore, the creation of five leaderboards allowed to incite the competition, where different quests such as Quizzes and Exercises are explored. Awarding trophies to the best player and the best guild served the same purpose of providing the competition and rewarding players for the effort made throughout the experience. We sought with the competitiveness between the Guilds to make the elements motivate each other. The XPs and Ranks were the mechanisms used for comparison on leaderboards, but it is important to remember that the Avatars, as they are being unlocked with the rise of ranks by the players, allow them to "spice up" the other lower rank players.

3.3   Aesthetics of the LS

Aesthetics is the last point of the MDA framework; in this step the challenge was to trigger emotional responses to the players with the creation of the dynamics explored on the LS platform. The platform is able to trigger different sensations depending on each student. The addition of gamification in LS sought to create a group of active students and that cooperate with each other to improve their knowledge. The gamification also sought to reach out to students through challenges and a new teaching experience.

The improvement of the visual aspect of the platform allowed to improve the different stimuli to the players. The design of the graphic interfaces deserved special attention in the development of the LS, in order to improve the experience of using the platform. For example, the Forum on the LS platform was developed with xenForo, a licensed forum software, which enabled the rapid availability of a set of social engagement features, alerts, profile personalization, and activity statistics valued by students.

4   Results Analysis

The results analysed in this section correspond to the data obtained from the students' use of the platform and their answers given in the final questionnaire of the curricular unit of version 3 of the LS. Version 3 was used in the Data Warehouse curricular unit (SIAD I) of the first semester of the 2017–2018 academic year, between September 24, 2017 and January 29, 2018, with 132 students enrolled. This curricular unit was taught simultaneously to four distinct courses, two master's and two bachelor's degrees. Data using the current version 4 cannot yet be analysed since the experiment only ends in early July 2018. In version 3 there was a great interest of the students towards the platform where 93% of students (123 of 132) participated in this learning experience. From the questionnaires about 96% of the students enrolled in the platform used it until the end of the semester. One of the reasons that allowed these high values in the commitment comes from the fact that the LS participation contributes to the final grade of the curricular unit as it is emphasized by some students in the questionnaires, "is another obligatory platform that conditionate the grade". In another sense, the reason why the (few) students did not use the platform until the end of the semester was the lack of time.

4.1 Evaluation of Mechanics in the LS: XPs and Types of Quests

The acceptance of the participation in the LS counting as 10% of the grade of continuous assessment obtained great discrepancy of opinions, as shown by Fig. 5. Half of the players agree and feel that the value given by their participation in the platform is fair. Further affirming that "*integrating the 'game' in the grade is another factor encouraging students to use the platform although it is not the main one. Despite not having a considerable weight, it is enough*" or that "*allowed to implement the LS and motivate students to participate without a very high impact to put into question the diversion effect of gamification*". Some additional comments received in the questionnaires reflect what we initially planned as "*that by being*

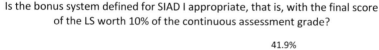

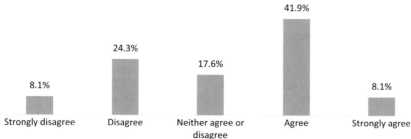

Fig. 5 Student satisfaction with the bonus system in LS version 3

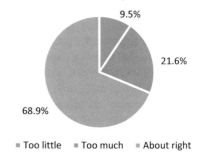

Fig. 6 Students' view of the number of elements present in LS version 3

The gamification elements (Leaderboard, Rank, XPs, Quests, Avatar, Badges, Trophies, Last Chance) used in the LS platform were:

9.5%
21.6%
68.9%

■ Too little ■ Too much ■ About right

part of the grade, even if only with 10%, it is an extra motivation for students to participate in the various proposed activities and often without realizing it, was beneficial to them. For example, quizzes help students to realize their weaknesses and what they have to learn to overcome them. The exercises help to study so that while preparing for the final test the student does not have to be remembering everything from the beginning since he/she has been practicing". The remaining students who did not agree with the value have different reasons: some feel that the 10% does not reflect the time spent and/or the effort made, while others feel that it should not count at all for the course grade and could just be a bonus to the grade.

Regarding the mechanisms used in the platform, they were perceived as sufficient (69%), yet 22% of responses considered them as excessive, as shown in Fig. 6.

The available quests were well-received by the students with the exception of the Forum. When analysing the data obtained by the LS platform, it was possible to verify that students performed on average 73% of the quests available, where the quests of the Practical Assignment type had the highest percentage of achievement, about 96% (this is a mandatory quest for continuous evaluation). The remaining quests obtained the following achievement values of Class Attendance 76%, Quizzes 88%, Exercises 48% and Forum 37%. These values show that fewer students participated in the forum and in the exercises, but this theme will be detailed later. We also tried to confront the students about their main motivation (for the grade or the game) to perform the different types of quests and more than 77% said to be for the grade. Still in this question none of the students claimed to participate in the LS only or mostly for the game. However, Fig. 7 shows that the XPs assigned were not consensual, many felt that the XP distribution was fair, others felt that the points earned did not represent the effort made.

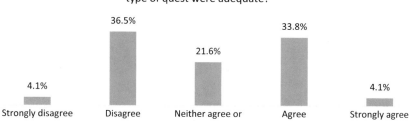

Do you consider that the values of Experient Points (XP) assigned to each type of quest were adequate?

Fig. 7 Students' opinions on the distribution of XPs for each *quest* type in LS version 3

4.2 Forum Rating

The Forum-type quest was the most controversial; several answers reported that the forum should not be evaluated. Many have expressed their displeasure by stating that their doubts were common to those of other colleagues and did not feel the need to expose their difficulties in comments on the forum. One of the comments that addresses this subject was the following: "*We are between 60 and 70 students, many of the doubts that have arisen are probably common to other colleagues, however, only one will have the 'opportunity' to ask in the forum without being considered SPAM. The same goes for those who want to help clarify these doubts. Even if several colleagues know the answer, only one will have the opportunity to clarify it in the forum without being considered SPAM*".

In this study it was observed that students did not explore the Forum in the way it was intended, i.e., by sharing other sources of information and issues that started new discussions. Several badges have been created to expose the most valued objectives in the LS platform, but it was not enough to invigorate the Forum. It is noteworthy that only nine Forum-type badges were awarded, the majority (seven) were bronze, which translates to the lower difficulty of the proposed objectives. Of these nine badges, one bronze was attributed for having reached the 20 requested posts, another three also of bronze for having received 20 likes in their publications and the remaining three of bronze for having received a pin post in a relevant comment for the class. The remaining two badges were gold for having found and aided in correcting errors in the curricular unit material. In the latter case, the sharing was made directly to the coordinator of the curricular unit, but the intention was to use the Forum. However, despite that students were awarded the badges.

In spite of these numbers, version 3 was the experiment that presented better results in comparison to the previous versions of the LS, and more than 74% found useful the availability of the LS Forum for knowledge sharing (see Fig. 8). Some student comments state: "*I fully agree with how the forum is a great place to expand our knowledge about the curricular unit*" and "*because it allowed me to learn from the doubts of others and clarify my doubts*". The most negative aspects

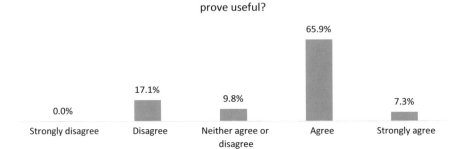

Fig. 8 Students' opinions about the availability of the forum in LS version 3

reported about the Forum are the delay in responding to questions. The aim of the Forum was not to be the teacher to answer all the questions raised, but rather to have a more fluid sharing of information among the students. This new form of cooperation and collaboration takes time to be assimilated by the students.

4.3 Evaluation of Mechanics in the LS: Last Chances, Badges and Trophies

As mentioned earlier, certain quests (Quiz, Exercise and Practical Assignment) need to be validated in order for students to earn XPs. Its validation was to determine the difficulty of each quest. When students were asked about this rule the vast majority (over 68%) considered it appropriate (see Fig. 9). However contrary opinions were received, the reason for their dissatisfaction was due to having to carry out and submit the challenges on an e-learning platform and have to validate them in the LS; they wanted a more centralized platform, as some students say:

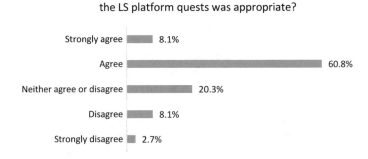

Fig. 9 Students' opinion about the need to evaluate quests in LS version 3

Table 1 Number of last chances performed by quest in LS version 3

Quests	N° of validations by last chance
Quiz 1	4
Quiz 2	14
Quiz 3	6
Quiz 4	2
Quiz 5	2
Exercise 1	9
Exercise 2	11
Exercise 3	6
Tutoring 1	27
Tutoring 2	38

"I find it strange that we have to go to the platform to evaluate the "quest" after completing it on another platform". This was a design option in version 3 and 4, not being the ideal it was the feasible, and in the future, it will be possible to perform all the *quests* inside the LS platform.

During the experiment it was found that students often performed the tasks but did not validate them and, ended up losing the XPs. The implementation of Last Chances was thus fundamental, and many students managed to regain XPs that they thought they had already lost as can be seen in Table 1. In version 3 of the LS no penalty was considered in the score of the "last chance" *quests*.

Badges were a mechanism that had less adherence on the part of the students, the average achievement of this element was 15%, a very low value. Most criticisms are based on the difficulty of achieving them. The most criticized badges were forum- and guild-related badges. Forum badges were criticized due to students' misunderstanding of what was valued and regarding the guild-related badges, students felt that they should not exist because they were dependent on each other. In the latter, dependence on the remaining members of the guild was intended to make students to push each other for improvement.

From Table 2 we can verify that the individual category was the one that obtained a greater number of assigned badges. However, its value is still much lower than desired. Still from Table 2 and Fig. 10 it is possible to understand that this mechanism will have to be further improved or explored in a different way. Once again, these values reflect the non-fulfilment of the objectives proposed for

Table 2 Average Badges earned by students by category in LS version 3

Categories of the Badges	Average of attributed Badges (%)
Individual	43.3
Guild	26.0
Forum	0.3
Final questionnaire	0

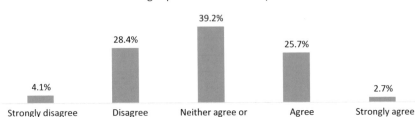

Do you consider that Badges and Trophies helped improve your learning experience with the LS platform?

Fig. 10 Students' opinions on the use of Badges and Trophies mechanisms in LS version 3

the Forum. The badge of the type "Final Questionnaire" was not awarded because the questionnaire ended up being performed (exceptionally) after the assignment of the grades for the participation in the LS, already in the beginning of the second semester.

4.4 Evaluation of Mechanics in the LS: Leaderboards and Ranks

The Leaderboards and their different dimensions are considered by the players (Fig. 11), more than 66%, as a source of motivation. Another data that demonstrates its importance is the average number of accesses by the students to the pages in the platform dedicated to the leaderboards that were on average about 52 accesses per student in 15 weeks.

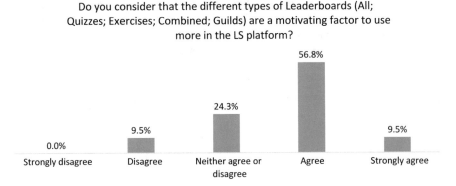

Do you consider that the different types of Leaderboards (All; Quizzes; Exercises; Combined; Guilds) are a motivating factor to use more in the LS platform?

Fig. 11 Students' opinions regarding the Leaderboard mechanism in LS version 3

Table 3 Distribution of the number of students by each rank in LS version 3

Ranks	N° of students by rank	Grade
Legendary	1	20
Master	7	18
Expert	70	15
Skilled	35	12
Rookie	6	10
Newbie	4	0

Table 3 shows the distribution of the number of students by each rank at the end of the curricular unit SIAD I. It is verified that the majority of the students have a grade equal or superior to 15 values (out of 20) in their participation in the LS. This value is quite positive. Some student comments point to the accentuated difficulty in level up, especially at higher levels. However, this differentiation of grades by the ranks was deliberately designed in the game, since the last ranks show "*master*" and "*legendary*" competences in the subject of UC, so they presuppose an extra effort to acquire solid knowledge in the subject taught.

4.5   Overall Evaluation of the Use of the LS

Finally, when students are asked if they would like to use the platform in another curricular unit, 69% said they would like it and the probability of using it if applied in another curricular unit rises to more than 74%. The values show a very positive impact on the motivation and/or commitment of students due to the gamification platform. This impact is also expressed from the values presented in Fig. 12, which shows the satisfaction of more than 70% of students with the use of an academic platform with elements of gamification. In addition to these data, a significant part

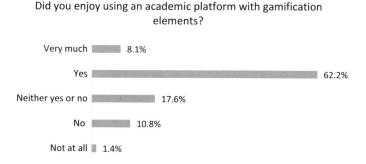

Fig. 12 Students' opinion regarding the use of the platform with gamification elements in the LS version 3

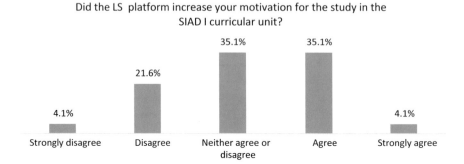

Fig. 13 Students' opinion about the motivation produced by the LS version 3

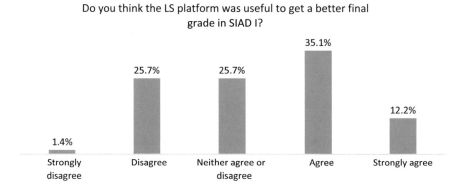

Fig. 14 Students' opinion on the impact on the grade for using the LS version 3

of the students still considered the platform as a motivational source for their study
(Fig. 13) and that allowed them to obtain a better grade in the curricular unit of
SIAD I (Fig. 14).

5 Conclusion

In this work it was possible to understand the steps that are necessary for the
construction of systems with gamification, based on the development of game
design and the taxonomy of these elements using the MDA framework. This paper
describes the mechanics and dynamics of a system with gamification in the scope of
the Learning Scorecard, a platform of Learning Analytics developed in a university
context, whose focus is to improve the commitment and motivation of the students
to improve their learning experience in a curricular unit. With the LS platform

currently being used, this paper presents an analysis of the impact of the use of this platform in a curricular unit of the first semester of 2017–2018 at ISCTE-IUL.

The evaluation of the use of the platform and the mechanics and dynamics introduced in the game design is very positive and encouraging in the continuation of the investigation around the improvement of gamification techniques of the Learning Scorecard.

The main difficulties encountered in the study were the lack of awareness of the objectives proposed for the Forum such as the sharing of relevant content and the need for faster student feedback. Although version 3 of LS has been an experience with much greater use of the forum compared to previous versions, there is still a lot of room to improve, and it is fundamental to increase students' motivation for sharing and collaboration through existing forum resources. Constant feedback was another of the problems encountered in this experiment. The large number of students and assignments available for students to complete with the need to be evaluated requires a huge effort on the part of the teachers to be able to give feedback to the students with brevity.

In systems where gamification techniques are applied, it is necessary to have the notion that the system must evolve continuously. So, the LS platform will have to seek to improve the game design using the historical data collected. The mechanics of Badges should be more explored, as students are not yet adhering to this mechanic. One of the most important points to be improved in the future, and also requested by the students, is the centralization of all the quests in the LS platform, improving especially the integration with the e-learning system. This is because the integration with the academic system of the university, for the attendance record is already solved.

References

Cardoso, E., Santos, D., Costa, D., Caçador, F., Antunes, A., & Ramos, R. (2016, November). Learning scorecard: Monitor and foster student learning through gamification. In *Proceedings of 2nd International Workshop on Educational Knowledge Management (EKM 2016)*. Bologna, Italy. Best paper award.

Cardoso, E., Costa, D., & Santos, D. (2017, June). Introducing the learning scorecard: A tool to improve the student learning experience. In *Proceedings of 23rd International Conference on European University Information Systems (EUNIS 2017)*. Münster, Germany. EUNIS Doerup E-learning Award 2017.

Deterding, S., Dixon, D., Khaled, R., & Nacke, L. (2011, September). From game design elements to gamefulness: Defining "gamification". In *Proceedings of the 15th International Academic MindTrek Conference on Envisioning Future Media Environments (MindTrek'11)*. Tampere, Finland.

Dicheva, D., Dichev, C., Agre, G., & Angelova, G. (2015). Gamification in education: A systematic mapping study. *Journal of Educational Technology & Society, 18*(3), 75–88.

Furdu, I., Tomozei, C., & Köse, U. (2017). Pros and Cons gamification and gaming in classroom. *BRAIN. Broad Research in Artificial Intelligence and Neuroscience, 8*(2), 56–62.

Hanus, M. D., & Fox, J. (2015). Assessing the effects of gamification in the classroom: A longitudinal study on intrinsic motivation, social comparison, satisfaction, effort, and academic performance. *Computers & Education, 80,* 152–161. https://doi.org/10.1016/J.COMPEDU. 2014.08.019.

Hunicke, R., LeBlanc, M., & Zubek, R. (2004). MDA: A formal approach to game design and game research. In *Workshop on Challenges in Game AI* (pp. 1–4). https://doi.org/ 10.1.1.79.4561.

Lee, J. J., & Hammer, J. (2011). Gamification in education: What, how, why bother? *Academic Exchange Quarterly, 15*(2).

Monterrat, B., Lavoué, E., & George, S. (2017). Adaptation of gaming features for motivating learners. *Simulation and Gaming, 48*(5), 625–656. https://doi.org/10.1177/1046878117712632.

Németh, T. (2015). *The definitions of gamification.* Retrieved from http://ludus.hu/en/gamification/ on May 6, 2018.

Prensky, M. (2001). *Digital natives, digital immigrants. From on the horizon* (Vol. 9, Issue 5), MCB University Press.

Regina, C., Losso, C., & Borges, M. C. (2015). Gamificação em Pesquisas em Educação: uma Revisão da Produção Acadêmica (in Portuguese). In *2nd Congress on Education with Technologies—Open and Flipped Learning* (pp. 1–21).

Sánchez-Mena, A., & Martí-Parreño, J. (2017). Drivers and barriers to adopting gamification: Teachers' perspectives. *Electronic Journal of e-Learning, 15*(5), 434–443.

Werbach, K., & Hunter, D. (2012). *For the win: How game thinking can revolutionize your business.* Wharton Digital Press. https://doi.org/10.1017/CBO9781107415324.004.

Zichermann, G., & Cunningham, C. (2011). *Gamification by design: Implementing game mechanics in web and mobile apps* (1st edition). O'Reilly Media.

A Dashboard for Security Forces Data Visualization and Storytelling

Miguel de Castro Neto⑩**, Marcel Nascimento**⑩**, Pedro Sarmento**⑩**,
Sara Ribeiro**⑩**, Teresa Rodrigues**⑩ **and Marco Painho**⑩

Abstract Being security assumed as a basic right of citizens in the current model of democratic rule of law, optimal resources allocation altogether with budgetary constraints are a key component. In fact optimal resources allocation and budgetary constraints oblige an increasingly careful strategic management, adapted to demographic reality. The SIM4SECURITY project aims to build a technological solution to support decision making regarding security, based on the development of a GIS model and in the implementation of demographic scenarios. This model will allow policy makers, leaders and forces of command units and services in the planning and rational affectation of resources adjusted to local dynamics in crime prevention and crime fighting. To communicate the SIM4SECURITY results and support decision making, a data visualization and storytelling approach was adopted by creating dashboards containing the various dimensions and perspectives of the information were elaborated and are presented. The obtained outcomes show that dashboards are an important visual tool in the decision-making process by providing meaningful insights regarding security and in the location-allocation of security forces.

M. de Castro Neto (✉) · M. Nascimento · P. Sarmento · S. Ribeiro · M. Painho
Nova Information Management School (NOVA IMS),
Universidade Nova de Lisboa, 1070-312 Lisbon, Portugal
e-mail: mneto@novaims.unl.pt

M. Nascimento
e-mail: m2016337@novaims.unl.pt

P. Sarmento
e-mail: psarmento@novaims.unl.pt

S. Ribeiro
e-mail: sribeiro@novaims.unl.pt

M. Painho
e-mail: painho@novaims.unl.pt

T. Rodrigues
IPRI-NOVA, Instituto Português de Relações Internacionais,
Universidade Nova de Lisboa, Lisbon, Portugal
e-mail: trodrigues@fcsh.unl.pt

© Springer Nature Switzerland AG 2019
I. Ramos et al. (eds.), *Information Systems for Industry 4.0*,
Lecture Notes in Information Systems and Organisation 31,
https://doi.org/10.1007/978-3-030-14850-8_4

Keywords Dashboards · Crime data · Demographic data · SIM4SECURITY

1 Introduction

Security is a fundamental right of citizens and is a complex phenomenon associated to a framework of unpredictable global emerging threats and uncertainties, that are hard to perceive and operationalize in the traditional model of security systems. This complexity forces the State to establish an appropriate institutional framework for internal security action and resources allocation (Teixeira et al. 2006), while population's safety becomes a central issue and demographics a strategic vector (Rodrigues 2014). Demographic projections were prepared (Bravo 2016) up to 2040, disaggregated by sex, year and municipality, revealing considerable changes on the Portuguese population in the next years. These new demographic trends can be described as a triple ageing phenomenon: less youngsters, a progressively older working population group, and a high increase of elderly population. If the latter can be seen as an improvement on the health system and the social and economic conditions in Portugal, with the consequent increase of the life expectancy, the demographic decrease of the other two age groups is very concerning, especially because such changes are not uniform throughout the territory. While in the country side there is a general decrease of population in all age groups, which originates the depopulation of the Portuguese rural areas, the urban areas see the decrease of young and working age groups and a serious increase of the elderly age group, in some cases ascending to 100% in the next 30 years. Besides the burden imposed to the social welfare system, with less taxpayers and more pensioners, implying a reformulation of this system, a review of the security forces distribution is of paramount importance, especially due to this new reality in the location of the senior population. In the rural areas, it is expected to observe more elders living alone or with other elders in isolated places (more vulnerable and facing ageing-associated diseases). In the urban areas, with different (weaker) relationships with neighbors and (higher) criminality patterns, elder will be more exposed to insecurity. The current allocation of security forces was defined in the 1990s. With the recent demographic and social changes in the Portuguese population, a new distribution model is required, to guarantee an adequate, proportional and effective response of the security forces to the population needs. Indeed, security is closely related with demographic and urban dynamics, new criminal realities and the risks of natural disasters.

This multiplicity of interlinked variables requires new approaches to deal with this complexity namely reinforcing technological competences and increasing capabilities regarding security intelligence. The SIM4SECURITY (Forecast and Spatial Analysis Model for Public Security, Ref. PTDC/ATPDEM/1538/2014) project aims to assist decision making process and optimize resources namely: (1) adequacy of police distribution according to citizens characteristics; (2) study of spatial and temporal dynamics of groups at risk and impact assessment in police offer; (3) deploying police forces; and (4) planning of the number and type of effectives needed for each region. Within this framework a dynamic database and model supported by a Geographic Information System (GIS) was developed to integrate georeferenced data and to provide the possibility of correlate data based on its geographic location. The value of GIS in the public security management arises directly from the benefits of integrating a spatial decision-making technology into a field with a solid need to address numerous critical spatial decisions. The necessary data sources, that sometimes are provided in different systems and operated by different agents, turn the task of GIS in a very challenging job.

A land use cover change model (LUCC) was also implemented to predict future urban populated land use. This study included the following objectives: to build LUCC maps, up to 2040, focused on the evolution of urban areas and in the transitions from the other land use classes to urban land use (Ribeiro et al. 2018); to create dasymetric maps (Petrov 2012) which allow the association to each type of land use, according to a given population density, the corresponding (projected) population; and, to determine the population living in the areas of responsibility of each police station. Additionally, this third objective allows, in conjunction with other GIS spatial analysis tools such as the calculation of distances by road network from each police station, the determination of the population living at a given distance, thus, identifying which of the police stations must be relocated to minimize that distance and improving the support to population. To prepare the spatial modeling of the LUCC maps, Ribeiro et al. (2018) used the Land Change Modeler (LCM), from TerrSet software. As input, LCM needs land use maps from two different periods in time, with the same characteristics. LCM analyses the changes, models the potential of transition, and makes the prediction of the future change, using a neural network (multi-layer perceptron). The demographic, crime and future scenarios development will be reinforced with visualization techniques to facilitate discussion and improve communication among stakeholders.

One of the visualization techniques that could be used to improve communication are dashboards and its concept has been proposed by analogy with other types of dashboards to promote the development of very practical types of information systems that have a direct impact for instance, in decision making (Adam and Pomerol 2008). Dashboards are defined as a visual display of the most important information needed to achieve one or more objectives; consolidated and arranged on a single screen so the information can be monitored at a glance (Few 2006). Indeed, dashboards are linked to the need to cut through the ever-increasing volumes of data available in the corporate information systems (Paine 2004). As dashboards combine different variables to reveal relations that would be difficult to identify when analyzing data separately, they are a good way to represent the information in the framework of SIM4SECURITY project. Dashboards leverage on visual information to support decision-making in multiple contexts, and they have been found helpful to increase awareness and support the decision-making process, thus improving the outcomes (Workman 2008). Regarding public security, they have been proposed to mitigate security related issues (Meynard et al. 2008; Posuniak et al. 2018; Reiter et al. 2016; Rodger and Pendharkar 2007), showing the importance to gather a succinct picture of the available indicators that authorities need to decide in the most adequate manner. Agencies implementing such tools can easily analyze statistical data to determine where crimes and traffic accidents occur, what types of crime are increasing and decreasing, and where community nuisances like vandalism and noise complaints commonly occur. Agencies can then use that data to shape agency policy and determine where to focus personnel and other crime-fighting resources.

The aim of this paper is to describe the data warehouse implementation that stores the data regarding the SIM4SECURITY project and present the dashboards elaborated with this data. The resulting dashboards are an effective way to support decision-makers to create insights about the demographic and crime data in the framework of SIM4SECURITY project, and to create location-allocation scenarios for security forces.

This paper is organized as follows. Section 2 portrays the description of the data collection and its interpretation. Section 3 shows the design and conception of the analytical model. The implementation of the dashboard is presented in Sect. 4. Some final considerations are included in Sect. 5.

2 Data Collection and Interpretation

To the development of the dashboard, Business Intelligence tools are used for the collection and management of transactional data and its transformation and usage in a multidimensional data model.

Concerning the data sources to be used for the development of the data model, the following information was collected:

- Demographic and social economic data obtained through Statistics Portugal (INE);
- Crime data by municipality obtained through Direcção-Geral da Política de Justiça (DGPJ);
- Police stations, location and allocation of police officers provided by Guarda Nacional Republicana (GNR);
- Demographic projections computed by researchers of NOVA Information Management School (NOVA IMS);
- Map of the Administrative regions of Continental Portugal (CAOP) obtained through the Directorate-General for Territorial Development (DGT); and
- Land Cover Land Use (LCLU) map for Continental Portugal for 2012 and LCLU map projections for 2030 and 2040, computed by researchers of NOVA IMS.

The socioeconomic data included in the data model refers to educational levels of population, labor indicators (employment and unemployment rates), social welfare system (social benefits, pensions, power of purchase, mean income, unemployment subsidies) and municipality budget for different activities (environment, sports, culture). Population data is disaggregated by age group, sex and is provided by municipality and parish (the lower level of the Portuguese administrative divisions).

Crime data from Portugal are publicly available from DGPJ (*Directorate-General for Justice Policy*). DGJP is the body, within the Ministry of Justice, responsible for the justice statistical data. Empowered by the National Statistics Institute, it is entrusted with the collecting, use, treatment and analysis of the justice statistical data as well as the dissemination within the national statistical framework. DGPJ provides official justice statistics, namely the crimes recorded by the different security forces, per year (since 1993), type of crime (levels 1—class, 2—subclass and 3—crime designation) and geographic location (NUTS, district and municipality). The level 1 (class type) distinguishes crimes as: crimes against people, crimes against property, crimes against cultural identity and individual integrity, crimes against life in society, crimes against the State, crimes against pet animals, and crimes typified in specific legislation. Each of these classes are divided in subclasses.

The data regarding police stations and the location and allocation of police officers was only provided by GNR, that is a police force that acts mainly in rural areas. The police stations data refers to theirs action areas (i.e. the parish or parishes that are patrolled by the police officers that belong to a certain police station), the hierarchy in which a police station belongs (i.e. *Comando, Destacamento* e *Posto Territorial*) the number of police officers allocated to a police station and the coordinates of a police station location.

The demographic projections refer to the data collected from the census 2011, that served as the basis to compute the demographic projections for 2030 and 2040 by parish. To compute the projections, the cohort-component method was used.

The administrative regions data is available from DGT (Directorate-General for Territorial Development). DGT is the national public institution responsible for the public policies of territorial management and urbanism as well by the creation and maintenance of reference geographic databases.

The LCLU map for 2012 is based on the Corine Land Cover 2012 provided by the European Environmental Agency (EEA) and is composed by eight LCLU classes. The LCLU projections for 2030 and 2040 were obtained using the Land Change Model (LCM).

After a filtering process, the indicators and attributes were selected, resulting in seven tables. In this filtering process the rational was to join the indicators regarding police, crime and demography, for its spatial location (i.e. by municipality or parish depending on the data availability). Through these tables with transactional data, the indicators and attributes were extracted, transformed and loaded in analytical tables through an extraction, transformation and load (ETL) process, that allowed the elaboration of a data warehouse. The indicators and the description of their attributes are presented in the following tables. In Table 1 are presented the attributes and respective description of police officers table.

The attributes and respective description of social economic data are presented in Table 2.

Table 1 Police officers table (Efectivos) (data privacy: private; source: GNR)

Attributes	Description
DICOFRE	Parish code
Actuação	Security force responsible for the parish
Comando	GNR *Comando* responsible for the parish
Destacamento	GNR *Destacamento* responsible for the parish
Posto	GNR *Posto territorial* responsible for the parish
PostoID	*Posto territorial* code
Efectivo	Number of police officers allocated to a *Posto territorial*
Longitude	Longitude of the *Posto territorial* location
Latitude	Latitude of the *Posto territorial* location

Table 2 Social economic table (socecon_data2011) (data privacy: public; source: INE)

Attributes	Description
Município	Municipality designation
DICO	Municipality code
Índice	Social economic index code
Valor	Social economic value

Table 3 Social economic metadata table (socecon_meta) (data privacy: public; source: INE)

Attributes	Description
Índice	Social economic index code
Description	Social economic index description

Table 4 Population table (pop_summary) (data privacy: public/private; source: INE/ NOVA IMS)

Attributes	Description
DICOFRE	Parish code
Nome	Parish designation
Pop_2011	Population by parish for 2011
Pop_2030	Estimated population by parish for 2030
Pop_2040	Estimated population by parish for 2040

In Table 3 are presented the attributes and respective description of social economic metadata.

The attributes and respective description of population data are presented in Table 4.

In Table 5 are presented the attributes and respective description of LCLU data.

In Table 6 are presented the attributes and respective description regarding crime data.

The crime metadata table is presented in Table 7.

Table 5 LCLU table (uso_solo) (data privacy: private; source: NOVA IMS)

Attributes	Description
DICOFRE	Parish code
Classe	Land cover/land use (LCLU) class
Area_Km^2	LCLU area in square kilometres
Area_ha	LCLU area in square hectares
Ano	LCLU reference year

Table 6 Crime table (crime_hist) (data privacy: public; source: DGPJ)

Attributes	Description
Território	Territorial unit nomenclature (NUTS I)
Distrito	District designation
Município	Municipality designation
Ano	Recorded year for the respective crime
Eventos	Number of occurrences regarding the respective crime
Índice	Intern nomenclature for the crime description

Table 7 Crime metadata table (crime_meta) (data privacy: public; source: DGPJ)

Attributes	Description
Classe	Class regarding crime classification (level 1 crime)
SubClasse	Sub class regarding crime classification (level 2 crime)
Crime	Crime designation and respective code (level 3 crime)
Descrição	Crime designation (level 3 crime)
Índice	Intern nomenclature for the crime description

3 Analytical Model Design and Conception

Before data can be structured as a data warehouse, it must be subject to an ETL process. The ETL process is composed by three steps in which data is manipulated, namely; (1) the extract step in which the data is extracted from the different source systems, making it accessible for further processing; (2) the transform step in which the data is subject to a set of rules to transform the data from the source to the target; and (3) the load step in which the data is loaded for a database.

In the extract step the data was gathered/provided from the different sources (described in the previous section) in the form of excel files (demographic, social economic, crime, police stations and demographic projections data), vector files for CAOP and land cover and land use for Continental Portugal.

For the data transformation the adequate tables structure was created for data storage using Visual Basic scripts. This process was particularly necessary for crime data obtained through DGPJ website, given that the initial data set was provided in a pivot table format. The demographic data was aggregated by age and sex to represent only the population total of the data for 2011 and projections for 2030 and 2040. To have a spatial representation of the allocation of police officers, demographic and crime, this data was joined to CAOP. The LCLU data for each parish was obtained intersecting this data with CAOP. The transactional tables were manipulated and transformed in analytical tables with the use of implemented scripts in SQL Server Integration Services.

These tables were then loaded in a data warehouse and the ETL process was concluded.

The data warehouse design was developed in a snowflake schema, composed by four facts tables (*Demografia–Demography*, *Crime*, *Território–Territory* e *Segurança–Security*) and seven dimensions tables (*Ano–Year*, *Socioeconómico–Socioeconomic*, *Crime*, *UsoSolo–LandUse*, *Postos–Stations*, *Município–Municipality* and *Freguesia–Parish*). In the dimensions tables the attributes and metadata were stored for each component of the data warehouse, while in the facts tables the metrics and indicators were stored, aggregated by type of transaction. The use of a snowflake schema allowed the removal of low cardinality attributes and allow the reduction of tables where is the need of an update if data are modified. As the spatial dimension was normalized into two lookup tables, this aspect allowed the representation of a hierarchy in separate tables (i.e. the hierarchy established in the spatial dimension between *Município–Municipality* and *Freguesia–Parish*). The dimension *Ano–Year* is linked with each one the four facts table. This dimension includes the years regarding demographic, territory and security data (i.e. data for 2011 and projections for 2030 and 2040) along with the years regarding crime recording (i.e. crime data between 1993 and 2016). The *Socioeconómico–Socioeconomic* dimension is linked to the *Demografia–Demography* fact table, including in this manner social and economic data provided by the last *census* relatively to 2011. The *Crime* dimension stores the classification and description of crime data and is linked to *Crime* fact table that stores the number of crimes. The fact *Território–Territory* table stores the area of each land use class (*Área por solo*) by hectar and is linked to to the dimension *UsoSolo–LandUse* that have the land use nomenclature used to describe land use in the framework of SIM4SECURITY project. The fact *Segurança–Security* table stores the number of inhabitants by parish along with the population density and the number of police officers by 1000 inhabitants and is linked to the dimension *Postos–Stations* that have the description of the police stations together with the respective operation parishes of each one. Two spatial dimensions were also defined namely *Município–Municipality* and *Freguesia–Parish*. The *Município–Municipality* dimension is linked to *Demografia–Demography* and *Crime* fact table that have their information aggregated to municipality level. The facts *Território–Territory* and *Segurança–Security* tables have their information disaggregated to parish level and are linked to the dimension *Freguesia–Parish*.

Figure 1 presents the snowflake schema of the data warehouse for the SIM4SECURITY project.

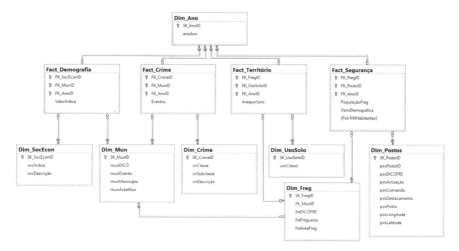

Fig. 1 SIM4SECURITY data model structured as a data warehouse

4 Dashboard Implementation

With the elaboration of the dashboard it is possible to create the analytical capabilities necessary to the visualization of metrics and variables combined in a dashboard. Dashboards allow the monitoring, visualization and analysis of critical information in decision support, in a simple and objective manner, allowing the revelation of relations that would be difficult to identify analyzing each dimension individually.

In the framework of SIM4SECURITY project six dashboard reports were elaborated using Power BI Desktop, as described below:

1. An overview report with a high-level perspective of the data under study, gathering the main facts stored in the Data Warehouse (Fig. 2).
2. A crime analytical report with in-depth analysis of the relevant metrics and the role of certain socioeconomic indicators as risk factors (Fig. 3).
3. A demographic analytical report with in-depth analysis of the relevant metrics and the evolution of demography throughout the country for the next years (Fig. 4).
4. A crime details report for a customized, low-level analysis, given the security coverage, location and year (Fig. 5).
5. A demographic details report for a customized, low-level analysis, given the land usage, location and year (Fig. 6).
6. A socioeconomic details report for a customized, low-level analysis, given the indices correlation to the main facts and location (Fig. 6).

The overview report "Visão Geral" portrayed in Fig. 2 shows the four different general themes contained in this dashboard framework: Crimes, population density,

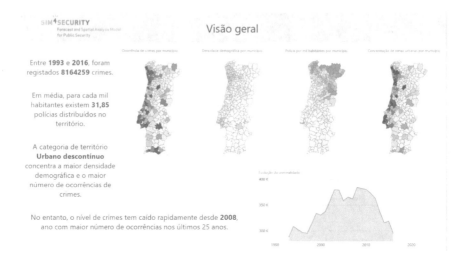

Fig. 2 Overview dashboard view

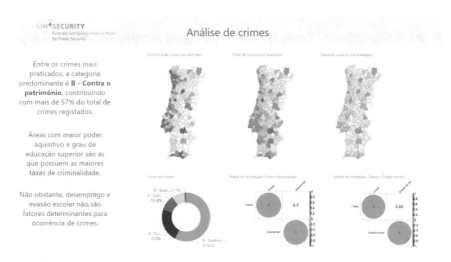

Fig. 3 Crime analysis dashboard view

police (per 1000 inhabitants) and the concentration of urban areas by municipality. On the left side of the dashboard it is possible to observe an overall summary from each of the themes displayed in the maps. On the bottom it is also possible to check the estimation of one of the above-mentioned themes through time, clicking on a municipality of a specific map theme.

Figure 3 shows the crime analytical report provided by the determination of correlations between the different socioeconomic indicators. In the provided Figure,

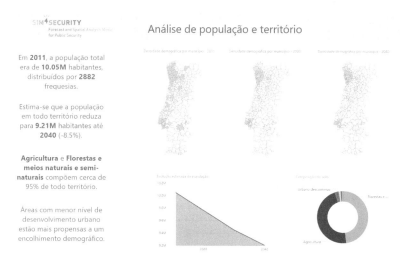

Fig. 4 Population and territory dashboard view

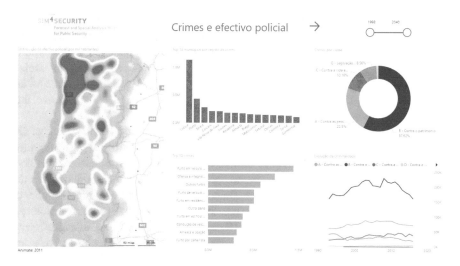

Fig. 5 Crime and security coverage details view

education levels and labor parameters are correlated with the crime occurrence. On the top, maps from the different indicators show the values of each by municipality. A pie chart on the bottom presents the percentage of each class, and correlation matrices between crime and school dropout and crime and unemployment rate are also depicted. Some remarks are provided in the left. The analysis can also be focused on one given municipality, by clicking on the map on the desired one.

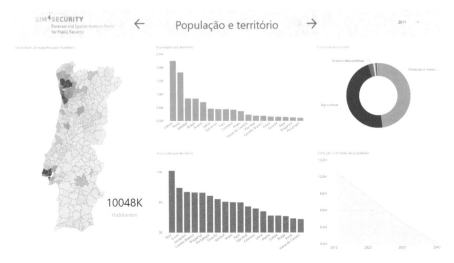

Fig. 6 Population and territory details view

Figure 4 provides the analysis of population throughout the territory. Maps of population density in three different time periods, 2011, 2030 and 2040, are shown in the top of the report. A chart of the population growth is depicted in the bottom, as well as some figures of the different land uses. A summary regarding population characteristics is presented on the left side of the report. By clicking in one of the municipalities in the maps, the interface changes to specifically characterize that indicated municipality.

Figure 5 gathers the relationships between criminality and security forces. On the left side of the report, an animated distribution of the security forces (provided in a ratio per 1000 inhabitants) is presented in time, where it is possible to observe the concentration of security forces in the north sea coast and in Lisbon areas. In the top of the report, a chart shows the top 10 municipalities with the highest number of recorded crimes (throughout time). A pie chart provided the crimes per class (in percentage). On the bottom, the top 10 crimes (by level 3—designation) with highest number of recorded crimes and the variation of level 1 class crimes are shown. With the exception of the latter, the other four views can be customized by the year of occurrence. This report can be incremented with additional data, specifically the criminality projections up to 2040, once they are finalized.

Figure 6 provides additional details to the population and territory indicators. The population density is shown by municipality in the left side. A bar chart indicates the population by district and a pie chart shows the distribution of the land uses in mainland Portugal (top). The bottom of this view reveals the area of each municipality and the variation of the population, provided by the demographic projections. In this view, it is possible to visualize these indicators in different time periods.

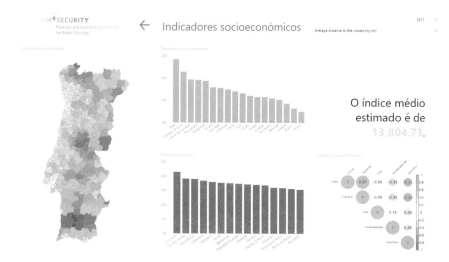

Fig. 7 Social economic indicators view

Finally, the details of the socioeconomic indicators are provided in the view presented by Fig. 7. This view is customized by the socioeconomic indicator and by the year. A map, on the left side, presents the distribution of the selected socioeconomic indicator, by municipality, throughout mainland Portugal. A bar chart, by district, shown the same indicator, in the corresponding average value, on the top, and by municipality, on the bottom. A correlation matrix is presented, providing the relation between the different data dimensions for the selected year. This graphical analysis is accompanied by some remarks, containing a summary of what is observed in the view.

The prepared dashboard enables additional analysis that previously could only be observed in separate, in the format of a paper report. It is now easier to look at different data displays (charts and the geographic distribution of a variable represented in a map) at a time, that can be customized by selecting the year or the specific desired indicator. Additional to this advanced analysis, the dashboard allows the simultaneous visualization of the different data dimensions and correlation among them.

It is relevant also to refer the analytical potential brought by the adoption of a business intelligence approach a dimensional database model since it support data navigation within the hierarchies of the different dimension (when available) as it is presented in Fig. 8 where it is possible to observe the drill-down capability within the crime type dimension.

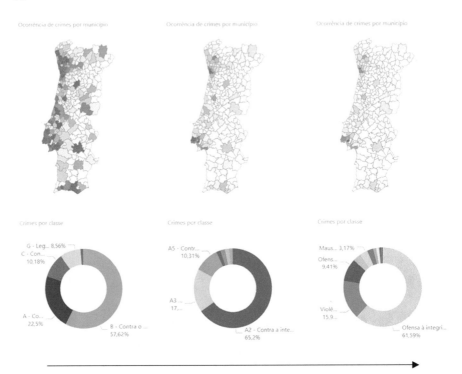

Fig. 8 Navigation within the crime type hierarchy

5 Conclusion

The distribution optimization of police forces along mainland Portugal territory is the main goal to be achieved in SIM4SECURITY project. To achieve this goal a GIS model was elaborated along with the development of future demographic and crime scenarios. The amount of data that was collected from different sources, represented a challenge in which for being able to have insights for decision making purposes, this data had to be subject to an ETL process. A data warehouse was then elaborated, where the data collected was stored. In order to support analytical capabilities this data warehouse is very important in various aspects namely to provide interconnection between the various dimensions and metrics of the variables in study and to feed the dashboards developed in the framework of the SIM4SECURITY project.

The multidimensional model approach adopted in the SIM4SECURITY project data warehouse was fundamental for data visualization and storytelling to support the dashboard construction and furthermore to allow its dynamic behavior which is critical for visual analysis and insights generation by manipulating and filtering the available facts under the different dimensions.

The resulting dashboards allowed a better understanding of the relations between crime and demographic variables and showed that they are a very useful tool that could aid in the decision-making process to optimize the allocation of security forces along the mainland Portugal territory.

The key points observed by these reports are:

- Crimes and population are in constant decline over the past years. Population is expected to shrink 8.5% by 2040, while crime is close to reaching an all-time low (considering the historical data collected for the past 25 years). These findings reinforce the high correlation shared between these two variables.
- GNR's security forces are mostly concentrated in the countryside, especially in northern Portugal (measured by one police officer per thousand inhabitants). Given that over 95% of the country's land usage refers to agriculture and forests, and the urbanization rate is relatively low, this phenomenon could be caused by the higher pace to which non-urban areas are being "depopulated".
- Urban areas are more likely to have higher crime rates. They also present higher purchasing power per capita and education levels. Meanwhile, unemployment and school dropout rates have shown no correlation to the crime phenomena.
- Over 57% of all crime records in Portugal refer to crimes against property. This category also showed higher variance throughout the years when compared to other crime categories.

Despite the interesting insights provided by the dashboards, the data used to elaborate them, and the data warehouse, several limitations were identified, namely: (1) the crime data is disaggregated only until municipality level, while population data is disaggregated to parish level; (2) the data regarding security forces is only for GNR, that have their main actuation areas in rural zones; (3) the DGPJ database have some year gaps regarding some crimes. Overcoming these limitations would certainly result in better insights retrieved from the dashboards since with the presently available data it is only possible to present information that can be useful in macro decision-making regarding crime (i.e. to adjust national and regional allocation of police forces).

For future developments it would be interesting to have crime records at parish level from both national Portuguese police forces (i.e. PSP and GNR), the number of police forces and the actuation areas for PSP also at parish level. With this additional data it would be possible to make the analysis at local level, providing a better disaggregated view for an optimized, efficient location-allocation of security forces.

References

Adam, F., & Pomerol, J. C. (2008). Developing practical decision support tools using dashboards of information. In F. Burnstein & C. W. Holsapple (Eds.), *Handbook on decision support systems 2* (pp. 151–173). Heidelberg: Springer, Berlin.

Bravo, J. (2016). *Projecções de População Residente a Nível Concelhio – Metodologia.* Universidade Nova de Lisboa, Information Management School, Novembro 2016.

Few, S. (2006). *Information dashboard design: The effective visual communication of data,* O'Reilly.

Meynard, J. B., Chaudet, H., Texier, G., Queyriaux, B., Deparis, X., & Boutin, J. P. (2008). Real time epidemiological surveillance within the armed forces; concepts, realities and prospects in France. *Revue D Epidemiologie et de Sante Publique, 56*(1), 11–20. https://doi.org/10.1016/j.respe.2007.11.003.

Paine, K. D. (2004). Using dashboard techniques to track communication. *Strategic Communication Management, 8*(5), 30–33.

Petrov, A. (2012). One hundred years of dasymetric mapping: back to the origin. *The Cartographic Journal, 49*(3), 256–264. https://doi.org/10.1179/1743277412Y.0000000001.

Posuniak, P., Kowalski, K., Wrobel, T., & Kresa, P. (2018). The equipment of a modern police patrol car and the safety of the crew. In *11th International Scientific and Technical Conference on Automotive Safety Proceedings,* April 18–20, 2018, Casta Papiernicka, Slovakia.

Reiter, R. M., Ganchenko, K., & Charalambidou, A. (2016). Requests and counters in Russian traffic police officer-citizen encounters face and identity implications. *Pragmatics and Society, 7*(4), 512–539. https://doi.org/10.1075/ps.7.4.01mar.

Ribeiro, S., Cabral, P., Henriques, R., Bravo, J., Rodrigues, T., & Painho, M. (2018). Modelação do crescimento urbano para a distribuição eficaz das forças de Segurança. O caso português. *Proelium, VII*(14), 39–62.

Rodger, J., & Pendharker, P. (2007). Lessons learned from testing, analyzing and problem solving an online military watchboard medical decision support system (MWMDSS) application: Potential implications for civilian and e-Government organizations, In Remenyi, D. (Ed.), *ICEG 2007: Proceedings of the 3rd international conference on e-Government,* p. 215, 3rd International Conference on e-Government, September 27–28, 2007, Montreal, Canada.

Rodrigues, T. (2014). Population dynamics. Demography matters. In *Globalization and International Security. An overview* (pp. 57–74). New York: NOVA Publishers.

Teixeira, N. S., Lourenço, N., & Piçarra, N. (2006). *Estudo Para a Reforma do Modelo de Organização do Sistema de Segurança Interna.* IPRI: Relatório preliminar.

Workman, M. (2008). An experimental assessment of semantic apprehension of graphical linguistics. *Computer Human Behavior, 24*(6), 2578–2596.

Shedding Light on Shadow IT: Definition, Related Concepts, and Consequences

Gabriela Labres Mallmann⑩, Aline de Vargas Pinto⑩ and Antônio Carlos Gastaud Maçada⑩

Abstract The use of Information Technology (IT) without formal approval and support of the IT department, called shadow IT, has challenged organizations to rethink ways of managing IT resources in order to cope with the use of unauthorized technologies in the workplace. We review the literature on shadow IT to shed light on this phenomenon, discussing the conceptual definition and types, the related concepts, and its consequences. This study, then, is an effort to better understand the phenomenon based on the existing literature. We provide contributions by enhancing the emerging body of knowledge on shadow IT, as well as by suggesting research gaps to be addressed in future research in order to advance on the topic.

Keywords Shadow IT · Workarounds · IT consumerization · BYOD · Literature review

1 Introduction

The organizational IT department is no longer the only provider of information technology (IT) used by employees in the business processes. Many individuals and workgroups have autonomously implemented and used technological solutions not provided by the IT department to perform work tasks. These unauthorized or unknown information technologies to the IT department used by employees to perform their work tasks has been called shadow IT (e.g., Haag and Eckhardt 2017).

G. L. Mallmann (✉) · A. de Vargas Pinto · A. C. G. Maçada
UFRGS, Porto Alegre, Brazil
e-mail: gabilmallmann@gmail.com

A. de Vargas Pinto
e-mail: alinevargas01@hotmail.com

A. C. G. Maçada
e-mail: acgmacada@ea.ufrgs.br

© Springer Nature Switzerland AG 2019
I. Ramos et al. (eds.), *Information Systems for Industry 4.0*,
Lecture Notes in Information Systems and Organisation 31,
https://doi.org/10.1007/978-3-030-14850-8_5

The magnitude of the phenomenon shadow IT is increasing over the last years because people are more familiar with technologies, which are readily available nowadays and, sometimes, free of charge. Thereby, it is easier for employees to adopt and use technologies beyond the ones provided by the organization. Consequently, it has been increasingly difficult for IT managers to administrate the growing variety of systems and the risks arising from it (Fürstenau and Rothe 2014). The Ponemon Institute, for example, argues that the average data breach in 2015 costs to businesses an average of $4 million, being 70% of unauthorized data access committed by the organization's own employees (Globalscape 2016). However, when an employee's action puts the organization at risk, there may be no malicious intent, but rather a need to be productive (e.g., Zimmermann et al. 2017; Mallmann et al. 2018a, b). Moreover, in some cases, employees are not aware of or do not understand the organization's information security policies (e.g., Haag and Eckhardt 2014; Silic et al. 2017).

Shadow IT is, then, gaining relevance in practice and attracting the attention of managers and researchers. Shadow systems and related concepts, such as workarounds, have received wide attention due to the popularization of cloud computing services (Müller et al. 2015), bring your own device policies (BOYD) (Miller et al. 2012), IT workarounds (Alter 2014), and other important trends in the IT consumerization scenario (Harris et al. 2012). Motivated by this context, this study aims to shed light on the shadow IT phenomenon, presenting and discussing its definition and types, related concepts and consequences of use. In that sense, this work contributes by answering, through a literature review, the following research questions: RQ1: What is the conceptual definition of shadow IT and how can the different instances of shadow IT be classified? RQ2: What concepts are relevant when investigating shadow IT and how are these concepts related? RQ3: What are the positive and negative consequences of using shadow IT?

Although shadow IT is not a new phenomenon, it can be considered relatively unexplored and the current knowledge is still limited and scarce (e.g., Silic et al. 2017; Haag and Eckhartd 2017). The academic literature on shadow IT is focused on exploratory studies, which mainly discuss the benefits and drawbacks of these technologies for companies (e.g., Fürstenau and Rothe 2014; Silic and Back 2014), as well as governance mechanisms to control these unauthorized technologies (e.g., Györy et al. 2012; Zimmermann et al. 2014). Thus, the need for a literature review on shadow IT is justified by the scarcity of theoretical-conceptual approaches in studying the subject (e.g., Haag and Eckhartd 2017).

We aim, thus, to gather the findings on shadow IT to contribute to the understanding of the phenomenon, which is crucial to advance the knowledge on the subject (Webster and Watson 2002). Another contribution of this study is to present the relation of shadow IT with related concepts. Haag and Eckhardt (2017) state that some concepts studied in the IS field share attributes with shadow IT, such as BYOD, IT consumerization and workaround, but it is important to recognize the aspects that differentiate them, allowing the characterization of shadow IT as unique and relevant concept. Finally, this study also may contribute to discuss some consequences that arise from the use of shadow IT once knowing the unauthorized technologies and its possible consequences can help mitigate risks by effectively redesigning existing workflows and/or technological systems (Vogus and Hilligoss 2016).

This article is organized in sections. Section 2 presents the literature review on the topic. Section 3 describes the method used. The analysis of the results is presented in Sect. 4. Next, the results are discussed, identifying research gaps and providing theoretical and practical contributions.

2 Related Work

The literature on shadow IT has gained relevance over the last few years. Since 2012, the number of published academic papers on the subject has increased considerably. The vast majority of studies on shadow IT are recent, being more than 70% of publications dated from the last four years (2014–2017). In this sense, the subject can be considered little explored yet, although it has gained notoriety in the academia over the years. The first articles on the subject discuss the emergence of shadow IT after the adoption of ERPs (Enterprise Resource Planning), for example, the creation and use of Excel spreadsheets to perform the work tasks instead of using the official ERP system implemented by organization (e.g., Jones et al. 2004; Behrens and Sedara 2004; Raden 2005).

From 2012, the studies have approached shadow IT at the organizational level, focusing on IT governance mechanisms to cope with the use of shadow IT in organizations, minimizing security risks (e.g., Györy et al. 2012; Zimmermann and Rentrop 2014; Fürstenau et al. 2017; Zimmermann et al. 2017). From 2014, studies have investigated shadow IT as a behavior that deviates from organizational policies, for example, by investigating motivations and antecedents that drive the use of shadow IT from the employee perspective, as well as the relationship between the use of shadow IT and individual performance (e.g., Haag and Eckhardt 2014; Haag et al. 2015).

The term shadow IT, although not recent, still lacks a widely accepted definition and a better understanding of what the phenomenon is and how it occurs inside organizations. The topic can then be considered relatively unexplored and the current knowledge is still limited (e.g., Silic et al. 2017; Haag and Eckhartd 2017). In addition, previous studies (e.g., Silic and Back 2014; Huber et al. 2017; Zimmermann et al. 2017) have proposed that there are many instances of shadow IT within organizations once shadow IT can be hardware, software or any other solution such as a spreadsheet, cloud services, or an employee-developed application. Thereby, the topic lacks a conceptual discussion, being necessary also to clarify the differences among related concepts and the consequences of the use (Haag and Eckhardt 2017).

2.1 Related Concepts

2.1.1 IT Consumerization

IT consumerization (ITC) represents the impact exerted by market technologies on organizations. Harris et al. (2012) argue that the popularization of devices and applications originating in the consumer sector is causing a second individual-oriented IT revolution. The presence of innovations from the consumerization sector are increasing within companies this tendency, called IT consumerization, has changed the way companies manage technology and continuously bringing new challenges for IT managers (Weiss and Leimeister 2012).

Weiss and Leimeister (2012) present a model of individual's expectations changes to explain the origin of the consumerization trend. According to these authors, what drives employees to use market technologies is an expectation of high-level user experience and their expectation of new application options by the organizational IT department. However, it is not always possible to IT department to provide new and many technological options to satisfy users, and whether the solution offered by the IT department failed in meeting employees' expectations, they tend to find and adopt consumer market technologies by their-selves. This tendency is more prominent among higher positions, such as managers and supervisors (Weiss and Leimeister 2012), and among a new generation of technology users, called in the literature as tech savvy or digital natives (Harris et al. 2012; Silic and Back 2014; Weiss and Leimeister 2012).

According to Harris et al. (2012), the ITC may have different definitions depending on the stakeholder. From the employee's perspective, ITC is related to individual use and familiarity with devices and applications of the user's personal life, which are seen as useful when used at work. From the perspective of the company's IT department, ITC is a vast amount of devices and applications used within the organization that may not be part of the sanctioned solutions list or that have not been formally approved by the IT department and can be seen either as a threat or as an opportunity. From the market perspective, ITC can be considered as any device or application that originates in the consumer market, and it is not, at least in the beginning, the target of the organization as a solution to be used together or replace the current information technology used by the company.

2.1.2 Workaround

Workaround is conceptualized by Alter (2014) as adaptations of the systems and resources provided by the company with the purpose to overcome constraints that make impossible or harder the completion of tasks in an effective way (Malaurent and Avison 2015). Workaround can be a strategy of using a system in a way that is not expected to be used or using alternative methods to solve an immediate and urgent problem (Azad and King 2008). Typical examples of workaround are the adjustment or manipulation of data to arrive at desired results (Alojairi 2017).

Many organizations consider that workaround is composed of temporary practices implemented to deal with uncertainties, for example, after a system's implementation, with the understanding that workarounds may decrease over time. However, pieces of evidence suggest that these practices actually evolve over time rather than disappear and may lead to the use of alternative technologies (Azad and King 2012). Many alternative solutions occur because the mandatory technology does not fit the work needs (Alter 2014). Consequently, an alternative solution may be necessary for employees to support their daily activities (Azad and King 2012) and facilitate user interaction when the official system is not well planned (Ferneley and Sobreperez 2006).

2.1.3 BYOx

The concept of Bring Your Own Anything (BYOx) can be related to the concepts discussed here since it concerns the adoption and use of technologies brought by the employee to the workplace. BYOx is a term that encompasses various BYO trends in organizations such as Bring Your Own Device (BYOD) and Bring Your Own Cloud (BYOC), etc. (e.g., French et al. 2014; Haag 2015).

The term BYOD is the most widely known and, therefore, the most discussed in the academic literature. BYOD is conceptualized as a policy that allows users to access work applications from their personal mobile devices (Dang-pham and Pittayachawan 2015). BYOD allows employees to bring their own computing devices to work and incorporate them into the organization's network rather than using company-owned devices (French et al. 2014). This can be considered a policy and strategy developed by organizations to deal with the tendency of employees to adopt and use their own solutions in the workplace.

2.1.4 Cloud Computing

By definition, cloud computing is a model that allows ubiquitous and convenient access over the Internet to a shared pool of configurable computing resources that can be quickly provisioned and released with minimal management effort or interaction with service providers (Mell and Grance 2011). The primary feature of cloud computing is the ability to acquire and manage data whenever the user requests (Lis and Paula 2015). Among the driving forces behind the use of cloud computing, we highlight the possibility of accessing application services without the need for any detailed or specific knowledge of the infrastructure used to deliver the features. Moreover, the services can be accessed virtually from anywhere using any device because applications are web-based (Shin 2015), allowing users to share information and knowledge more easily (Park and Ryoo 2013). The cloud services have brought revolutionary changes in the way solutions are designed, built, delivered, and managed. Therefore, given the facilities to access and use cloud resources, it enables a favorable scenario for users to adopt and use cloud services without the organizational IT department approval or support (Khalil et al. 2017).

3   Method

The research method of this paper is a literature review based on the guidelines proposed by Webster and Watson (2002). As shadow IT is still underexplored, a literature review can corroborate by creating a solid foundation for knowledge advance (Webster and Watson 2002). Thus, gathering knowledge from existing studies is essential for the evolution of the topic understanding.

Overall, we divided the research into two steps to achieve the objectives proposed by this study. First, we selected articles from several databases, considering the criteria of inclusion and exclusion. Second, the data collection and the analysis were performed based on three main categories. These steps are detailed below.

The articles search was carried out based on a research protocol. First, as suggested by Webster and Watson (2002), we performed a search in the leading journals of IS field ('AIS basket eight'). Next, we searched in scientific databases such as ScienceDirect, Web of Knowledge, Google Scholar, and EBSCO. We also searched in the databases of the Association for Information System—AIS Electronic Library (AISeL), which contains papers from the most significant conferences of Information Systems, such as the International Conference on Information Systems (ICIS) and the European Conference on Information Systems (ECIS). A broader source of articles is justified because most of the literature on shadow IT comes from international conferences, being necessary to expand the search to conferences as well. The number of publication on the topic has been increasing over the years. However, it still can be considered an emerging literature.

The following keywords were used to find the relevant articles: shadow IT and shadow systems, which should appear in the title, abstract or keywords. The following words served as exclusion criteria: workarounds, end-user-computing, and bring your own device (BYOD), because although they share similarities, they are different from the term shadow IT (Rentrop and Zimmermann 2012; French et al. 2014; Haag and Eckhardt 2017). Those concepts were used later, in the analysis, to identify the differences among shadow IT and related concepts.

Considering the research protocol, 50 relevant articles were selected that bring shadow IT as the central theme. The search was carried out between March and May 2018. Table 1 presents the articles selected according to the inclusion and exclusion criteria of articles.

We used Excel to tabulate and analyze data, dividing the analysis into three main categories. First, the definition and types, where we collected the definitions and approaches from previous studies, as well as instances of shadow IT. Second, the relationship among shadow IT and related concepts, where we gathered the characteristics of shadow IT that differentiate it from the other concepts. Third and last,

Table 1 Selected articles

Source		Number of articles
Journal	Network Security	2
	Computer & Security	1
	Information & Management	1
	Others (Computer Fraud & Security, CAIS, Journal of Information Systems, etc.)	9
	Total	13
Conference	AMCIS	8
	ECIS	7
	ICIS	5
	PACIS	5
	Others (ACIS, ICDS, BLED, ECKM, Confirm …)	12
	Total	37
Total		50

we identified the most prolific consequences of shadow IT in the literature, gathering positive and negative outcomes to organizations. Below we present our findings based on these three main categories.

4 Results

4.1 Conceptualizing Shadow IT

According to previous studies, shadow IT is defined as any hardware, software or services created, introduced and used by employees without explicit approval or even without the knowledge of the organization (Silic and Back 2014; Haag and Eckhardt 2017). Users implement shadow systems autonomously within the business units; consequently, these technologies have no technical or strategic relationship with the organization's IT service management (Zimmermann et al. 2014). Thereby, shadow IT represents the unauthorized or, sometimes, unknown technologies used by employees at work.

Another important point to define shadow IT is the user's intention to adopt unauthorized technology, defined by Györy et al. (2012) as well-intentioned, although it does not comply with organizational policies. The term "shadow" implies an illicit and malicious behavior. However, most shadow IT cases occur by convenience (Walters 2013). Thus, shadow IT is intentionally implemented by employees to perform and complete work tasks as a support solution to the business process, and not with malicious intentions such as to cause economic harm to the organization (e.g., Györy et al. 2012; Silic and Back 2014; Haag and Eckhardt 2014).

Differing from previous studies, recent investigations (e.g., Haag et al. 2015; Mallmann et al. 2018a, b) have addressed shadow IT from a behavioral approach. These studies are based on the concept called individual shadow IT usage proposed by Haag and Eckhardt (2014), which defines the use of shadow IT as the voluntary use of any IT resource that violates workplace standards as a reaction to perceived situational constraints with the intention of improving work performance without, however, harming the organization. This definition argues that shadow IT users act on their own with the primary goal of efficiently and productively performing their work tasks, which are adversely affected, for example, due to the malfunctioning of the organizational IT solution or inadequate instructions. These restrictions drive employees to deliberately bypass policies and accept potential security risks and damages to the organization's IT assets (Haag and Eckhardt 2014).

4.1.1 Instances of Shadow IT

First studies on shadow IT discuss the emergence of shadow IT after the implementation of Enterprise Resource Planning (ERP) (e.g., Jones et al. 2004; Behrens and Sedara 2004), mainly regarding the use of Excel spreadsheets instead ERP tools implemented by the company. However, due to technological advances, recent studies (e.g., Silic and Back 2014; Mallmann et al. 2018a, b) have presented other shadow IT occurrences, such as the use of social media and cloud-based services (e.g., Dropbox and Google Apps). Silic and Back (2014), for example, divide the types of shadow software found in their exploratory study into two groups: internal and external. Internal shadow software is software installed on organizational devices, while external shadow software is provided by external services such as cloud-based services.

The existing literature suggests that the occurrences of shadow IT may be applications, spreadsheets, cloud services, mobile devices, or a combination of these instances (e.g., Silic and Back 2014; Huber et al. 2016; Zimmermann et al. 2017). As an effort to clarify how individuals use shadow IT in the workplace, we sought in the literature how these technologies have been occurred in practice according to previous studies. Table 2 summarizes the four types of shadow IT based on the literature.

Four types of shadow IT have emerged from the literature review. The first one, called unapproved cloud services, represents unauthorized cloud services accessed through the internet (e.g., Fürstenau and Rothe 2014; Haag 2015; Walterbusch et al. 2017) that does not need to be installed on any device to be used. For example, the use of Dropbox to share content with colleagues or Skype for web to communicate with clients without permission of the IT department. The second type is unauthorized solutions developed and used by employees on organizational devices to perform their work tasks (e.g., Zimmermann et al. 2014; Zimmermann et al. 2017), which can vary from a simple Excel worksheet to a more complex application developed by employees to be used by a whole business unit. For example, the use

Table 2 Types of shadow IT

Shadow IT usage types	Description	Authors
Unapproved cloud services	Use of Internet-based Software and Software as a Service (SaaS) that are not approved or unknown by IT department. These systems are also called Mobile Shadow IT once it can be accessed outside the workplace (e.g., WhatsApp, Facebook, Skype for Web, Dropbox, Google Apps, etc.)	Rentrop and Zimmermann (2012), Györy et al. (2012), Fürstenau and Rothe (2014), Silic and Back (2014), Haag and Eckhardt (2014), Zimmermann, Retrop and Felden (2014), Huber et al. (2016), Walters (2013), Walterbusch, Fietz and Teuteberg (2017)
Self-made solutions	Use of solutions developed by employees on the company's computers to perform their work tasks. For example, an excel spreadsheet or an application developed by employees	Jones et al. (2004), Rentrop and Zimmermann (2012), Fürstenau and Rothe (2014), Zimmermann et al. (2014), Huber et al. (2016)
Self-installed applications	Use of software installed by employees to perform their work tasks, on the company's computers. For example, downloading and installing software available free of charge on the internet	Jones et al. (2004), Rentrop and Zimmermann (2012), Fürstenau and Rothe (2014), Zimmermann et al. (2014), Silic and Back (2014)
Self-acquired devices	Use of devices owned by employees. These devices are purchased directly from retail rather than being ordered through the official catalog of the IT department. It includes the use of applications in the employee's personal devices at the workplace (smartphones, tablets, notebooks, etc.)	Rentrop and Zimmermann (2012), Silic and Back, (2014), Zimmermann et al. (2014), Gozman and Willcocks (2015), Huber et al. (2016)

of an Excel spreadsheet developed for controlling, rather than using the company's official system.

The third type, called self-installed applications, is those unauthorized applications installed and used by employees on enterprise devices, for example, on computers, smartphones, or tablets provided by the organization (e.g., Jones et al. 2004; Silic and Back 2014). This type of shadow IT involves solutions that are generally available free of charge on the Web and need to be downloaded and installed prior to use, rather than accessed via the Internet. Finally, the fourth type represents the self-acquired devices by employees and represents the hardware layer of shadow IT. These are devices purchased, owned and used at work by employees, instead of company devices, without official permission or BYOD policy. This last type includes the use of applications on personal devices on the company's network (e.g., Rentrop and Zimmermann 2012; Zimmermann et al. 2017).

4.2   Shadow IT and Related Concepts

Haag and Eckhardt (2017) point out that shadow IT distinguishes conceptually from other related terms, such as bring-your-own-device (BYOD) and IT consumerization. While these concepts share similarities, there are crucial differences between them. Bellow, we discuss the relationship among shadow IT and related concepts, emphasizing the differences between them.

IT consumerization is a broader concept that encompasses different phenomena related to the use of consumer technologies in the workplace (Harris et al. 2012). The relationship between IT consumerization and shadow IT is due to the fact that consumerization encompasses both the consumer market technologies approved by organizational IT policies and technologies that are not yet included in these policies, that is unauthorized technologies that were not formally approved by the IT department, as it is the case of shadow IT.

Also under the concept of IT consumerization, the term workaround refers, in a broadly way, to conscious adaptations of work activities that are not expected or specified to be altered (Laumer et al. 2017). Haag and Eckhardt (2017) suggest three instances of alternative solutions. First is the non-IT-based workarounds, for example, use of paper to collect and process information. Second, the adaptation of mandatory IT solution and/or approved personal IT, using those solutions in different and unexpected ways, for example, using MS Word to convert and re-edit the content of PDF documents. Third and last, shadow IT, for example, the use of unapproved IT and/or approved IT changed in unapproved ways, for example, by using Dropbox instead of the official cloud-based services to store and share organizational information.

Thus, shadow IT is a type of workaround, although not every workaround is necessarily a shadow IT since workaround encompasses additional features that go beyond shadow IT. Shadow IT is technology-related, as its concept suggests, while workaround may also be related to non-IT devices (e.g., paper). In that sense, workaround is a broader concept that encompasses other instances, including shadow IT, and both terms can be classified as work deviance behavior that deviates or violates organizational policies (e.g., Haag and Eckhardt 2017). Another difference is, according to Lund-Jensen et al. (2016), related to the temporal aspect because workarounds tend to be temporary practices, while shadow IT used to be long-term practices used in daily activities.

In turn, BYOx is a concept often confused with shadow IT. The difference between the two concepts is crucial because it refers to the compliance or not with the IT security policies. In the context of BYOx, the technology brought to the workplace by employees is allowed by the organization through policies developed in conjunction with the IT department (e.g., Dang-pham and Pittayachawan 2015). For example, BYOD policy allows users to bring and use their own devices in the workplace. In the context of shadow IT, however, the solution used by employees is generally unknown by the IT area, and, therefore, neither approved nor supported by the company's IT department (e.g., Rentrop and Zimmermann 2012).

Silic and Back (2014) argue that in the current technological context, where smartphones are being increasingly used at workplace as the case of BYOD policies, shadow IT is becoming even more critical at different organizational levels, also motivated by the fact that users believe they are not doing anything wrong. Therefore, the consequence of BYOx policies in the context of shadow IT is to facilitate the emergence of these unauthorized technologies because the adoption of BYOx policies can increase IT complexity in managing the growing number of devices and applications used by employees, allowing numerous occurrences of shadow IT at work.

Finally, cloud computing emerges as a relevant concept in the context of shadow IT. In addition to mobile devices from the consumer market, Haag and Eckhardt (2015) argue that cloud-computing services have made shadow IT accessible also to people without much IT knowledge since the services are quite simple and intuitive to users, and usually it is delivered free of charge via web browsers. For this reason, many studies (e.g., Silic and Back 2014; Mallmann et al. 2018a, b) present cloud-based services as the primary occurrence of shadow IT, often used by employees in the workplace without authorization from the IT department.

4.3 Consequences of Shadow IT

Although the term "shadow" implies illicit and malicious behavior that jeopardizes the organizational IT security, most shadow IT cases are caused by convenience (Walters 2013). Previous studies suggest that employees use shadow IT to assist them when they are performing their tasks, but not with malicious intention (e.g., Győry et al. 2012; Haag and Eckhardt 2014). Thus, a broader discussion about the positive and negative consequences of the use of shadow is important to understand the impact to organizations.

Productivity and individual performance stand out in recent research as benefits of using shadow IT to perform work tasks (e.g., Silic and Back 2014; Haag and Eckhardt 2014; Haag 2015; Haag et al. 2015; Fürstenau et al. 2017). Empirical studies (e.g., Haag et al. 2015), suggest that shadow IT leverages individual productivity, improving employee work performance. Also related to employee performance, studies have found that employees often use shadow IT to communicate and collaborate at work (e.g., Shumarova and Swatman 2008; Silic and Back 2014), as well as to share information and knowledge among colleagues, clients and external partners (e.g., Steinhüser et al. 2017; Mallmann et al. 2018a, b). In that sense, improvements in communication and collaboration are some of the elements that can lead to increased productivity and individual performance of shadow IT users.

Shadow IT is also often related to innovation, being considered a legitimate driver of IT solutions and process innovation (Fürstenau and Rothe 2014). Haag et al. (2015) argue that the use of shadow IT question the importance of employees autonomy for the emergence of innovative behaviors within organizations because the use of shadow IT seems to be a manifestation of creativity and personal innovation. Thus, the literature also suggests an innovative side of shadow IT driven by employees (Fürstenau and Rothe 2014; Györy et al. 2012; Fürstenau et al. 2017; Singh 2015).

The individual performance improvements, in turn, can have impacts on the organization as a whole. Singh (2015) argues that IT managers who manage shadow IT, instead of just trying to avoid it, can see improvements in organizational performance due to the introduction of users innovations since employees are more satisfied with the tools they use to perform work tasks. Similarly, the empirical findings from Haag et al. (2015) show that, at the individual level, shadow IT users can be valuable to organizations because they are more goal-oriented, effective, and try to find long-term solutions. Thus, managers should also take into account the positive outcomes of using shadow IT, such as employees' productivity improvements and, consequently, organizational performance (Haag and Eckhardt 2015).

The downside of shadow IT, however, persists despite the potential benefits. Many employees are not aware they are deviating from IS policies, jeopardizing the organizational information security (Walters 2013; Silic and Back 2014; Silic et al. 2017). Security risks, therefore, are among the main concerns cited in the literature (e.g., Haag and Eckhardt 2015; Silic and Back 2014). By using shadow IT such as cloud-based applications to upload organizational data without the company's knowledge, it can imply in several security issues, such as information leakage, data loss, data privacy, compliance, etc.

5 Discussion and Final Considerations

This study aimed to review the literature on shadow IT in order to shed light on the phenomenon, presenting and discussing its definition and instances, related concepts and consequences. This section discusses the results, pointing out research gaps on the topic, as well as providing theoretical and practical contributions.

The literature on shadow IT so far has focused on identifying which unauthorized technologies are being used within companies (e.g., Silic and Back 2014), the investigation about employees motivations to adopt these technologies (e.g., Haag and Eckhardt 2015), and governance forms to control shadow IT (e.g., Fürstenau and Rothe 2014). These studies collaborate, primarily, to define shadow IT and its types. Based on the existing research, the present study discusses the conceptual definition of shadow IT, its types and consequences. In addition, the study discusses the differences between shadow IT and related concepts to clarify the unique characteristics of the phenomenon, as suggested by Haag and Eckhardt (2017).

Results suggest that when employees bring technology from the consumer market to use at work and this technology is not in line with organizational policies it can be characterized as shadow IT. Shadow IT, thus, is part of IT consumerization phenomenon, which is different from BYOx policies. These policies, such as BYOD, allow employees to use their own solutions to accomplish their job tasks, within a range of predefined options by the IT department. In short, while shadow IT is a deviant behavior, BYOx is a policy that allows employees to bring and use personal devices and solutions at work (e.g., French et al. 2014). Workarounds, in turn, is also a behavior that deviates from IT norms. However, it is broader than shadow IT because it also includes non-technology based solutions. Finally, cloud-based services are not necessarily shadow IT, but it does relate because many shadow IT used by employees are cloud services due to the ease of accessing and using these services and low barrier costs.

Regarding the consequences, the results suggest that there is still a divergence in the literature about the positive and negative outcomes of shadow IT. Information security risks, data leakage and loss, privacy risk, and compliance are among the main concerns cited in the literature (e.g., Haag and Eckhardt 2015; Silic and Back 2014). In this sense, previous studies (e.g., Haag and Eckhardt 2015) point out the need to balance the pros and cons of shadow IT. Therefore, further studies about the impacts of using shadow IT, such as organizational performance, innovative features, and security issues, would aid to clarify the consequences of shadow IT to mitigate the risks arising from its use and enhance its benefits.

5.1 Research Gaps by Level of Analysis

Previous studies have suggested that shadow IT emerges at the employee level (e.g., Györy et al. 2012; Fürstenau et al. 2017), but can be used by an individual or a group of individuals, emerging an individual and/or collective level of shadow IT usage. However, this perspective at different levels needs further research, including a group-level approach, in addition to the individual level, to understand how the working groups collectively support the use of shadow IT and what are the consequences for the group (Haag and Eckhardt 2017). Studies on shadow IT at the individual level have been developed since 2014 (e.g., Haag and Eckhardt 2014; Haag et al. 2015). Those studies have been analyzing shadow IT as a behavior, called shadow IT usage, as a manner to understand what drives individuals to deviate from IT policies and use shadow IT at work. In line with Haag and Eckhardt (2017), we could not find studies at the collective level of analysis, which suggests the necessity for further studies at group-level to understand the use of shadow IT among work groups, for example, the widespread of shadow IT usage among teams and departments.

The literature also provides evidence for a relationship between the use of shadow IT and age or generation. The dependence on technology for social interaction is increasing, especially among digital natives (Turkle 2011), changing the way we socially interact and bringing many consequences to individuals, organizations, and society. Previous studies have suggested that the use of consumer-based technologies is more prominent among younger generations, called tech-savvy, millennials or generation Y (e.g., Weiss and Leimeister 2012; Turner 2015). Thus, age can be a potential factor in understanding user behavior regarding technology. A generational study on the use of shadow IT can add valuable information about individual behavior in a postmodern society.

At the organizational level, issues such as IT governance should be associated with shadow IT. Studies at this level can seek management practices to deal with the use of unauthorized technologies in the workplace through IT governance approaches, for example, to reduce information security gaps and reduce the risks of overhead in IT infrastructure of the company by users (e.g., Győry et al. 2012).

5.2   Theoretical and Practical Contributions

This study provides theoretical and practical implications for the emerging knowledge on shadow IT. Although not recent, shadow IT is still understudied in the IS literature. This study contributes, in this sense, by providing a conceptual discussion about shadow IT and its use. The article also provides conceptual contributions by discussing the differences between shadow IT and related concepts, clarifying the characteristics of shadow IT. In addition, the article discusses the consequences of using shadow IT that are still few explored and unknown.

We also provide some practical contributions. Managers should pay attention to the fact that the main reason for the emergence of shadow IT is the complete or partial absence of appropriate IT solutions that meet employee requirements (Walterbusch et al. 2017). Thereby, knowing the types of shadow IT and its consequences is also a good opportunity for IT managers to understand users' expectations and their technological needs to provide suitable technologies to perform their tasks. Moreover, shadow IT literature discusses a wide range of consequences, from performance improvements and innovative solutions to security and compliance risks. Thus, organizations must find ways to balance the positive and negative outcomes of shadow IT according to the context of each organization.

Finally, this study is an effort to better understand the phenomenon through a literature review and suggest research gaps to advance the knowledge on the topic. As a limitation of this research, we point out the limited number of articles in journals that bring shadow IT as a central topic. Most of the studies on shadow IT are from conferences, showing the necessity of theoretical and conceptual advances on the phenomenon.

References

Alter, S. (2014). Theory of workarounds. Communications of the association for information systems. 34(55), 1041–1066.

Alojairi, A. (2017). The dynamics of IT workaround practices a theoretical concept and an empirical assessment. *International Journal of Advanced Computer Science and Applications, 8*(7), 527–534.

Azad, B., & King, N. (2008). Enacting computer workaround practices within a medication dispensing system. *European Journal of Information Systems, 17*(3), 264–278.

Azad, B., & King, N. (2012). Institutionalized computer workaround practices in a Mediterranean country: an examination of two organizations. *European Journal of Information Systems, 21* (4), 358–372.

Behrens, S., & Sedera, W. (2004). Why do shadow systems exist after an ERP implementation? Lessons from a case study. In *Pacific Asia conference on information systems (PACIS)*.

Dang-Pham, D., & Pittayachawan, S. (2015). Comparing intention to avoid malware across contexts in a BYOD-enabled Australian university: A protection motivation theory approach. *Computers & Security, 48,* 281–297.

Ferneley, E. H., & Sobreperez, P. (2006). Resist, comply or workaround? An examination of different facets of user engagement with information systems. *European Journal of Information Systems, 15*(4), 345–356.

French, A. M., Guo, C., & Shim, J. P. (2014). Current status, issues, and future of bring your own device (BYOD). *Communications of the Association for Information Systems*, 35(10), 191–197.

Fürstenau, D., & Rothe, H. (2014). Shadow IT systems: discerning the good and the evil. In *Twenty-second European conference on information systems*, Tel Aviv.

Fürstenau, D., Rothe, H., & Sandner, M. (2017). Shadow systems, risk, and shifting power relations in organizations. *Communications of the Association for Information Systems, 41,* 43–61.

Globalscape. (2016). Be afraid of your shadow: What is "shadow IT" and how to reduce it. Disponível em: https://www.globalscape.com/resources/whitepapers/shadow-it-guide. Acesso em: 05 março 2018.

Gozman, D., & Willcocks, L. (2015). Crocodiles in the regulatory swamp: Navigating the dangers of outsourcing, SaaS and Shadow IT. In *Proceedings of the thirty-sixth international conference on information systems*, Fort Worth.

Györy, A. A. B., Cleven, A., Uebernickel, F., & Brenner, W. (2012). Exploring the shadows: IT governance approaches to user-driven innovation. In *Proceedings of european conference on information systems*. Paper 222.

Haag, S., & Eckhardt, A. (2014). Normalizing the shadows–The role of symbolic models for individuals' shadow IT usage. In *Proceedings of the thirty-fifth international conference on information systems*, Auckland.

Haag, S. (2015). Appearance of dark clouds?-an empirical analysis of users' shadow sourcing of cloud services. In *Wirtschaftsinformatik* (pp. 1438–1452).

Haag, S., & Eckhardt, A. (2015). Justifying shadow IT usage. In *Proceedings of the 19th Pacific Asia conference on information systems*, Singapore.

Haag, S., Eckhardt, A., & Bozoyan, C. (2015). Are shadow system users the better IS users?– Insights of a lab experiment. In *Proceedings of the thirty-sixth international conference on information systems*, Fort Worth.

Haag, S., & Eckhardt, A. (2017). Shadow IT. *Business & Information Systems Engineering* (pp. 1–5).

Harris, J., Ives, B., & Junglas, I. (2012). IT consumerization: When gadgets turn into enterprise IT tools. *MIS Quarterly Executive, 11*(3).

Huber, M., Zimmermann, S., Rentrop, C., & Felden, C. (2016). The relation of shadow systems and ERP systems—Insights from a multiple-case study. *Systems, 4*(1), 11. https://doi.org/10. 3390/systems4010011.

Huber, M., Zimmermann, S., Rentrop, C., & Felden, C. (2017). Integration of shadow IT systems with enterprise systems—a literature review. In *Proceedings of the twenty-first Pacific Asia conference on information systems*, Langkawi.

Jones, D., Behrens, S., Jamieson, K., & Tansley, E. (2004). The rise and fall of a shadow system: Lessons for enterprise system implementation. In *ACIS 2004 Proceedings* (p. 96).

Khalil, S., Winkler, T. J., & Xiao, X. (2017). Two Tales of Technology: Business and IT Managers' Technological Frames Related to Cloud Computing.

Laumer, S., Maier, C., & Weitzel, T. (2017). Information quality, user satisfaction, and the manifestation of workarounds: a qualitative and quantitative study of enterprise content management system users. *European Journal of Information Systems, 26*(4), 333–360.

Lis, T., & Paula, B. (2015). The use of cloud computing by students from technical university-The current state and perspectives. *Procedia Computer Science, 65,* 1075–1084.

Lund-Jensen, R., Azaria, C., Permien, F. H., Sawari, J., & Bækgaard, L. (2016). Feral information systems, shadow systems, and workarounds–A drift in IS terminology. *Procedia Computer Science, 100,* 1056–1063.

Mallmann, G. L., Maçada, A. C. G., & Oliveira, M. (2018a). The influence of shadow IT usage on knowledge sharing: An exploratory study with IT users. *Business Information Review, 35*(1), 17–28.

Mallmann, G. L., Maçada, A. C. G., Eckhardt, A. (2018b). We are Social: a social influence perspective to investigate shadow IT usage. In *Proceedings of European conference on information systems,* Portsmouth, UK.

Malaurent, J., & Avison, D. (2015). From an apparent failure to a success story: ERP in China—Post implementation. *International Journal of Information Management, 35*(5), 643–646.

Mell, P., & Grance, T. (2011). The NIST definition of cloud computing. Disponível em http://faculty.winthrop.edu/domanm/csci411/Handouts/NIST.pdf.

Miller, K. W., Voas, J., & Hurlburt, G. F. (2012). BYOD: Security and privacy considerations. *It Professional, 14*(5), 53–55.

Müller, S. D., Holm, S. R., & Søndergaard, J. (2015). Benefits of cloud computing: Literature review in a maturity model perspective. *CAIS, 37,* 42.

Park, S. C., & Ryoo, S. Y. (2013). An empirical investigation of end-users' switching toward cloud computing: A two factor theory perspective. *Computers in Human Behavior, 29*(1), 160–170.

Raden, N. (2005). Shedding light on shadow IT: Is excel running your business. *DSSResources. com, 26.*

Rentrop, C., & Zimmermann, S. (2012). Shadow IT-management and control of unofficial IT. In *Proceedings of the 6th international conference on digital society* (pp. 98–102).

Silic, M., & Back, A. (2014). Shadow IT–A view from behind the curtain. *Computers & Security, 45,* 274–283.

Silic, M., Barlow, J. B., & Back, A. (2017). A new perspective on neutralization and deterrence: Predicting shadow IT usage. *Information & management,* (in press), 1–15. http://dx.doi.org/10.1016/j.im.2017.02.007.

Singh, H. (2015). Emergence and consequences of drift in organizational information systems. In *Proceedings of the Asia conference on information systems (PACIS).* Paper 202.

Shin, D. (2015). Beyond user experience of cloud service: Implication for value sensitive approach. *Telematics and Informatics, 32*(1), 33–44.

Shumarova, E., & Swatman, P. A. (2008). Informal ecollaboration channels: Shedding light on "shadow cit". In *Proceedings of LED 2008,* Bled, Slovenia.

Steinhüser, M., Waizenegger, L., Vodanovich, V. & Richter, A. (2017). Knowledge management without management—Shadow IT in knowledge-intense manufacturing practices. In *Proceedings of the 25th European conference on information systems,* Guimarães, Portugal.

Turner, A. (2015). Generation Z: Technology and social interest. *The Journal of Individual Psychology, 71*(2), 103–113.

Turkle, S. (2011). *Alone together: Why we expect more from technology and less from each other.* New York: Basic Books.

Vogus, T. J., & Hilligoss, B. (2016). The underappreciated role of habit in highly reliable healthcare. *BMJ Quality & Safety 25*(3), 141–146.

Walterbusch, M., Fietz, A., & Teuteberg, F. (2017). Missing cloud security awareness: investigating risk exposure in shadow IT. *Journal of Enterprise Information Management, 30*(4), 644–665.

Walters, R. (2013). Bringing IT out of the shadows. *Network Security, 2013*(4), 5–11.

Webster, J. & Watson, R. T. (2002). Analyzing the past to prepare for the future: Writing a literature review. *MIS Quarterly,* 26, xiii–xxiii.

Weiss, F., & Leimeister, J. M. (2012). IT innovations from the consumer market as a challenge for corporate IT. *Business & Information Systems Engineering,* 6, 363–366.

Zimmermann, S., Rentrop, C., & Felden, C. (2014). Managing shadow IT instances–a method to control autonomous IT solutions in the business departments. In *Proceedings of the Twentieth Americas Conference on Information Systems*, Savannah.

Zimmermann, S., & Rentrop, C. (2014). On the emergence of shadow IT-a transaction cost-based approach. In *Proceedings of the Twenty Second European Conference on Information Systems*, Tel Aviv.

Zimmermann, S., Rentrop, C., & Felden, C. (2017). A multiple case study on the nature and management of shadow information technology. *Journal of Information Systems, 31*(1), 79–101.

Public Procurement Electronic Platforms Assessment: Legal Requirements

Sandra Cunha, **Isabel Ferreira**, **Luís A. Amaral**
and **Pedro J. Camões**

Abstract Electronic public procurement (EPP) has been considered an important tool for promoting competition, simplifying procedures, and ensuring transparency in decision-making processes. In Portugal, EPP replaced paper-based pre-contractual procedures for communication and processing. Addressing this general issue, the authors designed and proposed TrivPlat, a free access tool for monitoring, managing, and evaluating electronic platforms of public procurement. This paper presents the TrivPlat project, reporting its development so far: the identification and characterization of legal requirements that electronic platforms for public procurement are required to follow in Portugal. Legal requirements may be grouped into four types: general operating rules, functional requirements, technical requirements, and safety requirements. The first phase of the TrivPlat project diagnosis is expected to result in the development of an aggregate evaluation framework for public procurement platforms in order to reach the fundamental principles: equality of treatment, confidentiality, traceability, effectiveness, compatibility, interoperability, security and general availability.

Keywords E-government · Electronic public procurement platforms · TrivPlat project

S. Cunha (✉) · I. Ferreira
IPCA, Barcelos, Portugal
e-mail: scunha@ipca.pt

I. Ferreira
e-mail: iferreira@ipca.pt

L. A. Amaral · P. J. Camões
Universidade do Minho, Braga, Portugal
e-mail: amaral@dsi.uminho.pt

P. J. Camões
e-mail: pedroc@eeg.uminho.pt

© Springer Nature Switzerland AG 2019
I. Ramos et al. (eds.), *Information Systems for Industry 4.0*,
Lecture Notes in Information Systems and Organisation 31,
https://doi.org/10.1007/978-3-030-14850-8_6

1 Introduction

Public procurement is increasingly regarded as an important potential instrument for achieving the goals of policy innovation strategies at the European Union level and in a range of European countries, namely as a technology policy instrument (Haugbølle et al. 2015; Georghiou et al. 2014; Edler and Georghiou 2007).

Electronic Public Procurement (EPP) is a crucial initiative of Governments' strategies given its impact on economic development (Ramanujam 2012; EC 2004, 2010; Amaral et al. 2003; Ferreira et al. 2014; Schoenherr and Tummala 2007; Tavares et al. 2009; Haugbølle et al. 2015). The Europe 2020 strategy includes EPP as one of the key policy instruments for smart, sustainable and inclusive growth (EC 2010).

With a focus on transparency, governments have made efforts to implement electronic public procurement (EPP), assumed as an important tool of digital governance and a key driver for innovation (Edler and Georghiou 2007). Among other advantages, public procurement has the potential to promote competition, more open decision processes, reduce corruption and reduce administrative burdens. In Portugal, EPP replaced paper-based pre-contractual procedures for communication and processing based on information technologies and systems. The organizational gains are recognized, particularly in the European context.

However, e-procurement platforms have limitations, which result in a number of constraints to evaluate the impact of public procurement in the creation of public value. Additional efforts are still necessary to efficiently promote a more transparent and accountable governance, enhancing thus the creation of public value through ICT.

Thus, the authors designed and presented TrivPlat, a free access tool for monitoring, managing and evaluating electronic public procurement. Trivplat is the result of a project approved for financing by the Portuguese Foundation for Science and Technology. The TrivPlat project is briefly presented in Sect. 2.

In essence, this paper aims to present the TrivPlat project and its contributions to the discussion of additional efforts necessary to implement a tool that efficiently promotes a more transparent and accountable governance, one that effectively secures public interest. It aims to contribute to the provision of information related to electronic public procurement and its perception, increasing transparency, promoting rational management of public resources and fight against corruption.

The relevance of these outputs is more prominent if we consider the current legal framework which allows the free choice of platforms, not only by public entities (as was previously the case) but also by economic operators. As part of TrivPlat, it is developed a benchmark model for the evaluation of public procurement platforms operating in Portugal, in order to compare the various supporting functionalities and the technical requirements, safety, usability and general rules of operation. This article aims to present the work in progress, the construction of the reference model, which, currently, is focused on the study and analysis of the legal framework.

The main results of the legal requirements for identification and characterization of electronic public procurement platforms are presented and discussed in Sect. 3.

Finally, the main conclusion is presented in Sect. 4.

2 TrivPlat—A Tool to Monitor, Manage and Evaluate Electronic Public Procurement

Effective use of EPP entails the development of technological tools, namely EPP platforms, which are an IT infrastructure that supports pre-contractual procedure phases legally envisaged for public expenditure. The development of Public Procurement Platforms (PPP) is handled by platform managing entities, which are in charge of technical management of system and computer apps necessary for electronic formalities, guided by vectors of security and confidentiality, safeguarding public interest. They may be public, private or public/private entities.

In Portugal, all technological development tasks are undertaken by private entities, which assume all risks of the technological project development. However, the performance of management entities is not always adequate (Oliveira and Amorim 2001; Ferreira 2016).

The introduction of PPPs has led to organizational changes and adoption of new procurement methods and strategies. There are also constraints caused by limitations on existing platforms in the Portuguese market (Ferreira and Amaral 2016). Limitations such as: (i) restricted view of organizational competency "managing public procurement"; (ii) lack of a cross-cutting view of the "managing public procurement" competence; (iii) fragile organizational culture and understanding; (iv) disarticulation between legislation and platform functionalities; and (v) technological solutions. The technological pitfalls are: (i) direct adjustment procedure and transparency paradox; (ii) case of qualified digital signatures; (iii) unqualified digital certificates; and (iv) high costs in access of platforms, diversity of work environments and functionalities of support to proceedings.

The limitations create problems for the competition principle, with particular impact on small and medium-sized enterprises. Who loses is the public purse and public interest. When a contractual procedure is initiated there is public interest to be guaranteed. There must be instruments that allow better management of public resources, crucial for decision-making.

It is critical to implement measures capable of technologically develop solutions more appropriate to the real needs of contracting entities and suppliers, eliminating technological limitations and pitfalls. These are also the objectives of the TrivPlat Project. Changes introduced by CCP should also be assessed, which is relevant especially at a time when Portugal is transposing the new Community Directive on EPP to a national level.

Notwithstanding the advances already achieved in Portugal, some problems persist that are symptomatic of the fragility of the public procurement platforms market. The promotion of a more competitive and transparent market for platforms is therefore decisive for a more open competition and its direct consequences on the economy.

The objective of this project is the development of an electronic tool, of free access, to monitor, manage and evaluate electronic public procurement, TrivPlat, structured in the following aspects: (i) to compare and evaluate public procurement platforms operating in Portugal, based on pertaining information, namely the functionalities and services provided, usability, turnover, costs for contracting entities and suppliers, users degree of satisfaction (a form of a trivago of public procurement platforms); (ii) to provide information on public procurement (electronic public procurement observatory), namely: who buys; what one buys; how regularly one buys; types of procedures adopted; proposal evaluation models; suppliers evaluation; (iii) to create an index of electronic public procurement (electronic public procurement measurement instrument); and (iv) to establish and stimulate a network of good practices (case studies and tutorials).

To achieve the desired result, and in order to guarantee discipline, accuracy and transparency, it is adopted the design research as the research methodology (Carvalho 2012; Baskerville and Myers 2002; Peffers et al. 2006; Livari 2007; Ferreira et al. 2011, 2012). Design Research is a form of research that aims to add knowledge associated with artifacts created, oriented to a purpose, answering to a felt necessity in real context (Carvalho 2012). Offermann et al. (2009) formalized a research process, structured in three stages: (i) identification and understanding of the phenomenon; (ii) solution design; and (iii) evaluation and construction of the artefact.

Thus, based on (i) the motivations for the study in this project; (ii) the objectives; and (iii) the expected result; and in order to guarantee accuracy and practical relevance following the guidelines presented by Offermann et al. (2009), the research project is structured in three main phases combined to obtain empirical evidence: a qualitative multi-method approach, information collection and analysis techniques. In a simplified manner, TrivPlat platform development will occur in 3 major activity phases that will follow each other during the period of 36 months: (i) diagnosis of the public procurement process in Portugal with focus on public procurement platforms; (ii) platform conception; and (iii) its implementation.

3 TrivPlat: 1st Phase—Diagnosis

3.1 Background

Electronic public procurement generally means replacing paper-based pre-contractual procedures for communication and processing based on information technologies and systems (EC 2004, 2010).

However, there are also potential problems that may hinder electronic public procurement adoption and, hence, transnational participation in electronic public procurement procedures (EC 2010): (i) inertia and fear by contracting authorities and suppliers; (ii) lack of standards in electronic public procurement processes (suppliers confronted with an electronic public procurement architecture composed by different platforms and devices); and (iii) costly technical requirements, especially for tenderers authentication.

In December of 2016, Jornal de Negócios reported the suspension of one of the largest public procurement platforms, Gatewit, managed by Construlink, for not complying with legally established requirements, namely improper collection of services to suppliers, which by law are free of costs. It should also be noted that the Portuguese Institute of Public Markets, Real Estate and Construction (IMPIC) and the National Security Office (GNS) notified the company of detected nonconformities after a first audit. The suspension decision follows a second audit, in which two authorities mentioned that the company had not taken the necessary corrective actions. As can be observed, performance of management entities is not always adequate. In addition to this problem, there is an emergence of platforms operating in the market without GNS accreditation nor licensing from IMPIC, as is the case of PortugalGov.com.

3.2   Research Plan, Methods and Activities

Considering the objectives of TrivPlat (a monitoring, management and evaluation tool), the construction of an evaluation benchmark for platforms operating in the market is decisive at this stage of the project. For this, it is necessary to make an analysis of the legal framework, focusing on the legal requirements regarding the development, management and licensing of existing platforms in Portugal. Thus the goal of this diagnosis phase is to achieve detailed knowledge of public procurement procedures, on the one hand, and of electronic platforms effectiveness to achieve their ends, on the other. In methodological terms, this knowledge will pass by the usage of 3 methods: (i) collection and systematization of legal rules that govern public procurement procedures; (ii) 15 structured interviews with key players in the procurement process; and (iii) collection and comparative analysis of public procurement data in EU countries.

In the first phase, diagnosis, four activities are planed (A):

- A1. Characterization of the public procurement process and electronic support platforms. This activity, at first, through a review and documentary analysis, will result in a report on the public procurement process as an instrument for implementing public policy aimed at improving the economic and social reality. Moreover, in a second moment, through a case study, it will also result in a report on public procurement platforms existing in the Portuguese market, focusing in, among other aspects, the description of support functionalities to the procurement process, technological specificities and associated costs for different stakeholders. A1 is decisive for definition of the evaluation benchmark of platforms, that is, for completion of A2.

- A2. Based on results obtained in A1, through analysis and interpretation of these results, the criteria underlying the definition of the dimensions that will support the evaluation benchmark of electronic public procurement platforms are defined. After this task, in a second moment, the benchmark is constructed. This activity will result in a set of platform comparison indicators. Completion of A2 will also generate decisive information, in part for construction of electronic public procurement measurement instruments, as defined in A3.

- A3. The objective of A3 is to construct measuring instruments for electronic public procurement. Thus, in a first stage, literature is reviewed around the network of concepts: electronic public procurement; transparency, corruption, electronic public procurement indexes; as well as the survey of existing indicators related to the subject under study. This activity will result in a set of indicators of electronic public procurement useful for: (i) researchers, making the accomplishment of empirical studies possible; (ii) government officials and civil servants, to substantiate decisions; (iii) private companies, that provide services, and suppliers of goods to the public sector, in order to delineate their market strategies; (iv) the general population, as a source of information and awareness of public procurement issues. The results obtained during A3 are, in part, inputs to A4.

- A4. Based on the results of previous activities (A1, A2 and A3), through analysis and interpretation, A4 aims to define the benchmark of good practices in electronic public procurement. This activity will result in the establishment of a collaborative and benchmarking network, which aims to stimulate dissemination of good practices in public procurement and to promote open innovation among the main players involved in the processes of electronic public procurement.

In this way, the following subsections are intended to present the main ideas and changes resulting from the new legal framework, identifying and summarily characterizing the main criteria to which the platforms must obey. With that information we intended to reach the first activities objectives.

3.3 The Actual Regulatory Framework

Public procurement rules in Portugal approved by Decree-Law 18/2008 of January 29, expressing a clear option for the dematerialisation of pre-contractual procedures and the adoption of other mechanisms that allow the optimization of electronic tools and Directives 2004/17/EC and 2004/18/EC, which promoted the progressive implementation of electronic contracting, have led to the creation of regulations for the operation of electronic platforms.

It was in this context that several diplomas were adopted in our country, of which we highlight the Decree-Law 143-A/2008 of 25 July, which transposed the principles and general rules that should be followed by the presentation of proposals and applications, Ordinance 701-G/2008 of July 29, which established the requirements and defined the functionalities to which the electronic platforms should follow and Ordinance 701-E/2008 of July 29, which approved the models of the technical data block, contract formation report, annual summary report and contract performance report.

Seven years after the CCP entry into force, with a view to transposing into national law the provisions of Article 29 of Directive 2014/23/EU of the European Parliament and of the Council of 26 February 2014, Article 22. and Annex IV to Directive 2014/24/EU of the European Parliament and of the Council of 26 February 2014 and Article 40 and Annex V of Directive 2014/25/EU of the European Parliament and of the Council of February 26, 2014, the Law 96/2015 of August 17, was published, regulating the availability and use of public electronic contracting platforms. This Law adds requirements that were dispersed in the legal system and revokes Decree-Law 143-A/2008 and Ordinance 701-G/2008. It also introduces a sanctioning framework. Thus, in Law 96/2015, the following are defined: (i) the requirements and conditions that electronic platforms must follow; (ii) the obligation of interoperability with the Public Procurement Portal and with other systems of public entities; and (iii) the supervision and sanctioning regime in case of breach of the stipulated legal rules.

In 2017, a further review of the CCP was made, through Decree-Law 111-B/2017 of August 31. This revision introduced a number of amendments, including, among others, the system of certain contracts, contract criteria, deadlines for submission of tenders, and provision of collateral, notably an extension of the use of public electronic procurement platforms. This decree also revokes Ordinance 701-E/2008 of 29 July.

Recently, Ordinance 57/2018 of February 26, regulated the operation and management of the Public Procurement Portal (BASE portal) and approved the data models to be transmitted to the BASE Portal. This decree shall enter into force simultaneously with the last revision of the CCP.

The portal BASE is designed to publish information regarding public contracts that are established under the Public Contract Code, which make it also a centralized tool to produce statistical information and public reports submitted to the European Commission. The information filled in the electronic platform for public procurement is transmitted to BASE. In this regard, they should follow a set of interoperability conditions with the Portal BASE in the following domains: (i) technical characteristics; and (ii) synchronization rule necessary to transfer data.

Thus, currently, the operation and management of electronic platforms follow, in legal terms, Law 96/2015 and Ordinance 57/2018. These diplomas include the functional, technical and security requirements, as well as the general rules for the operation of electronic platforms in procedures for the formation of public contracts.

3.4 Legal Requirements for Electronic Public Procurement Platforms: A Framework for the TrivPlat Project

The CCP's commitment to dematerialization of public procurement procedures and the consequent use of electronic tools in the formation of contracts is largely based on the role of electronic platforms, an essential part of the global architecture of the procurement process.

As defined in Law 96/2015, electronic platforms constitute a technological infrastructure consisting of a set of applications, means and computer services, which serve as support for public procurement procedures, by rolling out the various phases under direct command of the contracting authority and the interested parties or competitors, under the terms and within the limits previously established.

The free choice of electronic platforms for contracting entities and economic operators and the freedom of access to the pieces of public procurement procedures are freedoms enshrined in Law 96/2015, implying profound changes in the development, management and licensing of platforms. The interconnection and interoperability between electronic platforms, the technical credentials of the electronic platforms by the National Security Office and the licensing of the management entities of electronic platforms by IMPIC, I.P., are new challenges that arise.

As a result of this new understanding of the legislator, there is still another relevant aspect. The establishment of basic services provided by electronic platforms to economic operators is also defined: (a) access to procedures and parts of the procedure that have been published; (b) sending messages through the electronic platform; (c) sending of electronic mail messages to all of those involved at the stage of the ongoing public procurement procedure and, under the terms of the CCP, such communication is mandatory; (d) requests for clarifications and lists of errors and omissions; (e) the submission of applications, proposals and solutions; (f) pronouncements in prior hearing; (g) complaints and objections; (h) the contract decision; (i) the delivery of qualification documents; and, finally, (j) the visualization of all messages and notices created by the contracting entities which, according to the law, should be accessible.

The management entity (a legal entity that is able to exercise, under the terms of the Law, the activity of management and operation of electronic platforms) is responsible for making available the functionalities necessary for the application of legal provisions, in relation to electronic contracting in good conditions requirements, registration, reliability and sustainability. It also enhances the same legal diploma, that the interface with the users and all the communications and procedures carried out on the electronic platforms are written in Portuguese language, and an additional interface can be made available in other languages. These are the only references to the interface criteria and usability. That is, communications, data exchange and information processed through electronic purchasing platforms, as well as the respective archive, must comply with (i) the rules, (ii) requirements and (iii) technical specifications provided in the referenced law (Decree-Law 96/2015).

The legislation makes reference to 18 General Rules of Operation of Platforms, as evidenced in Table 1. It is important to point out that each of the 18 identified rules aggregate a set of sub-criteria, Given the complexity of the information, and extension of the same, in this article, we identify the rules by the maximum level of aggregation. This criterion was adopted in all the other tables presented in this article.

The General Rules are related with a set of fundamental rules to the procedure of purchasing process. The definition of a process manager on the platform, communication and notification rules, aspects related to the reference dates, loading of proposal documents, requirements for encryption of confidential documents, provision preliminary information sheet, list competitors, knowledge about the content of the proposals, making them available to juri members, among others, are some of the rules introduced by the legislator.

In functional terms, availability and free access and non-discrimination are two mandatory pillars that, in functional terms, platforms must obey. For example, the instruments to be used on electronic platforms and made available to economic operators, including products, applications and software, and their technical specifications, in order to avoid discriminatory situations, shall, inter alia: (i) be compatible with products in current use in the field of information and communication technologies, in particular the National Digital Interoperability Regulation (RNID);

Table 1 Operating general rules

Operating general rules (OGR)
OGR1: Conduct of procedures on electronic platforms (Article 60)
OGR2: Communications and notifications (Article 61)
OGR3: Documents provision (Article 62)
OGR4: Providing information on reference dates (Article 63)
OGR5: Requirements for proposal files (Article 64)
OGR6: Date and time of solution and proposal submission (Article 65)
OGR7: Components of each proposal (Article 66)
OGR8: Coding of tenders and identification of competing suppliers (Article 67)
OGR9: Upload proposals (Article 68)
OGR10: Documents encryption and classification (Article 69)
OGR11: Submission of proposals (Article 70)
OGR12: Sequence of proposals submission (Article 71)
OGR13: Ordering of tenderers and competitors (Article 72)
OGR14: Access to the content of applications, solutions and proposals (Article 73)
OGR15: Provision of proposals to the jury of the procedure or to the person responsible for the procedure if there is no jury (Article 74)
OGR16: Prior sheet for opening tenders and prior list of tenderers (Article 75)
OGR17: Opening tenders sheet and list of tenderers (Article 76)
OGR18: Negotiation and electronic auctions (Article 77)

(ii) indicate how to obtain the computer programs used, as well as their commands and instructions.

Table 2 identifies the fundamental functional requirements for such pillars to be secured. For example, in terms of minimum functional requirements, platforms should, among other things; (a) be based on open standards, in accordance with the RNID; (b) ensure that all messages are automatically available for viewing by those who have access to the phase of the ongoing procedure; (c) ensure the sending of e-mails to all stakeholders; (d) to guarantee the registration of any action carried out by the various registered users; (e) list, sort and export to XML format (Extensible Markup Language) and/or to ODF (Open Document Format), at all stages of the procedure, relevant information for management, reporting and monitoring, including metadata; (f) provide a report for verification and control of the flow of the procedure; (g) allow the parameterization of procedures with different contract criteria; (h) to support the execution of all procedures for the formation of public contracts, as provided for in the CCP; (i) allow aggregated downloading of all documents attached to messages submitted by economic operators; (j) allowing the use of authentication mechanisms and electronic signatures with qualified certificates issued by entities of the Trusted-Service Status List, namely the content of the ID card; (k) allow the realization of electronic auctions; (l) to ensure the possibility of auditing at any moment; (m) to ensure the verification of the characteristics of the qualified certificate in the electronic signature of documents; (n) allow the access, by the part of the Concorrence Agency, to data regarding the bids offered by economic operators.

It is worth noting that public adjudicators are free to introduce additional requirements in the documentation that supports the acquisition of electronic platforms, namely: (i) make available the pre-production environment for tests and initial training; (ii) allow the platform to be sheltered in a domain and sub-domain of the managing entity defined by the adjudicant; (iii) allow, through the Public Sector interoperability platform, the collection of information regarding the procedures under the National System of Public Procurement in order to monitor the bids offered by economic operators, in accordance with the terms to be defined later.

Another functional requirement is having a system that documents the various phases of the procedure, which provides the necessary functionalities to fulfill this

Table 2 Functional requirements

Functional requirements (FR)	
FR1: Availability and free access (Article 28)	
FR2: Non-discrimination (Article 29)	
FR3: Functional requirements (Article 30)	FR3.1. Minimum functional requirements
	FR3.2. Additional functional requirements
FR4: Flow of the procedure (Article 31)	
FR5: Denied access to the platform (Article 32)	
FR6: Information to interested parts (Article 33)	

obligation and keeps chronological information up to date until the contract act. This system should allow the identification, among other information, of: (i) the entity and the user that accessed the documentation that supports the proceeding; (ii) the exact date and hour of submission; (iii) the document sent, as well as the identification of the entity and the user that sent the information; (iv) the elapsed time of the communication. This system should be kept reliable and actual, including chronological information regarding the steps of the procedure until the adjudication stage.

Technical requirements, such as interoperability, compatibility, interconnection and data exchange between the electronic platforms and the Public Procurement Portal are identified in Table 3.

In order to allow the generalized exchange of data, namely between different formats and applications or between different levels of performance, the established and updated requirements must be respected, namely: (i) the scripting language for a web page; (ii) the level of accessibility for public pages; (ii) the protocol for guaranteeing the delivery of messages in the integration between two or more inter-governmental information systems of the Public Administration; (iii) assurance of the integrity and confidentiality of communications in the integration of two or more interagency information systems of Public Administration; (iv) the security of communication authentication in the integration of two or more interagency information systems of Public Administration; (iv) the type of electronic signature that all electronically signed documents must use. These, among others, are some of the requirements associated with TR1.

TR2 focuses on the interconnection of platforms with other fundamental platforms, directly and indirectly related to procurement processes, namely: (i) the Public Procurement Portal; (b) the Diário da República electronic portal; (iii) the National Public Procurement Catalog of ESPAP, I. P.; (iv) the Management of Financial and Budgetary Resources in shared mode (GeRFiP, of ESPAP, I.P.); (v) the solution that may be implemented by the Court of Auditors or by the entities of the National System of Internal Control of the State Financial Administration, within the scope of its competences in the area of auditing and control of public contracts; (vi) the citizen card authentication solution and the central authentication mechanism "autenticação.gov.pt"; (vii) the Protocol for the Standardization of Technical Information in Construction (ProNIC), managed by IMPIC, I. P.; (viii) the platform to be developed by the Competition Authority.

Table 3 Technical requirements	Technical requirements (TR)
	TR1: Interoperability and compatibility (Article 34)
	TR2: Interconnection with public platforms (Article 35)
	TR3: Interconnection between electronic platforms (Article 36)
	TR4: Data exchange between electronic platforms and the Public Procurement Portal (Article 37)
	TR5: Data to be transmitted to the Public Procurement Portal (Article 38)

One of the major technical challenges for the platform management bodies is to meet the interconnection and interoperability conditions necessary for economic operators to be able to freely choose the electronic platform, regardless of the one used by the contracting entity with which they wish to interact (TR3).

The electronic platforms for public procurement should transmit data to Portal BASE with regard the formation and execution of public contracts. This information and data should be codded and allow automatic treatment and is aimed to: (i) archive; (ii) perform statistical treatment; (iii) monitorization of information.

Finally, Table 4 highlights the necessary requirements in terms of security implementation and management.

Management entities implement an information security management system based on ISO/IEC 27001, ISO/IEC 27002, ISO/IEC 27005 and ISO/IEC 27033.

In sum, with respect to safety requirements, it is worth mentioning that public platforms for public procurement should support different access profiles for different users with different privileges, including at least: (i) safety administrator; (ii) systems administrator; (iii) systems operator; (iv) systems auditor. The platforms should be able to associate users to these profiles. They should also ensure that a specific user is not allowed to be associated to multiple profiles, according to

Table 4 Security requirements

Security requirements (SR)
SR1: Security implementation and management (Article 39)
SR2: User management, access profile and privileges (Article 40)
SR3: Systems and operations (Article 41)
SR4: Application security (Article 42)
SR5: Data integrity (Article 43)
SR6: Network security (Article 44)
SR7: Processing of personal data and free movement (Article 45)
SR8: Physical security (Article 46)
SR9: Identification and authentication (Article 47)
SR10: Access control (Article 48)
SR11: Management of cryptographic keys (Article 49)
SR12: Access logs (Article 50)
SR13: Archive (Article 51)
SR14: Backup and recovery (Article 52)
SR15: Information confidentiality (Article 53)
SR16: Electronic signatures (Article 54)
SR17: Chronological validation (Article 55)
SR18: List of electronic certification services (Article 56)
SR19: Electronic platform users authentication (Article 57)
SR20: Digital preservation (Article 58)
SR21: Preservation of electronic documents (Article 59)

the following criteria: (i) a user with profile of safety administrator is not authorized to assume the profile of systems auditor; (ii) a user with profile of systems administrator is not authorized to assume the profile of systems auditor.

4 Conclusion

EC (2010) considers that EPP technology has not provided expected solutions, however, investments in technological capacity for public procurement, like development of electronic platforms, have increased (EC 2010).

TrivPlat aims to develop a free access electronic tool to monitor, manage, and evaluate the public procurement platforms operating in Portugal. This is a relevant subject if we consider the Portuguese legal framework, and recently amendments, that establishes free choice of electronic platforms by public entities and economic operators.

In this paper we present the results of the work in progress of the 1st phase of the TrivPlat development. The main contributions here lies in the identification and brief characterization of the general, functional, technical and safety requirements for public procurement platforms.

The next step is to consolidate the construction of a platform assessment benchmark, based on the legal requirements and rules previously presented.

The authors are also studying, at this moment, the construction of a benchmark for evaluating the usability of platforms. In other words, the first phase of the TrivPlat project diagnosis is expected to result in the development of an aggregate evaluation framework for public procurement platforms (based on legal requirements, interface and usability criteria, as well as the overall process cycle from the identification of procurement needs to the evaluation of the execution of the contracts and their suppliers), in order to reach the fundamental principles: (i) Tenderers receive an equal amount of information at the same time (equality of treatment); (ii) Contracting authorities respect the confidential nature of information (confidentiality); (iii) Mechanisms are supported, in order to record all system events and user activities, as well as, attempts to gain access to sensitive information (traceability); (iv) Operation of the system improves competition conditions for the users (effectiveness); (v) Use of interoperable (compatibility) electronic means, generally available on the market or broadly used in MS, thus avoiding the use of country-specific or otherwise discriminatory technologies that restrict access to tendering procedures (interoperability); (vi) Use of technologies to ensure the secure communication of information and its storage in system data repositories (security); (vii) Use of technologies which are widely available and at low cost, as well as, mechanisms ensuring continuous operation of the system (general availability).

Acknowledgements This work has been supported by FEDER funds through the Operational Program for Competitiveness Factors—COMPETE and National Funds through FCT—Foundation for Science and Technology under the Project: nº 031171 and by COMPETE: POCI-01-0145-FEDER-007043 and FCT—Fundação para a Ciência e Tecnologia within the Project Scope: UID/CEC/00319/2013.

References

Amaral, L., Oliveira, J., & Teixeira, J. (2003). *e-Procurement: Uma reflexão sobre a situação actual em Portugal.* In APDSI (cords.) (pp. 46–50). Lisboa: Promoção e Desenvolvimento da Sociedade da Informação, APDSI. Available at http://repositorium.sdum.uminho.pt/handle/1822/850.

Baskerville, R., & Myers, M. (2002). Information systems as a reference discipline. *MIS Quarterly, 26*(1), 1–14.

Carvalho, J. A. (2012). Validation criteria for the outcomes of design research. In *A Pre-ECIS and AIS SIG Prag Workshop, IT Artefact Design & Workpractice Intervention, Barcelona, 2015.* Available at http://repositorium.sdum.uminho.pt/handle/1822/21713.

EC [European Commission]. (2004). *Public e-Procurement: State of the art, case studies on European Electronic Public Procurement Projects* (Vols. I and II). European Commission. Available at http://ec.europa.eu/idabc/servlets/Doc68cf.pdf?id=22176; http://ec.europa.eu/idabc/servlets/Docfd79.pdf?id=22175.

EC [European Commission]. (2010). *Livro Verde relativo ao alargamento da utilização da contratação pública eletrónica na UE.* http://ec.europa.eu/internal_market/consultations/docs/2010/e-procurement/green-paper_pt.pdf.

Edler, J., & Georghiou, L. (2007). Public procurement and innovation, *Research Policy, 36*(7), 949–963. Available at https://www.sciencedirect.com/science/article/pii/S0048733307000741.

Ferreira, I. (2016). *Modelo de gestão integrada dos contratos públicos eletrónicos orientados ao valor público.* Tese de Doutoramento apresentada à Escola de Engenharia da Universidade do Minho. available at http://repositorium.sdum.uminho.pt/handle/1822/41510.

Ferreira, I., & Amaral, L. A. (2016). *Public e-Procurement: Advantages, limitations and technological "pitfalls".* In United Nations University (Eds.), *Proceedings of the 9th International Conferences on Theory and Practice of Electronic Governance—ICEGOV2016. Montevideo, Uruguai,* 1–3 de março. Available at https://www.scopus.com/record/display.uri?eid=2-s2.0-84976353262&origin=inward&txGid=5804536443f47e63c01bcf0c9202eca6.

Ferreira, I., Cunha, S., Amaral, L. A., & Camões, P. (2014). *ICT for Governance in Combating Corruption: the Case of Public e-Procurement in Portugal.* In United Nations University (Eds.), Proceedings of the 8th International Conferences on Theory and Practice of Electronic Governance—ICEGOV2014. University of Minho, Guimarães, Portugal, 27–30 October. Available at https://dl.acm.org/citation.cfm?doid=2691195.2691265.

Ferreira, I., Ferreira, S., & Ramos, I., (2011). The relevance of results in interpretive research in information systems and technology. In *Proceedings of the Conference on Virtual and Networked Organizations Emergent Technologies and Tools (VinOrg'2011). Ofir, Portugal,* Julho 6 a 8. Available at https://www.scopus.com/record/display.uri?eid=2-s2.0-84865471851&origin=inward&txGid=74732e405ced5ba272c57c59de31dd73.

Ferreira, I., Ferreira, S., Silva, C., & Carvalho, J. A. (2012). Initial dilemmas in IST research: Design science and design research, a clarification of concepts. In *Proceedings of Iberian Conference on Information Systems and Technologies, CISTI'2012. Madrid, Spain,* 20–23 June. Available at https://www.scopus.com/record/display.uri?eid=2-s2.0-84869010261&origin=inward&txGid=be6826044d2a652354e95da7ab15c340.

Georghiou, L., Edler, J. Uyarra, E., & Yeow, J. (2014). Policy instruments for public procurement of innovation: Choice, design and assessment. *Technological Forecasting & Social Change, 86,* 1–12. Available at https://www.sciencedirect.com/science/article/pii/S0040162513002552.

Haugbølle, K., Pihl, D., & Gottlieb, S. C. (2015). Competitive dialogue: Driving innovation through procurement? *Procedia Economics and Organization, 21*, 555–562. Available at: https://ac.els-cdn.com/S2212567115002129/1-s2.0-S2212567115002129-main.pdf?_tid=22934758-0a9a-4ee2-98c5-cfb7847d7007&acdnat=1527756340_5f1f675f9b83e744616171dcd39dafb0.

Livari, J. (2007). A paradigmatic analysis of information systems as a design science. *Scandinavian Journal of Information Systems, 19*(2), 39–64. Available at: https://www.researchgate.net/publication/201168950_A_paradigmatic_analysis_of_information_systems_as_a_design_science).

Oliveira, L. M. S., & Amorim, P. P. (2001). Public e-procurement. *International Financial Law Review, 20*(3), 43–47. Available at: https://search.proquest.com/openview/943e4094bf9fa9c4931d755fc52f8846/1?pq-origsite=gscholar&cbl=36341.

Offermann, P., Levina, O., Schönherr, M., & Bub, U. (2009). *Outline of a design science research process*. In *Proceedings of the DESRIST'09, ACM*, 7–8 May. Available at: https://dl.acm.org/citation.cfm?id=1555629.

Peffers, K., Tuunanen, T., Gengler, C, Rossi, M., Hui, W., Virtanen, V., & Bragge, J. (2006). The design science research process: A model for producing and presenting information systems research. In DESRIST, Claremont, 24–25 February. Available at: http://geni15.wrsc.org/sites/default/files/documents/000designscresearchproc_desrist_2006.pdf.

Ramanujam, P. G. (2012). E-government: Strategies for successful e-procurement. *International Journal of Engineering and Management Sciences, 3*(1), 53–59. Available at: http://www.scienceandnature.org/IJEMS-Vol3(1)-Jan2012/IJEMS_V3(1)8.pdf.

Schoenherr, T., & Tummala, V. M. R. (2007). Electronic procurement: A structured literature review and directions for future research, *International Journal of Procurement Management, 1*(1/2), 8–37. Available at: https://scholars.opb.msu.edu/en/publications/electronic-procurement-a-structured-literature-review-and-directi-2.

Tavares, L. V., et al. (2009). *Estudos dos Impactos Tecnológicos da Contratação Pública Electrónica. Relatório final do Observatório de Prospectiva da Engenharia e da Tecnologia.* Lisboa: OPET.

Law

Lei n.º 96/2015, de 17 de agosto (Diário da República n.º 159/2015, Série I de 2015-08-17): Regula a disponibilização e a utilização das plataformas eletrónicas de contratação pública e transpõe o artigo 29.º da Diretiva 2014/23/UE, o artigo 22.º e o anexo IV da Diretiva 2014/24/UE e o artigo 40.º e o anexo V da Diretiva 2014/25/CE, do Parlamento Europeu e do Conselho, de 26 de fevereiro de 2014, revogando o Decreto-Lei n.º 143-A/2008, de 25 de julho. Available at: https://dre.pt/web/guest/pesquisa/-/search/70025051/details/maximized.

Decreto-Lei n.º 18/2008, de 29 de janeiro (Diário da República n.º 20/2008, Série I de 2008-01-29): Aprova o Código dos Contratos Públicos, que estabelece a disciplina aplicável à contratação pública e o regime substantivo dos contratos públicos que revistam a natureza de contrato administrativo. Available at: https://dre.pt/web/guest/pesquisa/-/search/248178/details/normal?l=1.

Decreto-Lei n.º 111-B/2017, de 31 de agosto (Diário da República n.º 168/2017, 2º Suplemento, Série I de 2017-08-31): Procede à nona alteração ao Código dos Contratos Públicos, aprovado pelo Decreto-Lei n.º 18/2008, de 29 de janeiro, e transpõe as Diretivas n.os 2014/23/UE, 2014/24/UE e 2014/25/UE, todas do Parlamento Europeu e do Conselho, de 26 de fevereiro de 2014 e a Diretiva n.º 2014/55/UE, do Parlamento Europeu e do Conselho, de 16 de abril de 2014. Available at: https://dre.pt/web/guest/pesquisa/-/search/108086621/details/maximized?p_p_auth=jwX26XeN.

Portaria n.º 57/2018, de 26 de fevereiro (Diário da República n.º 40/2018, Série I de 2018-02-26): Regula o funcionamento e a gestão do portal dos contratos públicos, denominado «Portal BASE» , e aprova os modelos de dados a transmitir. Available at: https://dre.pt/home/-/dre/114766031/details/maximized.

System Theoretic Process Analysis: A Literature Survey on the Approaches Used for Improving the Safety in Complex Systems

Saulo Rodrigues e Silva

Abstract Computer systems are becoming increasingly complex, especially interactive software systems, namely software user interfaces. The scientific community relies on different methods to assess their safety. This article provides an updated literature survey on hazard analysis approaches used to improve the safety of complex systems. To support the survey, we conceptualise complex systems, highlighting the challenge in terms of assessing their safety. We provide a brief overview on the approaches historically available to tackle issues in those systems, along with their most common methods. Finally, the article focuses in one method of a non-traditional approach, which is described in more details, along with some of its extensions, which seeks to improve the hazard analysis in complex systems.

Keywords Complex systems · High-assurance systems · Design requirements · Hazard analysis methods

1 Introduction

Critical interactive systems are those systems that the human operator interacts with. Failures in such systems have the potential to cause undesired or unplanned events, which Leveson (2011) characterises as accidents, with the potential for causing losses of different nature, such as social (e.g., threat or loss of human life), environmental (e.g., damage to the environment), financial (e.g. property damage), etc. Some examples of critical systems can be found in today's medical, aerospace, nuclear, financial and energy domains. To avoid undesired events, those systems need to provide safe operation. Although in general the design of critical systems demands full attention from system engineers and designers, special attention

Copyright held by the author.

S. R. e Silva (✉)
Universidade do Minho, Braga, Portugal
e-mail: saulo.silva@ifg.edu.br; id5541@alunos.uminho.pt

© Springer Nature Switzerland AG 2019

I. Ramos et al. (eds.), *Information Systems for Industry 4.0*,
Lecture Notes in Information Systems and Organisation 31,
https://doi.org/10.1007/978-3-030-14850-8_7

should be given to the design of their user interfaces, as problems in the way the human operator interacts with the system have the potential to lead the system to accidents with incalculable costs. This is because the human factor creates additional levels of complexity in the system design.

Due to the increasingly high level of automation in such systems (e.g., a high technological aircraft cockpit, sometimes also referred to as "glass cockpit"), the role of system operators (e.g., pilot) has changed. A previous condition in which the operator manually provides actions to change themselves the system operation modes (e.g., pilot manipulating the input controls required to change the aircraft's altitude) is being shifted to an abstract concept, in which the operator monitors several complex systems included in the automation (that acts as user interface for the system) that command the system's operation modes themselves. In the case of an aircraft, systems such as the Flight Management System (FMS) operate in discrete modes, meaning that as an outcome of the interaction, the automation either performs an action or it does not (Thimbleby 2010). As part of his/her work of piloting the aircraft, the pilot has the (limited) capacity to control the mode selection of such systems.

Several approaches have been historically used for tackling issues in critical interactive systems, to avoid problems that might arise when the human operator is monitoring the automation (e.g., *automation surprises*, where the system might react differently than the operator expects, causing surprise, confusion and uncertainty). This article provides an overview of such approaches, alongside their most common methods. It covers some historical definitions that intents to create the required context for explaining the traditional approaches and its methods. Finally, the article focuses in one method of a non-traditional approach, which is described in more details, as well as some of its extensions, aiming to improve the hazard analysis in complex systems. The evaluation procedure for the extensions is based on the analysis of works published in previous conferences about the surveyed method, as well as the search for prominent related works indexed in relevant scientific databases.

The article's main contribution is providing an updated literature revision on the Hazard Analysis (HA) methods, with focus on the safety of complex, software-based systems. For accomplishing that, the article is organised as follows: Sect. 2 provides a summary of Hazard Analysis approaches. Section 2.1 provides information on the traditional methods used for tackling problems in systems for more than 50 years. Section 2.2 provides information on the system theoretic approach, detailing the accident model that Systems Theoretical Process Analysis (STPA) is based on, as well as the method itself. The same section also provides an overview of the different extensions to the method, created for improving the detection of hazards in different kinds of systems. Section 3 concludes the article.

2 Hazard Analysis

For Rasmussen (1981), the potential for producing some undesired consequence is commonly referred to as "hazard". In his historical context, Hazard Analysis (HA) and Reliability methods were synonymous. Leveson (2011) defines them as techniques for identifying system failure modes, estimating their probability of occurrence so they can be eliminated or controlled during design or operations before damage occurs. Failure modes in this context are defined as the ways in which something might fail. Hazard Analysis methods have been used for many years (Song 2012) and in general are based on a traditional approach, whose main focus was frequently related with examining hazards caused by malfunctioning/failures in single components (hardware), present in systems.

As the complexity of the systems increase, a new unity of analysis is necessary. Systems-theoretic methods are used for examining and understanding complex socio-technical systems. They consider factors such as critical design errors or requirements flaws, which have the potential for causing an accident even if there is no component failure related with the flaws.

In order to make this difference between the traditional and non-traditional HA approaches clear, we can think about the existing difference between reliability and safety. In terms of system components, generally they can be considered reliable when their particular behaviour is verified, in other words, it complies with the design requirements and performs as designed, with no flaws or inconsistencies (errors) in their behaviour. In the perspective of Systems Theory (Zadeh 1962), however, although a component's implementation might be correct and reliable, its safety can only be determined by the relationship between the component and the other system components (Leveson 2011), that is, it can be unsafe even when performing as designed. Interactions problems that may arise during human interactions with the system, specially software systems, might present problems with those characteristics. This is because, although in general the specification of computer programs influences its safety (if some function in the software specification is not correct, the software behaviour is likely to present errors when that particular function is used), software based user interfaces might even have correct specification and yet behave unsafely, due to the complexity of the human operator's interactions with the system. In terms of HA, the old methods are not enough to guarantee the safety of computer systems because they do not consider the complexity of the human operator's interactions with the system (e.g., one could also consider the analysis of user interface's usability and safety properties for ensuring that the behaviour of the user interface is compliant with properties, capturing best practice in human-machine interface design).

We describe hereafter the two approaches and the analysis methods based on their assumptions.

2.1 Traditional Hazard Analysis Approach

Traditional methods for hazard analysis base their assumptions on the idea that hazards are the result of a sequence (chain) of events caused by the loss of functions in the system's components. Additionally, the effects of such loss of functions are propagated throughout the system. According to Leveson (2004), these methodologies may work well for losses caused by failures of physical components and for relatively simple systems. Henceforth we briefly describe some methods which implement the traditional Hazard Analysis approach.

FMEA Failure Modes and Effects Analysis (Bowles and Peláez 1995; NASA 1966) is a bottom-up method developed for the U.S. military and used for identifying failure modes and their causes, as well as for carrying out corrective actions to address them. The analysis, normalised in the Standard BS EN 60812:2006 (EN 2006), begins by identifying the system's components and their failure modes.

Then, the potential causes and effects of each failure mode are investigated. The outcome of the analysis is a set of scenarios triggered by a failure, namely, a safe and unsafe cause-effect chain of events. Both set of scenarios are analysed in similar levels of detail looking for unsafe scenarios, which in case of analysing non-hazardous failures, consumes time and does not add value to the analysis. The scenarios with highest probability of successful operation are selected for improving the system.

FMECA Failure Modes, Effects and Criticality Analysis (NASA 1966; Standard 1980) is a bottom up FMEA extension that in addition assigns a criticality ranking for each failure mode, which is based on Criticality Analysis (CA), a method for determining the significance of each potential failure for each component in the system's design, based on a failure rate and a severity ranking (Lipol and Haq 2011).

SFMEA Software Failure Modes and Effects Analysis (Reifer 1979) is another FMEA extension tailored for analysing software, by analysing how a software component (e.g., a variable, a function) might fail and how the detected failure propagates throughout the system and leads to a hazard. Because software components do not fail in the same manner as hardware components, the analysis is conducted by replacing the latter with the former. The analysis can be conducted at design level or code level and requires the detailed design documentation of the software, or the availability of the source code (Stadler and Seidl 2013).

SFMECA Software Failure Modes, Effects, and Criticality Analysis (Dehlinger and Lutz 2004; Lutz and Shaw 1999) is a bottom-up method based on hardware FMECA, tailored for finding potential software problems. The method can be used both in the design and requirements phase for tracking the propagation of anomalies from the causes (failure modes) effects in the software components to the system effects. SFMECA follows a similar analysis procedure such as SFMEA, which in summary starts by breaking the software into logical components (e.g., functions, variables), to predict the potential failure mode for each component on the overall system.

HAZOP Hazards and Operability Analysis (Lawley 1974) is an analysis technique originally designed by the Imperial Chemical Industries in the United Kingdom in the early 1960s, to help a multidisciplinary team looking for hazards in chemical processes, later normalised in the standard IEC 61882 (IEC 2001). The process of analysis begins by collecting all relevant system information. In consonance with the other approaches that rely on system information for the analysis, it is important that the system representation selected for documenting the system (e.g., a data-flow diagram in computer industry, or a piping and instrumentation diagram in process industry) is updated and leaves no ambiguity in the understanding of the system. "Attributes" are identified in the system representation (e.g., in a data flow diagram, attributes can be related with the rate of flow of data). The method uses a list of guide-words for identifying the intended behaviour and also stimulate the discussions among the team members about how the system attributes can deviate from normal operation. Thomas IV (2013) states that the simplicity of the method contrasts with the highly detailed system model required for identifying the parameters and apply the guideline words, which limits the application of the method to system models in advanced stages of design, as well as the number of potential solutions, since many important decisions have been made and solutions are usually related with minor changes such as patches or protection systems added to an existing design.

FTA Fault Tree Analysis (Haasl et al. 1981) is a top-down method used for investigating the causes of a high-level event, defined as the undesired system state or condition to be investigated. The method performs decomposition of the high-level event for creating lower-level events, which must occur to cause the higher-level event; the decomposition uses Boolean logic for identifying the possible combinations (lower-level) of basic causes for the undesired (higher-level) system state or condition. Since FTA works backwards for exploring and identifying ways in which the high-level event might emerge, a graphical hierarchical tree made of logical operators (e.g., *AND, OR*) is used in the analysis in order to demonstrate the relationship between the first event and its effect on the higher levels of the system; at each level of the tree, possible errors or failures that can trigger errors or failures in the higher-level are identified.

SFTA Software Fault Tree Analysis (Leveson and Harvey 1983) is a top-down hazard analysis method based on FTA, which applies the same methodology used for analysing hardware components, to the analysis of the software counterparts (e.g., functions). The analysis begins with an identified hazard, which must be defined using a method such as Preliminary Hazard Analysis (PHA). The starting point for the analysis is the software or functions responsible for controlling the system when the hazard occurred. The goal is to find specific failure modes or scenarios which can led to specific safety failures, or even demonstrate that the software is free of hazardous behaviour. As SFTA is based on FTA, the analysis uses a fault tree for documenting the analysis. At the top of the tree is the root event to be analysed. The logical operators *AND* and *OR* are used to describe the necessary preconditions of the next level of the tree.

ETA Event Tree Analysis (Kenarangui 1991) is a bottom-up method, which uses a visual tree structure, known as Event Tree (ET) for identifying all sequences of occurring events following an initial event. ETA uses similar Boolean logic as FTA for identifying whether the derived events from the root event in the tree (main event) are sufficiently controlled by safety procedures implemented in the system design, or can develop hazardous behaviour. Although dependent on an initial event, the method does not provide a way to identify it, therefore other methods are required for complementing the analysis. Other limitations are related with the method's assumption that the initial event occurred, providing no preventive measures to avoid it. Also the method considers the results of human actions as binary (success, failure), according to critics, a dangerous simplification that hides a great number of possible scenarios (Thomas IV 2013).

PHA Preliminary Hazard Analysis (Ericson 2005; Ericson et al. 2015) is a System Safety technique commonly used for identifying potential hazards at very early design level, when detailed design information is not available.

2.2 Systems Theoretic Hazard Analysis Approach

Currently there is only one hazard analysis method that is Systems-theoretic based, referred to as System Theoretic Process Analysis (STPA) (Leveson and Thomas 2013). This is a deductive (topdown) method, based on the STAMP accident model, both well funded on Systems and Control theory rather than reliability theory. The method targets failure of more complex systems, such as software intensive systems (systems that intensely make use of software) or socio-technical systems (systems that include human operators) (Leveson 2004). Although STPA is based on a accident model, the method can be applied early in the development phase, before an accident happens. It encourages the analyst exploring classes of aspects such as the human interaction related with complex, software intense, socio-technical systems.

Even though the goal of the article is not to meticulously discuss the method [the reader will find satisfactory information in Leveson's (2004) book and practical examples of the method's application in (Leveson and Thomas 2013)], we present STAMP and STPA briefly.

2.2.1 STAMP Accident Model

Systems-Theoretic Accident Model and Processes is a accident model that intends to understand the rules that govern the causes of an accident. The model is established on the top of three pillars: safety constraints, hierarchical safety structures and process models (Leveson 2004).

According to STAMP, events leading to losses (i.e., to an accident) happen due to insufficient enforcement in the system's safety constraints. More traditional accident models, such as Domino Theory (Heinrich et al. 1941) or the Swiss Cheese Model (Reason 1990), emphasise the prevention of failures in system's components to impede future accidents. STAMP shifts the unity of analysis from prevention of component failures to enforcing the system's behavioural safety constraints (Leveson 2011).

Figure 1 depicts a basic conceptual high level control structure, which is the representation/model of the system under analysis, containing the following elements:

- **Controller**—uses its information about the current state of the controlled process for determining if control actions are needed, and in that case, sends control signals to the controlled process. According to Leveson and Thomas (2013), an important issue on the design of an effective safety control structure is providing the feedback and inputs required for keeping the automated controller's model consistent with the actual state of the controlled process;
- **Process model**—is a representation the controller has of the controlled process, which includes information on how the controlled process operates (e.g., about sensors, actuators, displays, system variables, control actions) to affect the current state of the controlled process (Leveson and Thomas 2013);
- **Controlled process**—represents the automation being controlled by the controller (human operator, automated controller, or both). Responds to the control actions issued by the controller and provides feedback about the result of the operation;
- **Control action(s)**—the action(s) issued by the controller (that can be human or automated) towards the controlled process (that can be the automated controller or the controlled process) to affect the state of the system;
- **Feedback**—notifies the higher level (automated controller or human operator) about the result of the control actions in the lower level's controlled process.

According to Control Theory, the control structure's components are kept in state of dynamic equilibrium by feedback loops of information and control (Leveson 2011).

Fig. 1 A basic conceptual form of hierarchical safety control structure Adapted from (Leveson (2011)

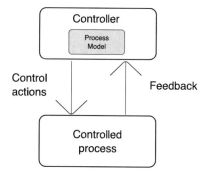

2.2.2   The STPA Method

STPA, short for System Theoretic Process Analysis (Leveson 2011), is a Hazard Analysis (HA) methodology based on the STAMP accident model, which considers the dangers that can arise during the operational phase of the system for establishing causal relations with problems.

The method can consider aspects of the environment where the system is inserted in the analysis, along with the human operators and their interactions while using the system. For this reason, working with a multidisciplinary team (e.g., designers, system engineers and human factors specialists, along with other multidisciplinary team members) during all the phases of the analysis is highly recommended.

One of the main contributions of STPA is providing a systematic way and clear guidance for identifying scenarios that could lead to hazardous system states involving unsafe interactions among components, even when they are operating according to their requirements. Leveson and Thomas (2013) states that hazardous components or unsafe interactions can be controlled through design.

In this method, design information from the system whose unsafe behaviour needs to be identified is provided as input. The design information might include:

– The system boundary;
– System and system components responsibilities;
– Knowledge the system components must have about the system;
– The system goals.

A working system, rather than a system design, may be used as source of information for the analysis. In such case, the responsibilities of the components comprising the system's control structure must be defined. Figure 2 presents the overall summary of the STPA analysis process. At the end of every engineering activity throughout the groups, output results are used as inputs for the next activity to be performed in the analysis.

Leveson categorises the engineering activities required for using the STPA method in three main groups: *fundamentals*, *step 1* and *step 2*.

2.2.3   The STPA Fundamentals

A number of early activities need to be performed in the early phase of the method's application, with the intention of collecting information about the system to be analysed, the safe behaviour to be enforced and the hazardous behaviour to be avoided (Leveson 2004, 2011). We summarise them hereafter.

Defining accidents. The first STPA activity necessary for conducting the analysis is related with agreeing/defining what an accident is. For instance, for an aircraft operation, monetary losses might not make sense. Instead, the definition of what an accident is in aviation domain must consider injury of persons. This definition is

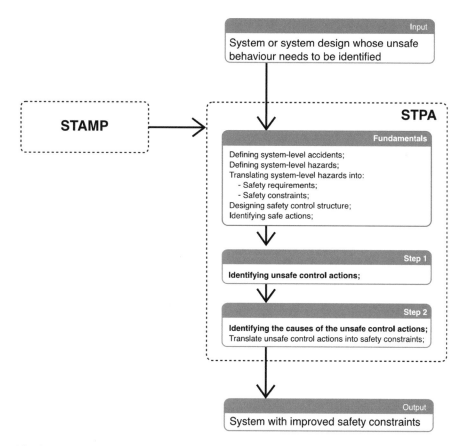

Fig. 2 STPA summary

implicit to different domains and need to be discussed with the stakeholders and customers, as there are different kinds of losses to consider. Government and specific agencies (e.g., Federal Aviation Administration—FAA, Food and Drug Administration—FDA, European Space Agency—ESA, etc.) might also be consulted, as they might have their own definitions of accident. One important aspect here, however, is that the definition of accident incorporates the system boundaries, derived from the system documentation, which must consider the difference between the control structure and the physical structure of the system.

Leveson, for instance, adopts a general accident definition, which includes general (material) losses, as well as human injury, as follows:

– *"Accident is an undesired or unplanned event that results in a loss, including loss of human life or human injury, property damage, environmental pollution, mission loss, etc.".*

Defining hazards The second STPA activity requires that practitioners agree on/ define the system hazards. For Leveson, a general hazards definition is as follow:

– *"Hazard is a system state or set of conditions that, together with a particular set of worst case environment conditions, will lead to an accident (loss)"*.

Leveson reminds us that the hazard should be within the system boundaries over which we have control (Leveson and Thomas 2013), because the result of the analysis will be able to affect the design. For instance, for an aircraft a hazard can not be weather, because we can not control the weather. Instead, a hazard can be to fly in areas of bad weather.

To assist the STPA practitioners in defining their own set of system-level hazards, the system documentation might contain useful information such as the system's goals. The practitioner can identify a small set of high-level system hazard at first, and refine them as the method evolves (Leveson and Thomas 2013). Practitioners can identify several hazards and work with them concurrently, as hazard scenarios identified in the analysis can be related with the same state or set of conditions.

Translating system-level hazards into requirements and constraints. The identified system-level hazards can be translated into design requirements [i.e., a specification of what should be implemented, descriptions of how the system should behave (Wiegers and Beatty 2013)] and the first safety constraints (namely, the safeguards that prevent the system from leading to accidents). According to (Masci et al. 2017), safety requirements can be formulated in natural language as the logical negation of the corresponding system-level hazards. For instance, if the system-level hazard "Pilot engages autopilot too early" is identified, a safety-requirement can therefore be defined as *Pilot must not engage autopilot too early*. Leveson states that this is a simple yet very important process, as engineers and system designers need that information in their standard engineering processes (Leveson and Thomas 2013).

Designing the control structure. The system engineering activities conducted so far, identifying the system-level accidents, hazards and safety requirements/ constraints are common activities to all safety engineering approaches, independent of which accident model or hazard analysis method is used (Leveson and Thomas 2013).

The first specific STPA effort that needs to be done is generating the control structure (sometimes also referred to as safety control structure, hierarchical control structure or functional control structure). The control structure is a relevant component in STPA as it allows illustrating not only the main elements that participate in the analysis, but it also illustrates their interrelations, i.e., what is the controller, what is the controlled process, what are the control actions and the feedback necessary for keeping the system working. Leveson states that using a control structure diagram is not standard in STPA, as the control structure might be represented using non-graphical notations. However, the graphical diagram is a documentation effort needed for performing STPA (Leveson and Thomas 2013), as the method provides a graphical diagram with guide-words registered for causal analysis.

After the control structure is designed, safe control actions required for keeping the system out of hazardous scenery can be identified, as they are issued by controllers towards the controlled process.

Identifying control actions. The control actions required for keeping the system out of hazardous scenery are potentially safe. The system-level requirements and constraints identified previously are an important source of information about the control actions. Another source is the model of the controlled process (system design), because it presents information about the boundaries of the system, which the STPA practitioner can use to help determine what control actions are needed. The model of the controlled process contains relevant information about the system, such as:

(a) The variables and states that are going to be monitored and/or changed;
(b) The control actions that must be provided by the controllers (automated, human or both) to operate the controlled process adequately. They are functions which monitor and/or change the system's variables and/or states. The control actions are also relevant for helping to identify the hazards that we want to avoid (unsafe control actions) and the safety control loop problems that may lead to the hazardous problems.

2.2.4   Identifying the Unsafe Control Actions (Step 1)

After performing the *fundamentals*, the next activity is *Step 1*, which consists in identifying unsafe control actions (UCA), namely, control actions that can lead the system to a hazardous behaviour. Usually UCA are result of inadequate enforcement of the system's safety constraints. For each CA, the conditions under which the control action may become inadequate are identified by the four general categories (Leveson 2011), as follows:

1. A control action required for safety is not provided or is not followed. E.g., a pilot does not engage the vertical mode of the autopilot;
2. An unsafe control action is provided that leads to a hazard. E.g., when engaging vertical mode, a pilot set wrong parameters for vertical speed.
3. A potentially safe control action is provided too late, too early, or out of sequence. E.g., when in descend mode, the pilot deploys flaps before airspeed is within safe values.
4. A safe control action required for safety is stopped too soon, or applied too long (for continuous or non discrete control action). E.g., the pilot pushes the aircraft side stick forward too long (which causes the aircraft to descend steeply).

Identifying UCA in STPA starts by analysing the previously identified control actions, using these categories.

2.2.5 Identifying the Causes of the Unsafe Control Actions (Step 2)

The objective of *Step 2* is to determine how the UCA identified in *Step 1* were caused. Although Leveson states that this step is not always performed in STPA analysis, due to the need of a more experienced analyst, she also states that it is in this phase that additional safety requirements are identified, as well as information is generated for assisting the designers in eliminating or mitigating potential hazardous behaviours (Leveson and Thomas 2013).

STPA provides a series of guide-phrases for helping the practitioner to identify the UCA causes not only by looking into failures or inadequate operation of individual components in the control structure, but also by finding scenarios and combinations of problems that could lead to unsafe control and hazards. Figure 3 presents a general representation of a control structure, along with the guide-phrases recommended by the method for determining the causes of the previously identified UCA.

The causes for unsafe control actions, according to Fig. 3, can be diverse and depends on which part of the control structure is being analysed, namely, the

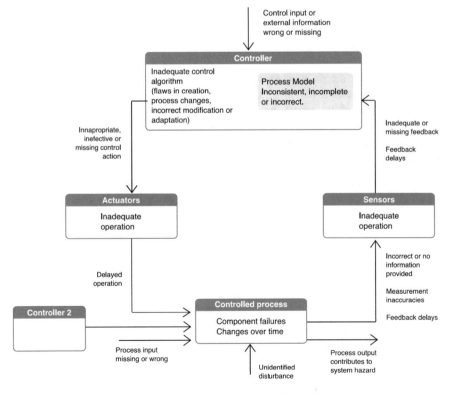

Fig. 3 Problems that can arise from the control structure leading to hazards according to Leveson (2011)

controller, the controlled process, the control action or feedback part. E.g., if a controller is being analysed, one assumption that can be made is that it takes too long to activate (provide a control action) an actuator, or commands its activation with the wrong control action. In general, these problems are divided in the following categories:

(a) Unsafe inputs—every controller in the hierarchical control structure is itself controlled by an upper level controller; in this process, input information or control actions coming from the upper controller may be missing or wrong, and compromise operations.

(b) Unsafe control algorithms—these are procedures designed for hardware controllers (e.g., engaging a hardware actuator) and procedures that human operators use (e.g., changing the system state). The procedures of the human operator are the ones they must follow to accomplish a goal in the system. They are created/affected by training and by feedback and experimentation over time (Leveson 2011). A hazardous control action will be caused, for instance, if the process changes and the algorithm that controls it was not updated, or if the control algorithm was inadequately designed (receives the correct command from the controller's model of controlled process but cannot execute it correctly).

(c) Inconsistent, incomplete or incorrect model of controlled process—automated controller(s) must have a model of the controlled processes that is consistent with the actual process or incorrect commands (control actions) might be sent causing a hazard.

(d) Incorrect information provided, measurement inaccuracies—the controlled process provides information for sensors keeping the system operating safely; incorrect or inaccurate information might cause hazards in the system.

(e) Issues with feedback—sensor(s) might create inadequate feedback, provide feedback with delays or not provide (missing) any feedback to the controller, and consequently cause hazards in the system;

Note that in the particular case of human controllers, the context and the environment where the activity is developed plays a relevant role in the decision making process. STPA recommends observing three categories of hazards issues related with human operators (Masci et al. 2017):

(a) Issues with feedback—in this case, feedback created inadequately, provided with delays or not provided (missing) by the automated controller to the human operator might cause hazards in the system, e.g., once the controlled process sends information to the sensors, the former send feedback with delays to the automated controller, which propagates the information with delays to the operator;

(b) Issues with mental model—the operator's understanding of how the system works is incorrect,
   e.g., operator's mental model of controlled process different from controller's model of controlled process;

(c) Issues with external information—wrong or missing procedures described in user manuals, or wrong information communicated to the operator.

After the unsafe control actions and their causes are identified, practitioners can enforce the first system safety constraints identified in Step 1 and continue the analysis to identify the scenarios leading to the hazardous control actions that violate the safety constraints. In order to understand the scenarios that may lead to hazards, the practitioner can make use of tools that range from tables or figures, to modelling and analysis tools, which provide relevant information about the system under analysis.

2.2.6 STPA Extensions

STPA's system representation is originally designed to fit the representation of different systems in domains ranging from aerospace and automotive (Castilho et al. 2018; Stringfellow et al. 2010), nuclear (Thomas et al. 2012), medical (Antoine 2013), cyber security (Young 2014) and energy (Rosewater and Williams 2015). Eventually though, STPA is being tailored to improve its capacity of analysis and hazards identification in a specific range of systems. This section introduces extensions to STPA, which improves the detection of hazards in hardware systems, software systems, as well as in the human operator analysis.

Stringfellow (2010) states that systems with flaws are operated in a state of high-risk. She proposed the *STAMP extension for Humans and Organisations using guideWords (SHOW)* for analysing how organisational factors, e.g., policies, might contribute to high-risk operations and affect safety in sociotechnical aerospace systems. The method uses STPA's structured approach for identifying design flaws, diagnosing policies that are resistant to pressures and contribute to high-risk operations, as well as allowing system decision-makers to predict how proposed or current policies will affect safety. A new set of guide-words is used in the STPA risk analysis, tailored for the identification and analysis of human and organisational factors and their role in accidents. The guide words are built upon individual error and organisational error taxonomies, identified with Grounded Theory (Robson and McCartan 2016).

Early Warning Sign Analysis (EWaSAP) (Dokas et al. 2013) is a STPA extension which adds two types of steps into the typical STPA control structure. In STPA the control structure provides, among other things, safety constraints for enforcing the system safety on the levels below and feedback indicating how the system safety was enforced. The first type of step added by the extension aims to establish a form of cooperation between the system being analysed and the system surrounding it, and for exchanging information about safety that might constitute early signs of flaws. The second type of step aims at analysing the early signs indicating the presence of flaws in the control structure of the system in focus, or the violation of its design assumptions that can contribute to losses, during the operational phase of the system. The method also introduces the notion of *awareness actions*, responsible for enforcing the transmission of early warning signs to other controllers within or outside the system, when a controller identifies factors contributing to losses in the system. Typical awareness actions transmits (i) *all clear*, (ii) *warnings*, (iii) *alerts* and (iv) *algedonic* signals (a special transmission for informing the controller at highest levels about a serious detected condition).

Thomas IV's (2013) approach for extending STPA provides a rigorous procedure that systematically helps to identify hazardous control actions based on the combination of process model context variables and context values. The *context* is the condition in the system and environment that make action (or inaction) hazardous. A combinatorial testing algorithm is also introduced, responsible for performing a STPA analysis using the context variables and values to produce the context tables. The context table gathers those information and allows other types of risk identification, based on the context of the control action. The approach also formalised STPA and STAMP using logical and mathematical structures that can be used by automated tools, and a method for using the results of the hazard analysis for generating formal safety requirements.

As Yang (2014) remarks the importance of software requirements as one of the most important elements during Software Safety Test Process, he proposes a framework of software safety testing based on Systems Theory, for improving the test analysis over the test approaches based on single components failure methods. The *Software Safety Test Requirements Elicitation based on STPA* approach uses the causal scenarios identified in the STPA's causal analysis and the safety requirements identified after the STPA's risk analysis, for generating the safety test requirements. Next, safety test requirements are used for designing specific safety test cases, implementing the safety test that are used for verifying the realisation of the system software requirements.

Leveson et al. (2014) also extends the STPA human controller, integrating two new causal factor categories based on principles from ecological psychology and cognitive models. The extension updates two parts of the STPA control structure. The detection of flawed feedback is included for verifying the operator's ability to understand feedback correctly. In the same work an action component is included, responsible for identifying actions that are appropriate for manipulating controls of the user interface.

STPA for Software-Intensive Systems (STPA SwISs) is an approach by (Abdulkhaleq et al. 2015, 2016). In short, it comprehends mainly tree parts: (i) deriving software safety requirements at the system level using STPA, (ii) creating a model of the safe behaviour from the STPA results using a UML state-chart notation and (iii) verifying the functional requirements on the model of the software, at the design and implementation levels, using formal specification.

Masci et al. (2017) proposes an extension that refines STPA's standard causal factors categories with 16 new categories, specialised in improving the analysis of user interfaces in medical devices, in terms of safety and usability. The categories are used in different parts of the STPA control structure, namely, the Feedback component, the human operator's Mental model component and in the External information component. The categories are derived from usability heuristics user interface design guidelines, defined in medical device usability standards (ANSI/ AAMI HE75 and ISO 62366-1).

France (2017) proposed STPA-Engineering for Humans, an extension for improving how the method analyses human errors. In order to accomplish that, the system model/representation is updated, adopting a new model of the human operator, which relies on three new components. (1) Control Action Selection captures the human controller's goals and how the decisions are made based on the mental models. (2) Mental Model verifies the knowledge the user has of the system and environment for capturing flaws. (3) Mental Model Updates analyses the human experiences and expectations and how they can affect the system use. This provides a high-level characterisation of human information processing, which intends to improve the characterisation of the human operator's mental models. As a result, it helps to create more robust causal scenarios that explore problems related to the human operator, and allows designers and human experts to discuss how to consider the role of the human operator in the system under analysis. The approach is tested in a realistic case study from automotive industries.

3   Conclusion

The field of Human Computer Interaction (HCI) owes a lot to the traditional hazard analysis methods, for the development of extensions for analysing software based systems, as well as user interfaces of those systems, aiming to ensure the safety of interactive software systems. However, we are entering in a new era of computing systems. Emerging complexity of software systems used for operating systems that used to be simpler (e.g. highly technological "self-driving" cars and "glass cockpit's" airplanes) are providing new challenges in terms of assessing the interaction among the human operators and those systems.

By combining human factors considerations along with the rigour of the engineering discipline in the analysis, STPA provides a flexible framework for analysing complex interactive systems. The method is being tailored to accommodate different kinds of systems, this way extending the range and depth of the analysis, including complex interactive systems. This work is theoretical, therefore future work includes moving to a realistic case study, which will provide us with a test-bench suitable for testing the approaches and present a comparison between them.

Acknowledgements We acknowledge Conselho Nacional de Desenvolvimento Científico e Tecnológico (CNPq) and Instituto Federal de Educação, Ciência e Tecnologia de Goiás (IFG) for the support, as well as Dr. José Creissac, Dr. Paolo Masci,Dr. João Fernandes and Dr. Orlando Belo for the valuable insights.

References

Abdulkhaleq, A., Vost, S., Wagner, S., & Thomas, J. (2016). An industrial case study on the evaluation of a safety engineering approach for software-intensive systems in the automotive domain.

Abdulkhaleq, A., Wagner, S., & Leveson, N. (2015). A comprehensive safety engineering approach for software-intensive systems based on STPA. *Procedia Engineering, 128*, 2–11. In *Proceedings of the 3rd European STAMP Workshop October 5–6, 2015*, Amsterdam.

Antoine, B. (2013). *Systems theoretic hazard analysis (STPA) applied to the risk review of complex systems: an example from the medical device industry*. (Ph.D. thesis, Massachusetts Institute of Technology).

Bowles, J. B., & Peláez, C. E. (1995). Fuzzy logic prioritization of failures in a system failure mode, effects and criticality analysis. *Reliability Engineering & System Safety, 50*(2), 203–213.

Castilho, D. S., Urbina, L. M., & de Andrade, D. (2018). Stpa for continuous controls: A flight testing study of aircraft crosswind takeoffs. *Safety Science, 108*, 129–139.

Dehlinger, J., & Lutz, R. R. (2004). Software fault tree analysis for product lines. In *Proceedings Eighth IEEE International Symposium on High Assurance Systems Engineering*, pp. 12–21. IEEE.

Dokas, I. M., Feehan, J., & Imran, S. (2013). Ewasap: An early warning sign identification approach based on a systemic hazard analysis. *Safety Science, 58*, 11–26.

EN, B. (2006). *60812: 2006 analysis techniques for system reliability. Procedure for failure mode and effects analysis (FMEA)*.

Ericson, C. A. (2005). Event tree analysis. *Hazard Analysis Techniques for System Safety*, 223–234.

Ericson, C. A. et al. (2015). *Hazard analysis techniques for system safety*. Wiley.

France, M. E. (2017). *Engineering for humans: a new extension to STPA* (Ph.D. thesis, Massachusetts Institute of Technology).

Haasl, D. F., Roberts, N., Vesely, W., & Goldberg, F. (1981). *Fault tree handbook*. Technical report, Nuclear Regulatory Commission, Washington, DC (USA). Office of Nuclear Regulatory Research.

Heinrich, H. W. et al. (1941). Industrial accident prevention. a scientific approach. In *Industrial accident prevention. A scientific approach* (2nd ed.).

IEC, B. (2001). *61882: 2001: Hazard and operability studies (hazop studies). Application guide*. British Standards Institute.

Kenarangui, R. (1991). Event-tree analysis by fuzzy probability. *IEEE Transactions on Reliability, 40*(1), 120–124.

Lawley, H. (1974). Operability studies and hazard analysis. *Chemical Engineering Progress, 70* (4), 45–56.

Leveson, N. (2004). A new accident model for engineering safer systems. *Safety Science, 42*(4), 237–270.

Leveson, N. (2011). *Engineering a safer world: Systems thinking applied to safety*. MIT press.

Leveson, N., & Thomas, J. (2013). *An STPA primer*. Cambridge, MA.

Leveson, N. G. et al. (2014). *Extending the human controller methodology in systems-theoretic process analysis (STPA)* (Ph.D. thesis, Massachusetts Institute of Technology).

Leveson, N. G., & Harvey, P. R. (1983). Software fault tree analysis. *Journal of Systems and Software, 3*(2), 173–181.

Lipol, L. S., & Haq, J. (2011). Risk analysis method: FMEA/FMECA in the organizations. *International Journal of Basic & Applied Sciences, 11*(5), 74–82.

Lutz, R. R., & Shaw, H.-Y. (1999). Applying adaptive safety analysis techniques (for embedded software). In *Proceedings of 10th International Symposium on Software Reliability Engineering, 1999*, pp. 42–49. IEEE.

Masci, P., Zhang, Y., Jones, P., & Campos, J. C. (2017). A hazard analysis method for systematic identification of safety requirements for user interface software in medical devices. In *15th International Conference on Software Engineering and Formal Methods (SEFM 2017)*, volume LNCS, vol. 10469, Springer. Springer.

NASA, N. (1966). S. Administration. Procedure for failure mode, effects and criticality analysis (FMECA), RM 63TMP-22. *NASA, Tech. Rep.*

Rasmussen, N. C. (1981). Methods of hazard analysis and nuclear safety engineering. *Annals of the New York Academy of Sciences, 365*(1), 20–36.

Reason, J. (1990). *Human error.* Cambridge university press.

Reifer, D. J. (1979). Software failure modes and effects analysis. *IEEE Transactions on Reliability, 28*(3), 247–249.

Robson, C., & McCartan, K. (2016). *Real world research.* Wiley.

Rosewater, D., & Williams, A. (2015). Analyzing system safety in lithium-ion grid energy storage. *Journal of Power Sources, 300,* 460–471.

Song, Y. (2012). *Applying system-theoretic accident model and processes (STAMP) to hazard analysis* (Ph.D. thesis).

Stadler, J. J., & Seidl, N. J. (2013). Software failure modes and effects analysis. In *Reliability and Maintainability Symposium (RAMS), 2013 Proceedings-Annual*, pp. 1–5. IEEE.

Standard, U. M. (1980). MIL-STD-1629A. *Procedures for Performing a Failure Mode, Effect and Criticality Analysis.* Department of Defense, USA.

Stringfellow, M. V. (2010). *Accident analysis and hazard analysis for human and organizational factors* (PhD thesis, Massachusetts Institute of Technology).

Stringfellow, M. V., Leveson, N. G., & Owens, B. D. (2010). Safety-driven design for software-intensive aerospace and automotive systems. *Proceedings of the IEEE, 98*(4), 515–525.

Thimbleby, H. (2010). *Press on: Principles of interaction programming.* The MIT Press.

Thomas, J., Lemos, F., & Leveson, N. (2012). Evaluating the safety of digital instrumentation and control systems in nuclear power plants. *NRC Technical Research Report 2013.*

Thomas IV, J. P. (2013). *Extending and automating a systems-theoretic hazard analysis for requirements generation and analysis* (PhD thesis, Massachusetts Institute of Technology).

Yang, C. (2014). Software safety testing based on STPA. *Procedia Engineering, 80,* 399–406.

Young, W. E. (2014). STPA-SEC for cyber security mission assurance. *Eng Syst. Div. Syst. Eng. Res. Lab.*

Zadeh, L. A. (1962). From circuit theory to system theory. *Proceedings of the IRE, 50*(5), 856–865.

Wiegers, K., & Beatty, J. (2013). *Software requirements.* Pearson Education.

A Demonstration of an Application of the Bertrand Network: Guessing the Distribution of Buyers Within the Market

Murillo Henrique Pedroso Ferreira(ⓘ) **and João Paulo Pereira**(ⓘ)

Abstract Bertrand and the Cournot model are one of the most used model for modeling competition between companies. This paper presents a work-in-progress that studies the application of the recently developed Bertrand Network model by using it in a reverse manner: first it is considered that firms are competing in equilibrium, then, after analyzing how companies are choosing prices, it is calculated which distribution of buyers would lead to that equilibrium. An unreal example is presented to help to understand the model. Furthermore, a formula is suggested to expand the networked model to allow a mix of duopolies and oligopolies.

Keywords Nash equilibrium · Bertrand network · Market competition · Expanded Bertrand network · Market expansion

1 Introduction

In the last years there have been researches to expand the classic Cournot and Bertrand market model to one version that considers a network competition, where firms can compete over different markets against different firms at the same time (Bose et al. 2014a, b; Motalleb et al. 2017; Abolhassani et al. 2014). Recent models expanded the idea of a single oligopoly model, where multiple firms compete for one market share (Bimpikis et al. 2014), since nowadays companies are even able to compete in multiple markets and react in real-time due to online analysis tools (Babaioff et al. 2014).

M. H. P. Ferreira · J. P. Pereira (✉)
Polytechnic Institute of Bragança, Bragança, Portugal
e-mail: jprp@ipb.pt

M. H. P. Ferreira
e-mail: murillo.hpf@gmail.com

J. P. Pereira
UNIAG (Applied Management Research Unit), Bragança, Portugal

© Springer Nature Switzerland AG 2019
I. Ramos et al. (eds.), *Information Systems for Industry 4.0*,
Lecture Notes in Information Systems and Organisation 31,
https://doi.org/10.1007/978-3-030-14850-8_8

Antoine Augustin Cournot and Joseph Bertrand have introduced the first model for studying the duopoly competition where. In the first one, firms can only choose quantity of a good to supply to the market (leaving the price to be determined by an auctioneer (Kreps and Scheinkman 1983)), while in the second one, firms can choose price as a strategy (Abolhassani et al. 2014).

Both tools have been used for investigating competitive markets, while Bertrand model are more suitable for price competition (Babaioff et al. 2014; Kasbekar and Sarkar 2012). Cournot competition is being used for modeling markets like electricity, where vendors decide for quantities rather than prices (Abolhassani et al. 2014), e.g., (Barquin and Vazquez 2008; Jing-Yuan and Smeers 1999; Yao et al. 2004). The Bertrand Network model has been proposed by Guzmán (2011) and it has been expanded in other works (Babaioff et al. 2013, 2014, 2016). All of them being an expansion of the classic model that has been widely used in pricing competition (Babaioff et al. 2014).

In the existing Cournot Network Competition (Bimpikis et al. 2014), an arbitrary number of firms can compete in the same market. This model allows to predict the reaction of other firms in case of one vendor decides to join one existing market share, as well as predict whether it is profitable for two firms to merge or not.

The main field of study of the authors is to offer a tool to analyze the chance of success to one vendor if he tries to expand to another market, in special, expanding to a market in another country (an international expansion). In the study, firms are competing using prices in several markets. The authors are currently working in another improvement for the Bertrand Networked Model (Babaioff et al. 2013), which contains several profs that asserts the existence of a Nash Equilibrium in any graph but has a limitation: only two firms can compete against each other in the same shared market. In the existing model, all buyers in each market share buy from the firm that asked for the lowest price. Firms cannot price discriminate, which means that each of them will ask for the same price for both shared markets that they are participating in and the captive market (if he has one). It is assumed that all companies sell a homogeneous good, so buyers are only interested in the lowest price (these properties have been kept).

The goal is to allow more firms to compete for one market. Since the main field of study is to evaluate whether is it profitable for a firm to join an existing market or not, it is required to allow at least 3 vendors to compete at the same market share (the firm that wants to expand, as well as two others that were already competing), which is not possible in the existing model. The attempt to expand the existing model uses the same basic structure: a hypergraph where each node represents firms, and hyperedges that represents shared markets. In addition, it is currently being worked on a practical application of the Bertrand Network model for this study, which is believed to be from little to no work that used the model that has inspired this work, in contrast to the Cournot Network model., e.g., (Bose et al. 2014a, b; Cai et al. 2017; Motalleb et al. 2017).

This paper presents one of the possible applications of the existing model to verify why companies are pricing in one specific way. Furthermore, it is shown one more evidence that, for each oligopoly market in the Expanded Bertrand Network, each vendor does not do better than ignoring the existing of such market share since the competition will be too aggressive between the two small vendors, as has already been proved by Guzmán (2011).

The remainder of this paper is structured as follows. Section 2 shows the Bertrand Network model, to understand its structure. Since there is a lack of a practical usage of the Bertrand Network in a real case, Sect. 3 presents how to apply the existing model in a real scenario. Section 4 shows an expanded formula from the existing model, that is, Eq. (7), as well as an illustrative example to better understand the formula, leaving the remaining section for discussion of the future work.

2 Existing Model

This warm-up example will be useful to understand the structure of the Bertrand Network. Consider the following competition among three vendors: the firm f_1 sells devices to users that are interested in high-performance and has a captive market $\alpha_1 = 20$ that represents the set of buyers that will buy from the firm f_1 no matter the price, as long it is not higher than 1 (loyal buyers). The firm f_2, on the other hand, sells devices to buyers that are interested in both high and low performance devices (participating in two different markets). Finally, the firm f_3 are only interested to sell to buyers that are interested in low-performance devices. After this, buyers were categorized into three different markets.

The firm f_1 competes for the market $\beta_{1,2} = 150$ against f_2, while the firm f_3 competes for the market $\beta_{2,3} = 185$ against f_2. Neither f_2 nor f_3 has a set of loyal buyers, therefore, $\alpha_2 = \alpha_3 = 0$.

In the given example, f_1 faces a tradeoff between extracting the maximum surplus from its captive market by asking for the monopolized price of 1 and lowering the price to increase the likelihood of winning market share $\beta_{1,2}$. On the other hand, f_2 must decide for a price that, at the same time, will extract the maximum surplus from both shared markets.

Figure 1 shows the competition network and the *equilibrium sketch* for the network. An *equilibrium sketch* is defined as a specification of the finitely bounded pricing range (support) for every seller i and the set of sellers that has an *atom* at 1. (Babaioff et al. 2013) has formally defined it in **Definition 5.1** and any support can be set, as well as any set of sellers with an atom at 1 can be chosen, but the results from the *equilibrium sketch* must satisfy the properties in **Definition 5.2**.

From the results in Babaioff et al. (2013, pp. 7–8), the unique *Nash Equilibrium* (N.E.) for this topology is that each company must mix its pricing strategy by following its support (see Fig. 1) and randomize by following its Cumulative Distribution Function (CDF). To each company be indifferent in choosing any price that falls within its support, the utility level for each vendor must be the same by pricing at $x \in [t_m, t_n]$ (where $0 < t_m \leq t_n \leq 1$ are the boundary points of its support,

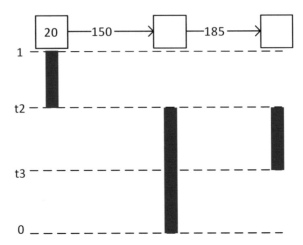

Fig. 1 Example of competition. Nodes represent firms, each hyperedge represents a market share. Captive markets are represented with a weight within the node, in which an empty node represents a captive market of size zero. Thick lines represent the pricing strategy of each firm that falls within their support, as a subset of $[0, 1]$. The black circle represents an atom at 1. It is said that when a firm has an atom at 1, the firm chooses the price of 1 with a positive probability

for a network that has at least one firm with an nonzero captive market). Formally, the following must hold:

$$u_1(t_1) = u_1(t_2) = u_1(x) \quad \forall x \in [t_2, t_1]$$
$$u_2(t_1) = u_2(t_2) = u_2(t_3) = u_2(x) \quad \forall x \in [t_3, t_1] \qquad (1)$$
$$u_3(t_2) = u_3(t_3) = u_3(x) \quad \forall x \in [t_3, t_2]$$

By working with the equalities above, it is possible to find the CDF function that represents the probability of each firm to choose the price of *at least* x. The utility level of each firm is defined by Babaioff et al. (2013) as follows:

$$u_i(x, F_{-i}) = u_i(x) = x \left(\alpha_i + \sum_{j \in N(i)} \beta_{i,j} \overline{F}_j(x) \right) \qquad (2)$$

where $N(i)$ is a set of neighbors of i, $\beta_{i,j}$ is the weight of the edge that connects i and j, α_i is the size of the captive market of i and $\overline{F}_j(x)$ represents the inverse CDF function (CDF for short), the mixed pricing strategy for the firm j. The inverse CDF is a nonincreasing linear function in x^{-1} which can be explicitly found for every $x \in [0, 1]$ by working with equalities in (1). For a detailed description of how to find the explicit CDF function for every firm i (for the same graph), see Babaioff et al. (2013, pp. 7–8) (Fig. 2).

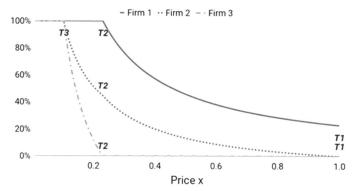

Fig. 2 Optimal Inverse Cumulative distribution function for each firm after working with the equalities defined in Eq. (1). This represents the expected behavior for each firm. For instance, Firm 1 has the chance of 100% of choosing the price of 0.2 for higher, which means that it is not expected to see Firm 1 asking for the price lower than 0.2

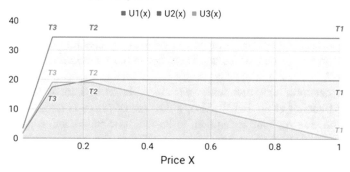

Fig. 3 Utility level for each company. Note that between the pricing range that fall within the support of each firm, the utility level is the same

For this example, by working with the equalities in (1), it has been found that $t_1 = 1$, $t_2 = 0.2294520548$, and $t_3 = 0.102739726$. Those values are the optimal pricing ranges for each firm i that allows mixing where none of the firms can deviate to another CDF function (pricing strategy) or to another pricing ranges to get a better payoff. In the Fig. 3, it is possible to see that f_2 is more likely to succeed in this scenario by having the highest utility level.

3   Applying the Model in a Reverse Manner

To verify if it is profitable for a firm to join an existing market, it is needed to apply this model to one existing network and then, simulate an entrance from some firm (see Fig. 5 for an illustrative example). Comparing the results will show information such as:

- Changes in pricing decision of each firm (reaction);
- Expected profit of each firm before and after the entrance of a firm in the network.

It is important to comprehend how buyers are distributed over market shares. This allows an analyst to understand the potential changes of each market in the network by repeating the process over time, tracking what is happening to the markets. If the result from the model shows that the number of buyers in a market has fallen, it may suggest that the market is in decline.

While the existing Bertrand Network model allows to go from the size of markets to the optimal ranging prices for each company, it is suggested to do the opposite in this study. If the distribution of buyers is not known, it will not be possible to repeat the calculations like the one briefly shown in the Sect. 2. The remainder of this section shows how to use the model to discover proportion of buyers from each market.

First, one must model the competition network by checking who is competing against whom and in which market. Then, figure out the *equilibrium sketch* of the built network because it is not known any algorithm that can give the equilibrium of any given network, although the *equilibrium sketch* is known for some graph structures (Babaioff et al. 2013). Also, a data set of prices is needed, so an information of prices over time is required to known how sellers are pricing.

It is assumed that the companies are playing the price competition game rationally, i.e., are indeed following their best CDF to choose prices within the optimal pricing range.

Recalling the Sect. 2, the same graph structure is modeled, but now the market sizes are assumed to be unknow and it will be shown that it is possible to get similar results from the original example by only knowing the prices that each firm was choosing.

3.1   Collecting Prices

Consider that prices were collected from day d_1 to d_n and let $P_{i,k,j}$ be the j-th price from the k-th day of the i-th firm. Let P_i be the non-decreasing sorted set of prices from the i-th firm. Finally, let P be the union of every P_i.

As the existing model use prices in $[0, 1]$, let the collected prices be mapped from $[0, M]$ to $[0, 1]$, where M is the highest price collected. Formally, let $f: P \to [0, 1]$.

Recalling the graph presented in the Sect. 2, the *equilibrium sketch* defines that the seller f_1 is pricing in $[t_2, t_1], f_2$ in $[t_3, t_1]$ and f_3 in $[t_3, t_2]$. Therefore, t_1 must be the greatest value in P, t_3 the minimum and let t_2 be the minimum value of f_1.

Let $C_i(x)$ be the number of elements in P_i that are lesser than x. To calculate the probability of randomly choosing the value of x or higher from the data set, let $\overline{F}_i(x) = \frac{|P_i| - C_i(x)}{|P_i|}$.

3.2 Assumptions

Suppose that an analyst has collected a data set that shows the following information:

- $t_1 = 1$ as it would be in any equilibrium (Babaioff et al. 2013);
- f_1 chooses the price of 1 with positive probability (has an *atom* at 1). Consider that after analyzing the data set, it has been found that the probability for f_1 to choose the price of t_1 or higher is $\overline{F}_1(t_1) = 0.23$, like in the original example (see Fig. 2);
- With similar reasoning, $\overline{F}_2(t_2) = 0.45$;
- $\overline{F}_1(x) = \overline{F}_2(x) = \overline{F}_3(x) = 1 \quad \forall x \leq t_3$ since every firm are choosing prices higher than t_3;
- $\overline{F}_2(t_1) = \overline{F}_3(t_2) = 0$ by claiming the results from Babaioff et al. (2013, p. 9), *Lemma 4.2* that states: *"Fix any valid tie breaking rule. In any network and any equilibrium, no two sellers who share a market both have an atom at the same positive price"*;
- $\overline{F}_3(x) = 0 \quad \forall x \geq t_2$ since t_2 is the higher price for f_3.

Note that the CDF for each company has been defined at the boundary points in their support, which would be possible by observing a data set (Fig. 4).

3.3 Calculating the Market Share from Prices and CDFs

Now, the calculation must be started by defining the following equalities that in equilibrium must be satisfied (see Eq. (1)).

$$u_1(t_1) = u_1(t_2)$$
$$t_1 * \alpha_1 = t_2 * \left(\alpha_1 + \beta_{1,2} * \overline{F}_2(t_2)\right)$$
$$\frac{t_2}{t_1} = \frac{\alpha_1}{\alpha_1 + \beta_{1,2} * \overline{F}_2(t_2)} \tag{3}$$

Fig. 4 Hypergraph in which
only the prices are known.
Note the question marks,
indicating that the market
sizes are unknown

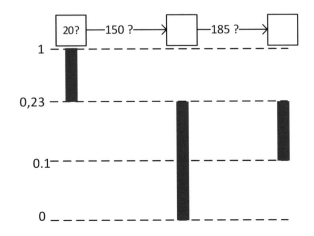

$$u_2(t_1) = u_2(t_2)$$
$$t_1\left(\alpha_2 + \beta_{1,2} * \overline{F}_1(t_1)\right) = t_2\left(\alpha_2 + \beta_{1,2}\right) \tag{4}$$
$$\frac{t_2}{t_1} = \frac{\alpha_2 + \beta_{1,2} * \overline{F}_1(t_1)}{\alpha_2 + \beta_{1,2}}$$

$$u_2(t_2) = u_2(t_3)$$
$$t_2 * \left(\alpha_2 + \beta_{1,2}\right) = t_3 * \left(\alpha_2 + \beta_{1,2} + \beta_{2,3}\right) \tag{5}$$
$$\frac{t_3}{t_2} = \frac{\alpha_2 + \beta_{1,2}}{\alpha_2 + \beta_{1,2} + \beta_{2,3}}$$

$$u_3(t_2) = u_3(t_3)$$
$$t_2 * \left(\alpha_3 + \beta_{2,3} * \overline{F}_2(t_2)\right) = t_3 * \left(\alpha_3 + \beta_{2,3}\right) \tag{6}$$
$$\frac{t_3}{t_2} = \frac{\alpha_3 + \beta_{2,3} * \overline{F}_2(t_2)}{\alpha_3 + \beta_{2,3}}$$

To be able to calculate the proportion of each market, the following equalities will be used:

$$\alpha_1 = a * \beta_{1,2}$$
$$\alpha_2 = b * \beta_{1,2}$$
$$\alpha_3 = c * \beta_{1,2}$$
$$\beta_{2,3} = k * \beta_{1,2}$$

This will simplify the calculations since now it will be possible to find the ratio of each market over $\beta_{1,2}$ (chosen by convenience, note that every shared market will be greater than 0, otherwise that market share would not exist). From Eq. (3):

$$t_2 = \frac{a * \beta_{1,2}}{a * \beta_{1,2} + \beta_{1,2} * \overline{F}_2(t_2)}$$

$$t_2 = \frac{a}{a + \overline{F}_2(t_2)}$$

$$a = t_2 * \left(a + \overline{F}_2(t_2)\right)$$

$$a - t_2 * a = t_2 * \overline{F}_2(t_2)$$

$$a = \frac{t_2 * \overline{F}_2(t_2)}{1 - t_2}$$

Since 'a' only uses constant values, from now on 'a' can be treated as a constant value. Proceeding with (4):

$$t_2 = \frac{b * \beta_{1,2} + \beta_{1,2} * \overline{F}_1(t_1)}{b * \beta_{1,2} + \beta_{1,2}}$$

$$t_2 = \frac{b + \overline{F}_1(t_1)}{b + 1}$$

$$t_2 * b + t_2 - b = \overline{F}_1(t_1)$$

$$b * (t_2 - 1) + t_2 = \overline{F}_1(t_1)$$

$$b = \frac{\overline{F}_1(t_1) - t_2}{t_2 - 1}$$

From Eq. (5):

$$\frac{t_2}{t_3} = 1 + \frac{\beta_{2,3}}{\alpha_2 + \beta_{1,2}}$$

$$\frac{t_2}{t_3} = 1 + \frac{k}{b + 1}$$

$$k = \left(\frac{t_2}{t_3} - 1\right) * (b + 1)$$

Finally, from Eq. (6):

$$\frac{t_3}{t_2} = \frac{c + k * \bar{F}_2(t_2)}{c + k}$$

$$\frac{t_3}{t_2} * c + \frac{t_3}{t_2} * k - c = k * \bar{F}_2(t_2)$$

$$c * \left(\frac{t_3}{t_2} - 1\right) = k * \left(\bar{F}_2(t_2) - \frac{t_3}{t_2}\right)$$

$$c = k * \frac{\bar{F}_2(t_2) - \frac{t_3}{t_2}}{\frac{t_3}{t_2} - 1}$$

This concludes the calculation and now it is possible to find the buyer distribution over the network that would lead to the same pricing range and CDF in the original example by just setting a value for $\beta_{1,2}$. Note that there are many possible values for $\beta_{1,2}$, and each of them will lead to different utility levels. By choosing $\beta_{1,2} = 150$, let see the value of the other markets that would be found by using the results that was calculated:

$$\alpha_1 = 20.16233766$$
$$\alpha_2 = 0$$
$$\alpha_3 = 0.0455$$
$$\beta_{2,3} = 195$$

Note that those results are very close to the first example in Sect. 2. By calculating every market size as a ratio over one of them (in this case every market size was being calculated over $\beta_{1,2}$) it is possible verify, for T being the total of buyers that will be distributed over the structure:

$$\alpha_1 + \alpha_2 + \alpha_3 + \beta_{1,2} + \beta_{2,3} = T$$
$$a * \beta_{1,2} + b * \beta_{1,2} + c * \beta_{1,2} + k * \beta_{1,2} = T$$
$$\beta_{1,2} = \frac{T}{a + b + c + k}$$

Similar reasoning can be applied for other networks. It is worth noting that the price and CDF values have been rounded at the beginning of this section, thus the approximated results for each market share.

4 Expanded Bertrand Network

To show what is willing to achieve, consider the Fig. 5.

First, it is stated that any market which is being shared for more than two firms are called oligopoly shared market. The meaning of $N(i)$ has changed to be the set of shared markets that are being shared to exactly 2 vendors. Now the Eq. (2) is expanded to one form that considers the mix of duopolies and oligopolies.

$$u_i(x) = x * \left(\alpha_i + \sum_{k \in N^o(i)} \beta_k * \sigma_{-i,k}(x) + \sum_{j \in N(i)} \beta_{i,j} * \overline{F}_j(x) \right) \qquad (7)$$

where $N^o(i)$ is the set of the neighboring oligopoly shared markets of i, β_k is the size of the oligopoly shared market k and $\sigma_{-i,k}(x)$ represents some combination of the CDFs of all vendors that are participating in the oligopoly shared market k excluding the firm i, as a subset of $[0, 1]$. Essentially $\sigma_{-i,k}(x)$ tries to represent the combination of the pricing strategy of all competitors of i in the oligopoly k.

That said, the attempt to define the aggregated function of CDFs for oligopoly markets is shown below. To let the utility function be linear (like in the original model), let the aggregated function be the average sum of all the CDFs. Consider any oligopoly k with n firms and let $H(k, y)$ be a hash function that returns the index of the y-th firm in that oligopoly k, for $1 \le y \le n$:

$$\sigma_{-i,k}(x) = \frac{\sum_{y=1}^{n} \overline{F}_{H(y)}(x) - \overline{F}_{H(i)}(x)}{n - 1}$$

For the sake of simplicity, k has been omitted from $H(k, y)$. The belief that, in any oligopoly with at least 2 firms that has a captive market, **Lemma 4.2** from Babaioff et al. (2013, p. 9) does not apply is shown below.

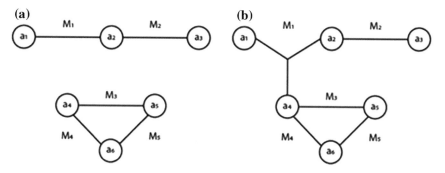

Fig. 5 Two connected components of the hypergraph in **a** representing two different market networks and **b** an expansion attempt of the firm f_4 to join the market share M_1

Conjecture 1 *Fix any network composed by one oligopoly shared market with at least 2 firms that has a positive captive market. There exist more than one firm that does choose 1 with positive probability.*

Assume that **Lemma 4.2** does apply. Sort the firms and label them from 1 to n such as $\alpha_1 \geq \alpha_2 > \alpha_3 \cdots \geq \alpha_n \geq 0$. Then, if f_1 has an *atom* at 1, the following holds:

$$\sigma_{-1}(1) = 0$$

Then:

$$\sigma_{-1}(1) = \frac{\sum_{j=2}^{n} \overline{F}_j(1)}{n-1}$$

$$\sum_{j=2}^{n} \overline{F}_j(1) = 0 \tag{8}$$

Which is true since none of the firms has an atom at 1. Therefore, for every $1 < i \leq n$:

$$\sigma_{-i}(1) = \frac{\overline{F}_1(1) + \sum_{j=2}^{n} \overline{F}_j(1) - \overline{F}_i(1)}{n-1}$$

$$\sigma_{-i}(1) = \frac{\overline{F}_1(1)}{n-1}$$

Thus, For every $1 < i \leq n$:

$$u_i(1) = \alpha_i + \beta * \sigma_{-i}(1) \Rightarrow u_i(1) = \alpha_i + \beta * \frac{\overline{F}_1(1)}{n-1}$$

For the firm n there exist a minimum price t_2 that allows mixing, thus the following must hold:

$$u_n(1) = u_n(t_2)$$

$$\alpha_n + \beta * \frac{\overline{F}_1(1)}{n-1} = t_2 * \left(\alpha_n + \beta * \frac{\overline{F}_1(t_2)}{n-1}\right)$$

$$\alpha_n + \beta * \frac{\overline{F}_1(1)}{n-1} = t_2 * \left(\alpha_n + \beta * \frac{1}{n-1}\right)$$

$$t_2 = \frac{\alpha_n + \beta * \frac{\overline{F}_1(1)}{n-1}}{\alpha_n + \beta * \frac{1}{n-1}}$$

Every firm that will mix must be mixing at the same interval $[t_2, 1]$, so none of them can deviate and ask for a price that will allow him to win the shared market with probability one (Babaioff et al. 2013; Guzmán 2011).

$$t_2 = \frac{\alpha_i + \beta * \frac{\overline{F_1}(1)}{n-1}}{\alpha_i + \beta * \frac{1}{n-1}}$$

$$\frac{\alpha_n + \beta * \frac{\overline{F_1}(1)}{n-1}}{\alpha_n + \beta * \frac{1}{n-1}} = t_2 = \frac{\alpha_i + \beta * \frac{\overline{F_1}(1)}{n-1}}{\alpha_i + \beta * \frac{1}{n-1}}$$

This is only possible if $a_n = a_i$ for every i, contradicting the assumption that each firm may have different sizes of captive markets. This suggests that another firm might be choosing the price of 1 (which would lead to $\sigma_{-i}(1) > 0$ for another $i > 1$), or some firm is choosing the price of 1 with negative probability, from the equality in Eq. (8).   ∎

This concludes the belief that **Lemma 4.2** must be reworked, in addition to another prof by Guzmán (2011) that asserted that the duopoly model is the solution of the oligopoly model, but with a different aggregated function.

5 Conclusions and Future Work

This paper has presented one way to use the model for guessing the distribution of buyers over one competition network. As stated before, the information that can be gather from the proposed attempt to show how this model is very important and can be useful in analyzing the attempt of one company to join in another market.

It is now needed to apply this to a real case, detailing how it would be possible to identify the CDF for each firm at every boundary point of firms support. It is also needed to provide one formal prof for the Conjecture 1 (if true).

References

Abolhassani, M., Bateni, M. H., Hajiaghayi, M., Mahini, H., & Sawant, A. (2014). *Network cournot competition*. Lecture Notes in Computer Science (pp. 15–29).

Babaioff, M., Blumrosen, L., & Nisan, N. (2016). Networks of complements. In *The 43rd International Colloquium on Automata, Languages and Programming (ICALP)*. Retrieved from https://www.microsoft.com/en-us/research/publication/networks-of-complements/.

Babaioff, M., Lucier, B., & Nisan, N. (2013, June). Bertrand networks. In *Proceedings of the Fourteenth ACM Conference on Electronic Commerce*. https://doi.org/10.1145/2482540.2482564.

Babaioff, M., Nisan, N., & Paes Leme, R. (2014). Price competition in online combinatorial markets. In *Proceedings of the 23rd International Conference on World Wide Web* (pp. 711–722). Seoul, Korea: ACM. https://doi.org/10.1145/2566486.2568016.

Barquin, J., & Vazquez, M. (May, 2008). Cournot equilibrium calculation in power networks: An optimization approach with price response computation. *IEEE Transactions on Power Systems, 23*(2), 317–326. https://doi.org/10.1109/tpwrs.2008.919198.

Bimpikis, K., Ehsani, S., & Ilkiliç, R. (2014). Cournot competition in networked markets. In *Proceedings of the Fifteenth ACM Conference on Economics and Computation* (pp. 733–733). Palo Alto, California, USA: ACM. https://doi.org/10.1145/2600057.2602882.

Bose, S., Cai, D. W., Low, S. H., & Wierman, A. (2014a). The role of a market maker in networked cournot competition. In *arXiv: Computer science and game theory* (pp. 4479–4484). Retrieved October 5, 2018, from http://dblp.uni-trier.de/db/journals/corr/corr1701.html.

Bose, S., Cai, D. W., Low, S., & Wierman, A. (2014b). The role of a market maker in networked cournot competition. In *53rd IEEE Conference on Decision and Control* (pp. 4479–4484). https://doi.org/10.1109/cdc.2014.7040088.

Cai, D., Bose, S., & Wierman, A. (2017). On the role of a market maker in networked cournot competition. Obtido de https://arxiv.org/abs/1701.08896.

Guzmán, C. L. (2011). Price competition on network. *Banco de México*.

Jing-Yuan, W., & Smeers, Y. (1999). Spatial oligopolistic electricity models with cournot generators and regulated transmission prices. *Operations Research, 47*(1), 102–112. https://doi.org/10.1287/opre.47.1.102.

Kasbekar, G. S., & Sarkar, S. (January, 2012). Spectrum pricing games with spatial reuse in cognitive radio networks. *IEEE Journal on Selected Areas in Communications, 30*(1), 153–164. https://doi.org/10.1109/jsac.2012.120114.

Kreps, D. M., & Scheinkman, J. A. (1983). Quantity Precommitment and bertrand competition yield Cournot outcomes. *The Bell Journal of Economics, 14*, 326–337. https://doi.org/10.2307/3003636.

Motalleb, M., Eshraghi, A., Reihani, E., Sangrody, H., & Ghorbani, R. (2017). A game-theoretic demand response market with networked competition model. n *2017 North American Power Symposium (NAPS)* (pp. 1–6). Morgantown, WV, USA: IEEE. https://doi.org/10.1109/naps.2017.8107253.

Yao, J., Oren, S. S., & Adler, I. (2004). Computing Cournot equilibria in two settlement electricity markets with transmission constraint. In *37th Annual Hawaii International Conference on System Sciences.* https://doi.org/10.1109/hicss.2004.1265176.

The Potential of Tag-Based Contextualization Mechanisms to Leverage the Sale of Regional Products and Promote the Regions Through Products

Carlos R. Cunha⬚, Vítor Mendonça⬚, Aida Carvalho⬚ and Elisabete Paulo Morais⬚

Abstract In small and rural regions, where we can many times find top quality products, there is, many times, a greater difficulty in promoting their products. This difficulty begins in the nature of the companies that manufacture these products. These companies are typically family-owned or small-sized, not having large capacity to carry out very elaborate marketing strategies. They often depend of the tourist attractiveness of the regions themselves to leverage their sales. This paper discuss the challenges for the promotion of regional products and rural regions, review the role of smartphones and the main tag-based contextualization mechanisms and their potential for leverage the sale of rural regional products and, finally, presents a cooperation-based conceptual model, where are combined contextualization-tags and mobile devices to promote regional products, leverage sales and promote rural regions by attracting new visitants, making regional products a window-mechanism to the promotion of rural regions heritage and tourism-related services.

Keywords Rural regions · Rural products · Model · Tag-based contextualization · Promotion

C. R. Cunha (✉) · E. P. Morais
Applied Management Research Unit (UNIAG), Polytechnic Institute of Bragança, Mirandela, Portugal
e-mail: crc@ipb.pt

E. P. Morais
e-mail: beta@ipb.pt

V. Mendonça
Polytechnic Institute of Bragança, Mirandela, Portugal
e-mail: mendonca@ipb.pt

A. Carvalho
Centro de Investigação, Desenvolvimento e Inovação em Turismo (CiTUR),
Polytechnic Institute of Bragança, Mirandela, Portugal
e-mail: acarvalho@ipb.pt

© Springer Nature Switzerland AG 2019
I. Ramos et al. (eds.), *Information Systems for Industry 4.0*,
Lecture Notes in Information Systems and Organisation 31,
https://doi.org/10.1007/978-3-030-14850-8_9

1 Introduction

Local Products, Quality and Typicity (LPQTP) of Trás-os Montes have a set of much more real features that confer authenticity. Often, referred to as typical, regional, artisan, among others, can be more respected, bringing together producers, consumers and regions. Given their distinctive characteristics, they can respond to the dynamics and challenges of promoting the territory, ensuring the achievement of new quality standards in the creation of a brand that is recognized by the demand.

The LPQTP, are easily identified by their geographical origin and can be in the context of economic and social restructuring one of the most fruitful potential development alternatives in rural areas (Ribeiro and Martins 1996).

Currently, associated with tradition, innovation and creativity, they have been positive developments as a result of use of ingredients (natural and artificial) of varied and complex chemical composition, for preserving, blush, gasify, among many others, increasing the terms of shelf life (Treager et al. 2007) in compliance with EU regulations and certifications.

In Portugal, the Protected Designation of Origin (DPO), Protected Geographical Indication (PGI) and Guaranteed Traditional Specialty (GTS) protect the products, methods of production, assuring the consumer that the product has a different flavour and aroma and that was obtained or processed in a traditional way. They are a regional endogenous potential that attribute value to the territory, translating all the distinguishing characteristics of a place, a space and a region that generates and multiplies feelings of belonging and collective identity (Ribeiro and Martins 1996). When a consumer chooses a certified product, he or she understands that that product is different from a noncertified product because it is guaranteed to be socially more equitable, to cause less environmental impact, and is generally healthier. They have a specific positioning and distribution channel in specialty stores (national/international), meeting the new demands, needs and expectations of consumers (Bernart 1996). They are strategic assets of reputed value for the territories, but when they are acquired do not reflect and/or make available information on the characteristics of the territories as tourist destinations. This is, nevertheless, a differentiating product, the consumer, when he acquires them, does not know the local idiosyncrasies associated with the product as well as the local gastronomy, the landscape, human and monumental heritage of the region, churches, convents and monasteries, houses and palaces, squares and archaeological sites, historical centers, regional literature and music, among other patrimony of their territories of belonging. However, because of their authenticity, they can work more and better the territory component, ambassadors and facilitators of the communicational process as a promotional tool that can create attraction, influence in perception and induction, promoting a consumer persuasion effect on potential tourists, seeking to convert them into effective tourists. This effect, perhaps, to build a joint and holistic strategy to promote the rural environment and awaken in producers, technicians, politicians, legislators, researchers, entrepreneurs, among others, who wish to fight against desertification and depopulation of rural areas, thus combating asymmetries.

The rural tourism industry is characterized by small firms where a lack of trust and cooperation predominates (Correia 2006). These constraints have created problems in the rural tourism sector, reflecting the need for technical assistance to destinations and rural organizations to develop management strategies. Also, the shift from a basic rural economy to a new economic specialization involves experimentation, learning processes, new capabilities, new policies, adjustment and reconfigurations (Debashis and Amitava 2003). In the context of rural tourism is essential to create cooperation networks that favouring competitiveness and the complementarity of companies (Gao et al. 2007), allowing economic agents offer a wider range of products and services to its customers (Hall and Mitchell 2002). This reality shows, in our opinion, that any conceptual model to leverage sales and/or promotion system must be based on a cooperative approach and not by isolated individual organizations. Considering the context of tourism in rural regions, and especially in disadvantaged regions, where small economic operators are dominant, it is essential to create conditions and promote ways to increase their competitiveness. As such, any proposed models to leverage sales and promote regions, must support/create synergies among the small agents and promote cooperative arrangements, and consequently, increasing the capacity of installed response.

In this work we have used the Action Research method, one of the four that form the Applied Research methodology (action research, case-study research, ethnography and grounded theory), (Rapoport 1970), which is mainly focused on four stages: plan, action, observation, reflection and revision (Kemmis and Taggart 1988).

2 Mobile Devices and Tag-Based Contextualization Mechanisms

Mobile-devices, mainly smartphones, combined with their ability to access the Internet in an unexpansive way, are embedded in daily routines and represent the most common and widely used technology today. As such, educational level is not a serious barrier to their use. Studies have shown that in Portugal, at the end of 2017, the penetration of the mobile service amounted to 170.5 per 100 inhabitants. The penetration rate of mobile stations with effective use was 127.4 per 100 inhabitants. According to the Marktest Telecommunications Barometer data, 95.5% of Portuguese residents in the quarter were Mobile Telephone Service customers (ANACOM 2017). As a rule, "everyone carries at least one mobile-device". This wide availability makes them an ideal tool for interacting with information technology and on-demand services. This idea is reinforced by the current evolution trends in mobile-devices, which suggests an enormous potential that can be tapped to support enterprise information and services platforms, specially m-commerce, as discussed in (Mahatanankoon et al. 2005; Ngai and Gunasekaran 2007; Cunha et al. 2010) making them the key technology to access data services and support ubiquitous frameworks.

Tags, as a machine-readable representation of data (Gao et al. 2007), have been largely used to represent data and to link objects to digital information. There are several tag-based ID technologies, such as barcodes and radio-frequency identification (RFID) tags. The combination of 2D visual tags with an easy-to-use on-the-fly decoding system yields an effective, powerful and innovative way of providing real time contextualized information and on-demand services.

Found almost everywhere, 1D barcodes or simply barcodes are a tag-based ID technology that have the capability to store and represent data through parallel lines of different width. They are massively used in retail commerce, linking products to databases, making automatic management and accounting systems possible. Two-dimensional or 2D barcodes represent another step in the tag systems technological evolution. They have emerged as the natural way to encode large quantities of alphanumeric data and to link objects to web-based information and services, through the encoding of an URL (Parikh and Lazowska 2006; Rekimoto and Ayatsuka 2000; Toye et al. 2005). RFID tags are transponders that can be placed in one package or product, among others. It contains silicon chips and antennas that allows it to respond to radio signals sent by a transmitter base. Table 1 shows a comparison between different types of tag-based ID technologies.

The current trends in the evolution of smartphones have made built-in cameras a standard component and NFC support present in many models; as a result, almost all smartphones are portable decoding devices, transforming a low-cost widespread consumer electronics device into a visual or non visual inspection system.

Tags can be easily and inexpensively embedded in real-world objects and their decoding systems are based on image recognition algorithms. Because of their ability to handle more data per tag area, visual tags are replacing the well-known EAN13 barcodes. Putting together barcodes with information storage capabilities and smartphones as decoding systems represent a natural approach as a reliable mechanism to quickly look up information or initiate an object-specific action. In fact, visual 2D visual tags, NFC tags and mobile-devices are already used in several activities.

Tags can also provide an attractive and transparent way to enable user access to product-oriented contextualized information and services, as stated in (Gao et al. 2007), which allows the creation of innovative interface between companies and

Table 1 Comparison between common tag-based identification technologies (Cunha et al. 2010)

	Barcodes	2D Visual tags	RF tags
Strengths	Printable; Low-cost; Suitable for visual decoding	Printable; High data store capability; Low-cost; Suitable for visual decoding	Automatic non-visual reading: Can be decoded while inside objects
Weaknesses	Low data store capability; Decoding in dirty environments	Decoding in dirty environments	Not Printable; Cost; Reading problems; RFID portable decoder

customers: new Client Relationship Management (CRM) and Business-to-Consumer (B2C) tools allowing a rich multimedia experience by using smartphones and contextualization mechanisms, which allow for example, the use of augmented reality contents, sound and image in well defined geographic spots, thus significantly improving the understating of a given context or situation benefiting the B2C interactions.

The bridge between a site-specific action and the information system that provides the on-demand services is accomplished by the contextualization element, placed in the targeted objects. This translate the fusion-vision of physical and digital world.

3 Making Regional Products a Point of Entry for Rural Regions: Challenges and Opportunities

Smartphones are becoming a primary platform for information access and a primary application area for mobile applications is tourism. Understanding and exploring the capabilities of mobile channel is of great importance (Pesonen and Horster 2012). Also Wang et al. (2011) state that smartphones have a huge potential to influence in a significantly way the touristic experience. Mobile media are compelling channels for digital marketers and advertisers due to their potential to support one-to-one, one-to-many and mass communication both cheaply and effectively (Watson et al. 2013). In a complementary way, the use of contextualisation elements is already part of many products, however, presenting results that often fall far short of expectations. Lindsey et al. (2014) discusses the role of QR codes and wine apps in consumer wine purchases, stating that we must increase the utility of the QR code by providing deals, in the form of value, to the QR code users. In a study conducted by Yeong and Woo (2016), is discussed that the use of contextualization elements in gastronomic products can help marketers to develop effective strategies, as the results suggest that it is important to emphasize food information for consumers. The study findings demonstrate that consumer considers QR code for food traceability system to provide detailed information about foods and much information that helps them in their buying-decision.

Contextualization tag-based mechanisms have also strong implications for marketing in general, and especially in service marketing. From a marketing perspective tags, such as QR codes, can be used to promote brands and attract customers in new ways and be used in advertising and promotion in general (Mostafa 2015; Walsh 2009). There are also, in the field of heritage promotion, several untapped opportunities to regions. According Rujijan and Ralangarm (2015), tourists have use the ability of smart devices to scan contextualization tags that subsequently processed and rendered various information, including pictures, history and several details about historical places.

In our opinion, there is an untapped potential for combining mobile devices and contextualization mechanism for leverage regional products sales and, through them, promote and "sale" rural regions heritage and touristic services. This potential must be explored by a cooperative a cross selling approach.

4   Proposed Conceptual Model

In a context in which the strategic alliances, consolidated in interorganizational cooperation networks, affirm themselves as strategic, we propose, as presented in Fig. 1, the development of a Cooperative Marketplace System in order to promote and leverage the sale of products and/or services in rural spaces.

The system should allow the various cooperating agents (manufacturers, tourism operators, local government entities) to have access to a platform in which they share information about products, services, regional events, among others.

On the other hand, customers will have access to the information of a product from reading the identifier of that product. Therefore, the platform based, for example, on customer location and user behavior may provide access to other products, services and/or related events, promoting cross-selling practices and facilitating relationship management with customers in a cooperative manner.

The proposed model paradigm starts in the ability of put contextualization mechanisms in regional products (e.g. olive oil bottles, regional sausages, etc.). This possibility doesn't represent difficulties (e.g. almost all products already, have at least, 1D barcodes), and in many cases aren't expensive.

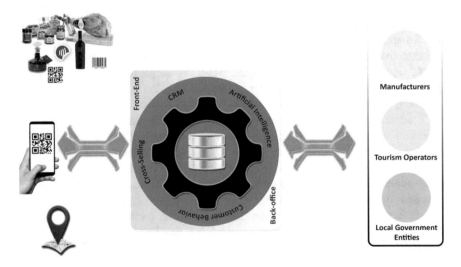

Fig. 1 Conceptual model: cooperative marketplace system

With today smartphones, that have the ability of decode the major contextualization tags, and that also have Global Positioning System (GPS), we can understand the product and the location interaction that clients are experience. With these two elements we can redirect "the client", through, native decoding applications or service-providers developed mobile applications (this scenario enable much more potentialities), to our cooperative marketplace. This proposed marketplace, intend to materialize a cooperative network combining local governmental entities, tourism operators, regional products manufacturers, among other. With this cooperative approach we can centralize the promotion of regional products, heritage and services related to tourism. This makes products a window to regions.

Such platform could represent and integrated approach capable to generate knowledge about the clients' expectations and one unique opportunity to an innovative CRM strategy. In rural regions, characterized by small players and several lacks related to financial and technological capabilities, we think that making products the window to promote regions and leverage the sales of regional products and services is the right path to take.

5   Conclusion and Final Remarks

This paper has discussed the role of regional products and considerate the context of tourism in rural regions, and especially in disadvantaged regions, where small economic operators are dominant, being essential to create conditions and promote ways to increase their competitiveness. As such, the model that we have presented intends to create synergies between the small agents and to promote cooperative arrangements, and consequently, increasing the capacity of installed response. In order to achieve this goal, we believe that it must be through the products that we can operationalize the leverage of the products themselves and the regions where they are inserted. Regions are fixed objects, yet their products travel the world. This R&D work will, in is next stage, develop a prototype platform to materialize the proposed model.

Acknowledgements UNIAG, R&D unit funded by the FCT—Portuguese Foundation for the Development of Science and Technology, Ministry of Science, Technology and Higher Education. UID/GES/4752/2016.

References

ANACOM. (2017). Relatório do Serviço Telefónico Móvel 3º Trimestre de 2017, Autoridade Nacional de Comunicações, Portugal, Relatório Técnico de 3º Semestre.
Bernart, E. (1996). Los nuevos consumidores o las nuevas relaciones entre campo y ciudad através de los produtos de la tierra. *Agricultura y Sociedad, no, 80–81*, 83–116.

Correia R. (2006). Wine, tourism and collective action. In *Proceedings of Academy of the 2nd World Business, Marketing & Management Development Conference*, (pp. 60–68). Paris, France.

Cunha, C. R., Peres, E., Morais, R., Bessa, M, & Reis, M. C. (2010). Contextualized Ubiquity: A new opportunity for rendering business information and services (extended version). *Journal of Theoretical and Applied Electronic Commerce Research*, *5*(3), 55–64. ISSN 0718–1876, Universidad de Talca—Chile.

Debashis, S., & Amitava, M. (2003). Pervasive computing: a paradigm for the 21st century. *Computer, 36*(3), 25–31.

Gao, J. Z., Prakash L., & Jagatesan R. (2007). Understanding 2D-barcode technology and applications in mcommerce—design and implementation of a 2D barcode processing solution, In *Proceedings of 31st Annual International on Computer Software and Applications Conference* (pp. 49–56). Beijing, China.

Hall C. M. & Mitchell R. (2001). Wine tourism in the Mediterranean: A tool for restructuring and development, *Thunderbird International Business Review*, Wiley, *42*(4), 445–465.

Kemmis S., & Taggart, R. M.(1988). *The Action Research Reader*, Victoria: Deakin University Press.

Lindsey, H. M., Wolf M. M., & Wolf M. J. (2014). Technological change in the wine market? The role of QR codes and wine apps in consumer wine purchases, *Wine Economics and Policy, 3* (1), 19–27, ISSN 2212-9774.

Mahatanankoon, P., Wen, H. J., & Lim, B. (2005). Consumer-based m-commerce: exploring consumer perception of mobile applications. *Computer Standards & Interfaces, 27*(4), 347–357.

Mostafa, A. (2015). The effectiveness of product codes in marketing, In *Procedia—Social and Behavioral Sciences*, (vol. 175, pp. 12–15). ISSN 1877-0428.

Ngai, E. W. T., & Gunasekaran, A. (2007). A review for mobile commerce research and applications. *Decision Support Systems, 43*(1), 3–15.

Parikh, T. S. & Lazowska, E. D. (2006). Designing an architecture for delivering mobile information services to therural developing world, (pp. 791–800). ACM, 2006, Edinburgh, Scotland.

Pesonen, J. & Horster, E. (2012) Near field communication technology in tourism, *Tourism Management Perspectives*, (vol. 4, pp. 11–18). ISSN 2211-9736.

Rapoport, R. N. (1970). The three dilemmas in action research, *Human Relations*, (pp. 499–513).

Rekimoto, J. & Ayatsuka, Y. (2000). Cybercode: Designing augmented reality environments with visual tags, In *Proceedings of DARE 2000 on Designing augmented reality*, (pp. 1–10). Denmark: Elsinore.

Ribeiro, M. & Martins, C. (1996). La certificación como estratégia de valorización de produtos agroalimentarios tradicionales: la alheira, um embutido tradicional de Trás-os-Montes. In *Agricultura y Sociedad*, 80–81, pp.313–334.

Rujijan, V. & Ralangarm, S. (2015). Temple information retrieval system using quick response code via mobile application, In *Procedia—Social and Behavioral Sciences*, (vol. 197, pp. 998–1005). ISSN 1877-0428.

Toye, E., Sharp, R., Madhavapeddy, A., & Scott, D. (2005). Using smart phones to access site-specific services. *IEEE Pervasive Computing, 4*(2), 60–66.

Treager, A., et al. (2007). Regional foods and rural development: The role of product qualification. *Journal of Rural Studies, 23*(1), 12–22.

Wang, D., Park, S., & Fesenmaier, D. (2011). The role of smartphones in mediating the touristic experience. *Journal of Travel Research, 51*(4), 371–387.

Watson C., McCarthy J., Rowley J. (2013). Consumer attitudes towards mobile marketing in the smart phone era, *International Journal of Information Management*, *33*(5), 840–849, ISSN 0268-4012.

Walsh, A. (2009). Quick response codes and libraries. *Library Hi Tech News, 26*(5/6), 7–9.

Yeong G. K. & Woo E. (2016). Consumer acceptance of a quick response (QR) code for the food traceability system: Application of an extended technology acceptance model (TAM), *Food Research International*, (vol. 85, pp. 266–272). ISSN 0963-9969.

Urban Intelligence for Sustainability

Miguel de Castro Neto and **João Sousa Rego**

Abstract A smart city can be seen as an urban space that takes advantage of information and communication technologies and data science to answer todays challenges, namely to become more efficient in services and infrastructures management and to deliver increased quality of life to the people who lives, works or visits the city, not forgetting the support to fight climate change. In this framework cities governments are nowadays under pressure and going through a digital transformation process that is translated in the proliferation of "Smart Cities" initiatives around the world as part of the strategic response to the challenges and opportunities of growing urbanization and climate change altogether with the emergence of cities as a space for social and economic development framed by an urgent need for global sustainability. In this work we will propose a concept of urban intelligence and its building blocks that result from the city digital transformation process which will lead to a paradigm shift leading to the city as a platform where urban planning and management for sustainability is supported by urban analytics and real time data.

Keywords Urban intelligence · Smart cities · Sustainability · City as a platform · Digital transformation

1 Introduction

Although we can find in the literature many "Smart City" definitions, we can say they all share the idea that a smart city is a urban space that takes advantage of information and communication technologies and data science to answer todays

M. de Castro Neto (✉) · J. S. Rego
Nova Information Management School, NOVA IMS Universidade
Nova de Lisboa, Lisbon, Portugal
e-mail: mneto@novaims.unl.pt

J. S. Rego
e-mail: jrego@novaims.unl.pt

© Springer Nature Switzerland AG 2019
I. Ramos et al. (eds.), *Information Systems for Industry 4.0*,
Lecture Notes in Information Systems and Organisation 31,
https://doi.org/10.1007/978-3-030-14850-8_10

challenges, namely to become more efficient in services and infrastructures management and to deliver increased quality of life to the people who lives, works or visits the city, not forgetting the support to fight climate change.

In fact today 50% of the world population lives in urban areas, a process of urbanization which tends to accelerate—estimating a population growth of 7–9 billion by 2050, which will represent 75% of the global population. Thus, although cities occupy only 2% of the earth land surface, are responsible for the production of 80% of global GDP and consume 75% of natural resources, produce 50% of global waste and emit 60–80% of greenhouse gases (UNEP 2017).

In this framework cities governments are nowadays under pressure and going through a digital transformation process to support higher efficiency resource usage that is translated in the proliferation of "Smart Cities" initiatives around the world as part of the strategic response to the challenges and opportunities of growing urbanization and climate change altogether with the emergence of cities as a space for social and economic development.

In this work we will propose a concept of urban intelligence that results from a digital transformation process which will lead to a paradigm shift where the city can be seen as a platform. In this city as a platform intelligent urban planning and management is supported by urban analytics and real time data. Furthermore, we will characterize what we believe are today the urban intelligence building blocks.

According to a recent landmark report released by the UN Intergovernmental Panel on Climate Change (IPCC 2018) urgent and unprecedented changes are needed to limit to 1.5 °C of warming temperatures.

This Report highlights the fact that the current levels of commitments are leading for a disastrous 3 °C of warming above the pre-industrial temperatures, but the limit of 1.5 °C is the highest that the world can take.

Keeping global warming below 1.5 °C means a decrease in people exposed to hot flashes, heavy rains, droughts, storms and floods, for example by allowing the rise in sea level to be 10 cm lower than expected by 2100, giving human and ecological systems new opportunities to adapt.

The 1.5 °C is the goal that give humanity the possibility for adaptation and mitigation, the development plan, the risks and the options for adaptation and mitigation, as a basis for policy development.

In order to achieve these objectives, there will be the need to change energy and transport systems, in an unprecedented way, being this two sectors the one more responsible and/or with more impact in the CO_2 emissions levels.

Cities cover less than 2% of the Earth's surface but consume 78% of the world's energy and produce 60% of all CO_2 emissions. Cities are one of the great opportunities to reach the defined objective, reaching quickly the scale factor of the measures to be taken.

The transport, because of the daily urban movements (house/work/house, of millions of people. The urban area consume large amounts of energy and the percentage of renewable energies is still too low to assure a decrease in the carbon emissions. *We can all reduce the pressure on our cities by consuming less, reusing what we can, and recycling the rest.* (Timothy Takemoto/Flickr)

2 Smart Cities

2.1 Smart City Definition

The concept of smart city, although not recent, remains diffuse and quite hetero-geneous. In general terms, it can be said that an smart city is a connected, knowledgeable and optimized urban space where the local administration uses information technologies to provide services and manage infrastructures, reducing costs, increasing security, and attracting investments, in a sustainable and resilient way, improving the quality of life of those who live, work or visit it.

Although the term has been gaining more popularity in the last two decades, to define what is a smart city is still a complicated task. There is neither a single definition to frame the concept smart city nor a one-size-fits-all definition (Albino et al. 2015), as we can see in Table 1 which reports some of the different meanings given to the concept by some authors.

In a more holistic perspective ISO (2014) defines intelligent city as one that can be described as a city that:

- It dramatically increases the pace of its sustainability and resilience;
- Fundamentally by improving (i) how it involves society, (ii) how it uses col-laborative leadership methods, (iii) how it works across disciplinary areas and city systems, and (iv) how it uses integrated data and technology;
- With a view to transforming services and quality of life for those who are in the city and for those who are involved with the city (who lives, who works and who visits).

Table 1 Smart city definitions (Fernandes 2017)

Definition	Source
Smart city as a high-tech intensive and advanced city that connects people, information and city elements using new technologies in order to create a sustainable, greener city, competitive and innovative commerce, and an increased life quality	Bakıcı et al. (2012)
Smart city generally refers to the search and identification of intelligent solutions which allow modern cities to enhance the quality of the services provided to aware citizens	Giffinger et al. (2007)
Smart Cities initiatives try to improve urban performance by using data, information and information technologies (IT) to provide more efficient services to citizens, to monitor and optimize existing infrastructure, to increase collaboration among different economic actors, and to encourage innovative business models in both the private and public sectors	Marsal-Llacuna et al. (2015)
The idea of a smart city is rooted in the creation and connection of human capital, social capital and information and communication technology (ICT) infrastructure in order to generate greater and more sustainable economic development and better quality of life	Manville et al. (2014)

The smart city results from the answer to the challenges posed by two mega-trends: urbanization and digital revolution. Thus, we can define an smart city as an interaction between technological innovation, organizational innovation and political innovation (Alawadhi et al. 2012).

With the objective of unifying and reach a consensus Anthopoulos et al. (2016) carried out a study where various smart cities models already proposed were analysed. The result was a unified smart city model that is composed by six dimensions that are recognized an agreed by many scholars, even with small variations. The six axes are: Smart Economy; Smart Mobility; Smart Environment; Smart People; Smart Living; and Smart Governance.

According to Khatoun and Zeadally (2016), the most widely adopted smart city reference model includes the six above referred dimensions, placing the citizen as the center of all the axes once they exist to meet their needs, as shown in Fig. 1.

In order to support the model of intelligent city presented, these authors defended it needs to be based on the following five components:

- **Broadband infrastructure**—a fundamental infrastructure that provides connectivity to citizens, businesses and organizations;
- **Electronic services**—involving ICT use to provide city services, including sales, delivery, and customer support;
- **Public Open Data**—means that the data can be freely used, reused and distributed by any person or entity;

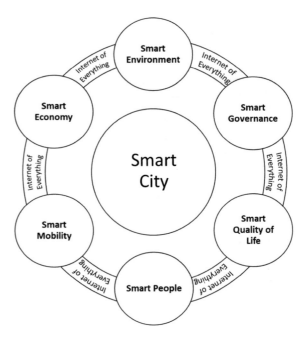

Fig. 1 Smart city model

- **Sustainable Infrastructures**—implies responding to the challenge of building and maintaining infrastructures in the city that are both socially, environmentally and economically sustainable;
- **Electronic Governance**—supporting the governance performance using electronic means to facilitate an efficient, rapid and transparent process of dissemination of information to the public and also to carry out administrative activities.

Concluding, we can say that the different smart city definitions share the idea that the growing sensing capabilities induced by the technology and connectivity evolution will play a major role in the process.

Altogether, the potential that the technologies today offer to collect huge amounts of data, launches the challenge of being created analytical capabilities and made available the necessary skills to promote their conversion into information and thus of value to the decision making process, to the creation of new products and services, and for more active and engaged citizenship.

According to the Strategic Policy Forum on Digital Entrepreneurship (2016), digital transformation doesn't only enable economic growth, but also the improvement of the quality of life for all citizens. Nevertheless it is fundamental to take into consideration the strategic role of cities and regions in leading a modern, smart transformation of their territories and the importance of a holistic approach, including a multitude of actors, in order to grasp all the digital opportunities offered by the transformation.

Based on the comparative analysis of 13 different European cities which pioneered digital transformation and restored spectacular economic growth, this forum produced a blueprint that identifies four main attributes through which stakeholders can truly help their cities and regions to go digital:

- Leadership and collaboration for a smart governance of the local digital ecosystem;
- Digital talent and entrepreneurs to accelerate the digital transformation process;
- Access to data and technologies for applied solutions to local challenges;
- Key Infrastructures and investments for digital launch-pads.

This focus on digital technologies is distinct from other potential levers of transformation in urban areas, such as political, social, cultural and economic—although there are and may be complementarities between them, or even specific aspects related to the compacting of the urban form of the cities and the events of their expansion (Ahfeldt and Pietrostefani 2017).

The following technologies are currently associated with this digital transformation process (Alawadhi et al. 2012):

- Analytical tools and applications, including "Big Data";
- Mobile tools and applications;
- Platforms on which we build and share digital capabilities;
- Social tools and applications;

- The Internet of Things (IoT), which include connected devices and smart grids.

These technologies together, often globally designated as Internet of Everything (IoE), are having a profound impact on cities transformation leading to the vision of the city as a platform, as we shall see below.

In fact, with the digital transformation, information will be the lever for changing the cities planning and management models, since a city that is better known is better managed, being a matter that is transversal to all the strategic domains of the city, from economy to social inclusion, from environment to urban regeneration, from risk management and prevention to urban-rural integration.

2.2   City as a Platform

The process of digital transformation that leads to the construction of the smart city is gradual, going through an evolutionary four stages process presented below (Telefonica 2016) where in our opinion the city as a platform will emerge in the end (Fig. 2).

According to this smart city evolution process, after an initial stage where a strategy is defined the cities will undergo a moment where different vertical initiatives will be developed (e.g. urban waste management, smart parking, public lighting, etc.). This will be a challenging stage since there is a real risk of creating information silos that will compromise the next evolution stages.

If the necessary conditions are present, the city can evolve to the third and connected stage where all the vertical projects will be linked together, data will flow transparently across the smart city infrastructure and urban intelligence can play its role in planning and managing the city creating the opportunity to move to the fourth stage where this capabilities and data are made available to the city stakeholders and value is created by new products and services that can boost economic growth.

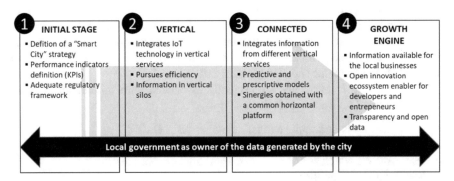

Fig. 2 Smart city evolution (Telefonica 2016)

It is in this context that we believe cities digital transformation will lead to the materialization of the city as a platform vision. In fact, cities can now use four asset classes, or tools—people, data, infrastructure and technologies—which can each interact in more fluid, synergistic ways than before and the convergence of these factors, among others, is prompting many people to begin to think about cities not just as places, but as platforms (Bollier 2016).

In the report "Smart Cities—The city as a platform for Digital Transformation" (Telefonica 2016), cities as a 'platform' should facilitate synergies, ensure interoperability with other services and promote innovation from open platforms and establishing a single digital market applications and services for citizens, businesses and visitors.

In this context of the city digital transformation that will support the evolutionary process referred above leading to the city as a platform we present below (Fig. 3) a proposal for a possible conceptual model of the smart city as a platform.

This approach sees the city as a platform that provides access to (open) data services and urban analytics based on collected or linked data and the Internet of Everything, to support three types of different functions: city planning and management by the municipality; development of products and services by entrepreneurs and companies; and provision of information and services to the citizen.

Thus, a fundamental point for the evolution of this concept is the establishment of a single and open infrastructure based on a horizontal platform standard. One example comes from the European Union that created the FIWARE (2016) platform, developed from the initiative "Future Internet", whose objective was to create an open ecosystem where it facilitated the creation and delivery of digital applications and services in different sectors at a reduced cost. This platform is already

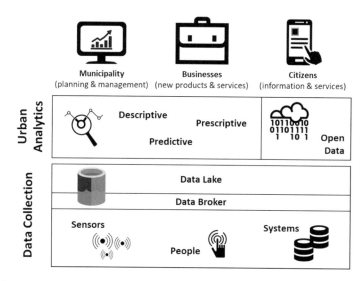

Fig. 3 Smart city as a platform

used in many European cities and is a middleware has an open API, in which it seeks to have the involvement of both users and those who do development, makes a standard platform with reusable solutions.

Nevertheless, digital transformation brings deep implications to city governance models (Bollier 2016), urban dwellers live their lives hyperlinked to numerous virtual spaces, the pulse of information in real time, with intelligent devices, remote access to databases and forms of participation in crowdsourcing and in this way, governance is no longer just the exercise of going to elections and manage the local authority to include the collection and information management from the citizens and from other sources, enriching the decision-making process with multiple layers of interaction, synergies, involvement and participation.

In this context is extremely relevant to refer the City as a Platform Manifesto[1] where is shared a common desire to improve the quality of life for people and the planet, knit local communities closer together, and offer a new economic agenda for local governments by using digital platforms. The responsible for the manifesto believe that, by itself, technology will not solve the challenges facing cities around the world since we need a shared collaborative framework between residents, the public and private sector to drive the desired outcome of sustainability, inclusivity and targeted innovation that benefits cities and their residents.

With this mindset and understanding, adapting and applying platform business model principles, they defend that cities can become regional or global knowledge hubs and innovation centres. Furthermore, cities that follow this path will become better places to live and be better equipped to manage urban challenges—with more insight, precision and transparency—since they will attract talent, create jobs and unleash innovation.

The City as a Platform Manifesto drives this future by adhering to the following principles when deploying city platforms managing the vast reservoir of data offered by sensor networks, enterprises, city agencies and residents:

1. City platforms must enable services that improve the quality of life in cities; benefitting residents, the environment, and helping to bridge the digital divide;
2. City platforms must bring together both public and private stakeholders in digital ecosystems;
3. City platforms must support sharing economy principles and the circular economy agenda;
4. City platforms must provide ways for local start-ups and businesses to innovate and thrive;
5. City platforms must enforce the privacy and security of confidential data;
6. City platforms must inform political decisions and offer mechanisms for residents to make their voices heard;
7. City platforms must involve the local government in their governance and curation, and are built and managed by the most competent and merited organisations;

---

[1]https://www.tmforum.org/smart-city-forum/city-platform-manifesto/.

8. City platforms must be based on open standards, industry best practices and open APIs to facilitate a vendor neutral approach, with industry agreed architecture models;
9. City platforms must support a common approach to federation of data or services between cities, making it possible for cities of all sizes to take part in the growing data economy;
10. City platforms must support the principles of UN Sustainable Development Goal 11: Making cities and human settlements inclusive, safe, resilient and sustainable.

3 Urban Intelligence

If the city evolution went through the above referred process and we are in the context of the city as a platform we can say that the necessary conditions are present to support what in fact we consider urban intelligence, which is only possible by an holistic and orchestrated augmented smart city approach.

In fact, the presence of the above referred signpost of a smart city don't automatically imply we are in a city where we have urban intelligence leading the planning and operational decisions.

Urban intelligence in our vision is much more than the efficient and optimized management of the different verticals which characterize the above referred third stage in smart cities evolution. In fact it is when we reach the connected city stage, where data and systems are fully integrated, that we have the opportunity to take full advantage of data science and big data to take city governance to a higher level of intelligence and to see urban analytics deliver their true value.

Using as an example public lighting we can think about a smart vertical solution vs a intelligent city solution. In the first (using a vertical approach and often referred as smart city best practice) we will take advantage of environmental sensors and traffic motion detectors to optimize public lighting management and the decision of switching lights on and off altogether with the light intensity will result from optimization models using the referred data sources. In the latter and in a urban intelligence approach, if we can take advantage of the city as a platform approach, the public lighting system planning and management will use not only the environmental sensors and traffic motion detectors to optimize public lighting management, but also real time data coming from other internal and external data sources. Amongst the examples we can present to illustrate this augmented smart city we can refer the use of data from other internal operational systems not related directly with the lighting system, e.g. automatically increase the illumination of a city square Friday evening from 18:00 until 24:00 because there is going to be held a pop-up market, or create dynamic connections with external systems that will influence public lighting, e.g., use real time data from the city emergency services or the police to adjust the lighting conditions in a specific moment and place as a reaction to accidents or crimes.

This is the real challenge we face today when it comes to create a real smart city —how can we build the city as a platform and take full advantage of the growing number of data sources by having an integrated and holistic approach to optimize urban planning and management using the potential of urban analytics and data science.

In this framework, real urban intelligence results from the possibilities created by the city as a platform approach and the integration of four asset classes, or tools— people, data, infrastructure and technologies—where the city governance is taken to a much higher level of efficiency translated into an augmented planning and management environment supported by big data and data science.

Going Back to Fig. 3, We Are in a Stage Where Real Time Data Integration in a City as a Platform Approach Will Support the Three Kinds of Analytics: Descriptive, Predictive, and Prescriptive Making Urban Intelligence a Critical and Powerful Leverage for City Governance.

4   Urban Intelligence Building Blocks

In order to build urban intelligence that ensures resource usage efficiency and more sustainable and inclusive cities, and at the same time boost entrepreneurship and technological start-ups in the creation of innovative products and services for new markets, thus promoting economic development, there is an inescapable challenge that we must overcome.

This challenge is city data, true fuel of urban intelligence that should collected or linked and released in the form of open data—data that can be used, modified, and shared by anyone for any purpose.

According to OECD (2015), the data produced in cities can be divided into three categories:

- Flows—Cities are structured by and pervaded with different types of infras- tructures (e.g. ICTs, transport, water, energy, waste networks) that facilitate movement and flows of resources, products, people and information across cities. Sensors embedded in urban infrastructures increasingly allow the digiti- sation and datafication of these flows.
- States—Urban inside spaces and outside environments are subject to constant natural and manmade changes. According to OCDE, the particular state of urban spaces and environments—the density of people, air temperature and quality, light and sound levels, etc.—is increasingly monitored by sensors, including cameras; through synoptic instruments such as satellites; or in continual observations from urban vantage points.
- Activities—Connected machines and devices used for both personal and pro- fessional activities in cities allow measurement of transaction, consumption and

communication patterns. According to OCDE these patterns include in particular:

1. People's activities, communication and interactions;
2. Interaction between people and their environment;
3. Interactions among components of their environments, such as communicating and autonomous machines and devices.

Furthermore and of critical importance when we want to understand the city metabolism and its dynamics, interactions and transactions of individuals and businesses with public institutions (e.g. tax records, land use, sales, inventories, public health, crime records, school outcomes, workforce development), with businesses (e.g. credit card payments, consumption behaviour, sales records), and individuals (e.g. social networking) create transactional data on activities in cities.

Also in the context of urban intelligence the spatial dimension plays a fundamental role since these data, created through the sensing, measuring and recording of flows, states and activities in cities, can also be distinguished by the extent to which they are location specific:

- data produced by stationary sensors embedded in urban infrastructures and environments, mostly describing flows and states in cities;
- geo-locational and geo-referenced data generated in cities, often from mobile devices and sensors, describing mainly the activities (actions, interactions, transactions) of connected people, machines and devices;
- and other data generated in cities that do not necessarily have geographic properties, e.g. data on financial transactions.

In this sense, we can identify in this process of digital transformation of cities leading to the city as a platform, where data is the new raw material, a set of building blocks of urban intelligence, as shown schematically in Fig. 4 and detailed below. On the one hand we have the open data with origin in the activity of the companies and collected from the sensors that they have to support their business or in the transactions that they carry out, on the other hand we have as data source the collective intelligence, that is the citizens, which has gained increasing relevance and which can either result from data collected actively or passively from the actions of the citizens.

Fig. 4 Urban intelligence building blocks

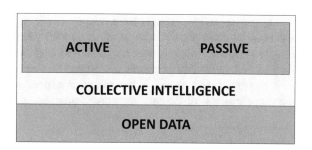

4.1   Open Data

An interesting aspect in this emerging class of smart cities is their evolution into data-opening initiatives. While the collection of mass data through sensors linked to a variety of physical infrastructures has always been a feature of the first generation of smart cities, the publication of such data as open data, or its integration with open data published by urban authorities in different aspects of management and life in the city, is a relatively recent phenomena (Ojo et al. 2015).

The ability to create, collect and process scattered data and make it available openly is the first and also the most ambitious and disruptive urban intelligence building block. Municipalities have a key role here and an opportunity to unleash processes of open innovation, co-creation and collective intelligence where citizens, companies, management and academia, as well as the third sector, will create new products and services, many of them still unimaginable, of high value added and capable of generating new markets. It is up to the municipalities to take the first step and launch open data initiatives (supported, at first, by the internal data sources and their projects based on IoT).

Open data is "data that can be used, modified and shared by anyone for any purpose" (Open Data Handbook[2]).

The Full Open setting (Open Knowledge International 2017) gives precise details about what this means. To summarize the most important:

- Availability and Access: the data must be available as a whole and have no more than a reasonable cost of reproduction, preferably downloaded over the internet. The data must also be available in a convenient and modifiable form;
- Reuse and Redistribution: Data must be provided in ways that enable reuse and redistribution, including combining with other data sets;
- Universal Participation: Everyone should be able to use, reuse and distribute—there should be no discrimination in the fields of action or against individuals or groups. For example, "non-commercial" restrictions that would prevent "commercial" use, or restrictions of use for certain purposes (e.g., education only), are not permitted.

The need for clarity about what it means to be open is closely related to interoperability. Interoperability is key to achieving the key benefits of data openness: drastic increase in the ability to combine different datasets together and the generation of new or better products and services (Khatoun and Zeadally 2016).

Open data has increasingly been seen as a defining element of smart cities and as such can be conceptually considered as a smart cities initiative, and it is important now to understand how open data initiatives impact the context of smart cities, as well as that smart city programs condition the associated open data initiatives.

By opening data on the environment, transport, education, health and so forth, municipalities can objectively support companies, start-ups, application developers,

---

[2]http://opendatahandbook.org/.

civil society organizations, among others, to find new and ways of dealing with urban problems.

Open data, not only governmental but also private companies open data, is an extraordinary and yet largely unexplored resource. While many organizations and individuals collect large amounts of data, government has a particularly significant role here, not only because of the quantity and relevance of the data it creates, collects and maintains, but especially because such data should by definition be public, since they were the result of government activity and as such should be available as open data.

Also private companies are becoming more important and relevant in this context since they are rapidly becoming the true repositories of relevant urban data.

In the case of urban intelligence, open data strategies allow cities to aspire to achieve four key objectives:

- Higher levels of transparency: allowing the citizen to understand, examine and question the action and decisions taken by the municipality requires information. The more open data becomes public, the more we encourage participation and improve the services we deliver;
- Citizens Engagement: to increase citizens' involvement in city development and services, in decision-making processes and in participatory debate, requires citizens to understand the context in which the municipality operates. Thus, giving citizens and their communities access to operational data from the municipality and, in particular, spatially relevant data (from their "neighbourhood") helps to encourage more active and informed participation;
- Service Improvement and Efficiency Gains: Providing open data will support and accelerate the sharing of data from the municipality and other entities with expected results in improving service and efficiency gains;
- Boost Economic Development: the release of data is now considered a "trigger" for the promotion of economic and community activity. Cities around the world have already found that the massive availability of open data enables local businesses and developers to create new applications, new products and services, opening the door to the emergence of new markets.

4.2 Collective Intelligence

Reality has showed that citizens engagement in cities governance is one of the most important trends in the construction of smart cities. This reality is also of paramount importance in the context of urban intelligence since citizens inputs are as we will show the most important building block in the city as a platform to foster urban intelligence.

The most relevant dimension of this citizens involvement as a urban intelligence building block is the so-called collective intelligence, which consists of adopting active or passive crowdsourcing processes, as we shall see, in order to better understand cities reality and at the same time create very efficient and effective mechanisms for collecting data.

4.2.1 Active

Active collective intelligence supports the possibility of taking advantage of citizens engagement through active participation using informal mechanisms fostered by social networks and information and communication technologies. In addition to collecting data that does not require an active contribution from citizens, there are currently a number of new processes and tools that allow citizens to choose how to contribute with data, namely event reporting tools and new data collection techniques.

Event Reporting Tools: Citizens have always had the possibility to make requests or make complaints, in most cases by telephone, in writing or at community meetings. However, this usually requires more time than the citizen is available to give and today there are a significant number of digital tools that make it easier and simpler for citizens to report occurrences adopting a "Fix my street" approach.

New data collection techniques: Traditionally, when we wanted to better understand some phenomenon that affected our citizens we would conduct an inquiry. These surveys, while having the virtue of being highly detailed, since they are planned and executed by specialists, do not give immediate answers and are too costly.

Thus, we have seen emerging new ways of collecting the opinion of citizens to incorporate in the planning and implementation of municipal policies, such as participatory budgets or ideas contests.

4.2.2 Passive

In this modality of collective intelligence use we take advantage of the sensing capacity leveraged by the data generated in a passive way by the citizens actions. Today we leave a digital trace of almost everything we do and respecting personal privacy through data anonymization we can generate extremely valuable insights about the city metabolism.

In this context, we can refer as an example how city governments can today use mobile phone metadata (location, nationality, model) or content published in social media and other forms of data available online to better understand citizens' behaviour, identify problem and create insights about potential solutions.

Citizens as sensors—The sheer number of people who live or work in cities and have mobile phones generate location data that is increasingly seen as a valuable resource for a wide range of purposes, from traffic modelling (people and/or vehicles), urban planning, management of interventions, public health policies, creation of business opportunities, etc.

Social media—Social media, and in particular social networks such as Facebook and Twitter, are increasingly viewed by governments as an relevant data source to opportunity to improve cities governance thanks to the increasing capacities to analyse feelings and quantify the "Value" of the issuer of opinion, since we can know today and in real time in great detail the opinions and reactions of citizens.

5 City Sustainability

A Smart City, being smart accordingly to earliest definition on the paper, as the ability to measure all data about her and to create localized measures, urban acupuncture, with direct impact and scale.

The International Organization for Standardization, given the importance of cities in sustainable development, has developed ISO 37120 which defines and establishes methodologies for a set of indicators to steer and measures the performance of city services and quality of life. The capacity of cities to achieve significant results in the development of sustainability, dictated their analysis and the constitution of indicators. Thus, emerges ISO 37120 Sustainable Development of Communities Indicators for city services and quality of life with 17 themes that characterize the cities and their indicators, allowing the systematic and independent control of the level of quality of life of each city Table 2.

Table 2 ISO 37120 sustainable development of communities indicators

Themes	Indicators
Economy	Unemployment rate in the city
	Estimated value of commercial and industrial properties as a percentage of the total assessed value of all properties
	Poverty risk rate after social transfers
	Percentage of full-time employees
	Youth unemployment rate (15–24 years)
	Number of enterprises per 100,000 inhabitants
	Number of patents registered per 100,000 inhabitants per year
Education	Actual female schooling rate
	Percentage of students completing the 1st and 2nd cycle of basic education: survival rate
	Percentage of students completing the 3rd cycle and upper secondary education: survival rate
	Pupil/teacher ratio in the 1st and 2nd cycle Real rate of male schooling
	Actual enrolment rate
	Number of individuals completing tertiary education per 100,000 population

(continued)

Table 2 (continued)

Themes	Indicators
Energy	Total residential electricity consumption per capita (kWh/year)
	Percentage of city population with authorized electricity service
	Energy consumption of public buildings per year (kWh/m^2)
	Percentage of total energy from renewable sources, such as a share of the total energy consumption of the city
	Total electricity used per capita (kWh/year)
	Average number of electrical interruptions per customer per year
	Average duration of electrical interruptions (in hours)
Environment	Concentration of fine particles (PM2.5)
	Particle concentration (PM10)
	Emissions of greenhouse gases in tonnes per capita
	Concentration of nitrogen dioxide (NO$_2$)
	Concentration of sulfur dioxide (SO$_2$)
	Concentration of Ozone (O$_3$)
	Noise pollution
	Change in the percentage of native species
Finance	Debt service ratio (debt service expense as a percentage of the revenue generated by the municipality itself)
	Capital expenditure as a percentage of total expenditure
	Own source revenue as a percentage of total revenues
	Taxes charged as a percentage of billed taxes
Fire response and emergencies	Number of fire fighters per 100,000 inhabitants
	Number of fire-related deaths per 100,000 inhabitants
	Number of deaths related to natural disasters per 100,000 inhabitants
	Number of volunteer and part-time fire fighters per 100,000 inhabitants
	Response time for emergency response services since initial call
	Response time to fire department since initial call
Governance	Participation of voters in the last municipal elections (as a percentage of eligible voters)
	Women as a percentage of the total elected to the autarchic bodies
	Percentage of women employed in local administration staff
	Number of convictions for corruption and/or bribery between local elected officials and local government officials per 100,000 inhabitants
	Representation of citizens: number of local elected representatives per 100,000 inhabitants Number of registered voters as a percentage of the population with voting age
Health	Average life expectancy
	Number of hospital beds per 100,000 inhabitants
	Number of doctors per 100,000 inhabitants
	Mortality rate of 0–4 years per 1000 live births
	Number of nurses per 100,000 inhabitants
	Number of mental health professionals per 100,000 inhabitants
	Suicide rate per 100,000 inhabitants

(continued)

Table 2 (continued)

Themes	Indicators
Recreational spaces	Area of recreational spaces of collective use in per capita building 13.2 Area of recreational spaces of collective use in the open air per capita
Safety	Number of police officers per 100,000 inhabitants 14.2 Number of homicides per 100,000 inhabitants Crimes against property per 100,000 inhabitants Response time to police since the distress call Violent crime rate per 100,000 inhabitants
Accommodation	Percentage of city population living in tents Number of homeless per 100,000 inhabitants Percentage of existing households without registered legal titles
Waste	Percentage of population of the city with regular collection of municipal waste Total municipal waste collected per capita Percentage of recycled urban waste Percentage of urban waste deposited in landfills Percentage of municipal waste incinerated Percentage of municipal waste burned in the open Percentage of urban waste deposited in an open dump Percentage of municipal waste managed by other means Production of hazardous waste per capita Percentage of hazardous waste in the city that is recycled
Telecommunications and innovation	Number of internet connections per 100,000 inhabitants Number of mobile phone connections per 100,000 inhabitants Number of landline calls per 100,000 inhabitants
Transportation	Extension of the high capacity public land transport network per 100,000 inhabitants Extension of the low capacity public land transport network per 100,000 inhabitants Travel in public transport per capita Individual vehicles per capita Percentage of people using a means of transport other than their individual vehicle in their daily commutes Motorcycles and mopeds per capita Extension of tracks and cycling lanes per 100,000 inhabitants Transport-related fatalities per 100,000 inhabitants 18.9 Direct commercial air links
Urban planning	Green area per 100,000 inhabitants Trees planted annually per 100,000 inhabitants Percentage of the area of the city with illegal urbanization Ratio jobs/housing
Residual waters	Percentage of population in the city served by a domestic wastewater collection system Percentage of untreated domestic wastewater in the city Percentage of domestic wastewater in the city receiving primary treatment Percentage of domestic wastewater in the city receiving secondary treatment Percentage of domestic wastewater in the city receiving tertiary treatment

(continued)

Table 2 (continued)

Themes	Indicators
Water and sanitation	Percentage of population of the city with service of water supply for human consumption
	Percentage of city population with sustainable access to protected water source
	Percentage of population with access to improved sanitation
	Total domestic consumption of water per capita (liters/day)
	Total water consumption per capita (liters/day)
	Average number of annual hours of interruption of water supply per family accommodation
	Percentage of water loss (unbilled water)

Also, the state of the art in the study against climate change by the academic community has found the city as a key element for the process.

"How cities can do so much locally" is presented by the article, "Intersecting Residential and Transport CO_2 Emissions" announced by MIT. The mission of MIT is to promote knowledge and educate students in science, technology, and other areas of knowledge that best serve the nation and the world in the 21st century.

The study examines the extent to which planning policies are complementary to the reduction of greenhouse gas emissions from power stations. To obtain the study, the researchers examined data, the environmental and demographic dimensions of 11 large US cities and then developed projection models according to the year 2030, based on a number of different policy scenarios.

Legal existence of higher energy efficiency for residential housing reduced as a residential subsidy by an average of 6% by 2030. However, houses should be adapted to render an additional 19% figure in households on average in the 11 cities.

6 Conclusions

In order for the urban intelligence vision to materialize, it is important to move from a logic of reactive urban management to a proactive logic, supported by its digital and knowledge-based transformation, broad data availability and constant updating of information. A cognitive city supported by urban intelligence in which planning and management is focused in providing quality of live to its citizens based on the empowerment of ICTs and advanced techniques of real-time data processing and analysis, in order to efficiently and sustainably operate the various subsystems that compete for life in cities. Urban intelligence generates efficiency, which contributes directly to the creation of more sustainable and resilient cities and to a better quality of life in an urban environment.

We defend that the construction of urban intelligence has as its foundations the digital transformation of the city and in the urban intelligence building blocks which will only succeed in a model of an intelligent city acting as a platform focused on the generation of knowledge, in the wide availability of data and in the permanent updating of the information, working in a collaborative network involving all the actors: government and local administration, companies, academia and citizens.

In this context we must refer the challenges we face today regarding personal data security and privacy, especially with the new Regulation (EU) 2016/679 of the European Parliament and of the Council of 27 April 2016 on the protection of natural persons with regard to the processing of personal data and on the free movement of such data. Although our vision of urban intelligence can coexist with the safeguard of the referred regulation by taking advantage of the data anonymization process, this will have to managed.

It is important to emphasize that the essential principles for an intelligent city will have to be to promote an increased transparency in governance, the generation of synergies with stakeholders (public administration, companies, academia and citizens), better quality of services on the part of the administration and service providers with a greater involvement and participation of citizens in governance and in the life of the city, together with the promotion of economic, social and environmental development, enabling citizens to establish themselves in a given territory, in a given community where fundamental requirements for their quality of life are guaranteed.

This last objective, economic development, is effectively the one that will ensure the sustainability of the solutions of urban intelligence found, because only by creating value and increasing the income of citizens and companies that coexist in urban areas will make it possible to succeed in the long term.

The transformation which is leading to the city as a platform concept is a real revolution and the challenge we face is the construction of this new analytical city today.

The UN Climate Report says that we need to reduce CO_2 emission, so that the temperature does not increase more than 1.5C. Cities were identified in this report has targets because urban areas are the most responsible for the biggest and persistent impacts in the CO_2 emissions.

The development of a smart methodology for the city planning and management is one of the key elements for achieving the objectives set by the Intergovernmental Panel on Climate Change (IPCC).

The ISO organization has released a new standard that re-enforces the relevants of the city in the fight against climate change. Giving policy makers and executer a hide range of data to measure and manage the fulfilment of the new smart city indicators and specific climate change impacts.

Cities are responsible for the production of a wide set of information that generates knowledge of the impacts in CO_2 emission. For example: pendulum movements. This real-time indicators, transformed into knowledge can be determinant for the set of new public policies that can impact positively in CO_2

emissions. The challenge is to interpreted this knowledge and be able to take real-time decisions with real impact in this fight. This is a change in the procedures of the traditional city management organization, that need to be able to recall and work the data in a smart way.

This new instruments show that the fight against climate change needs to have a local framework, within the urban areas. Using a smart city framework to manage and execute new policies that have a real and structural impact in CO_2 emissions. This new perimeter of public policies, the cities, is a much more efficient tool in the climate change war than regional, national, or European levels because they end specific problems and can have a direct impact in the CO_2 emissions.

In the one hand, this new paradigm of smart cities ask for a digital transformation in the means available for the city. On the other, a smart city asks for a change management approach project, adapting the organization (people, technology, process) to the new information, new data and new decisions being taken in a acupuncture way of policy making.

References

Ahfeldt, G. M., & Pietrostefani, E. (2017). *The compact city in empirical research: A quantitative literature review*. SERC Discussion Papers, SERCDP0215. Spatial Economics Research Centre, London School of Economics and Political Science, London, UK.

Alawadhi, S., Aldama-Nalda, A., Chourabi, H., Gil-Garcia, J. R., Leung, S., Mellouli, S., Nam, T., Pardo, T. A., Scholl, H. J., & S. Walker. (2012). *Building understanding of smart city initiatives* (pp. 40–53). 11ª IFIP WG 8.5. Kristiansand, Norway, September 3–6, 2012.

Albino, V., Berardi, U., & Dangelico, R. M. (2015). Smart cities: Definitions, dimensions, performance, and initiatives. *Journal of Urban Technology, 22*(1), 3–21. https://doi.org/10.1080/10630732.2014.942092.

Anthopoulos, L., Janssen, M., & Weerakkody, V. (2016). A Unified Smart City Model (USCM) for smart city conceptualization and benchmarking. *International Journal of Electronic Government Research, 12*(2), 77–93. https://doi.org/10.4018/IJEGR.2016040105.

Bakıcı, T., Almirall, E. & Wareham, J. (2012). A smart city initiative: the case of Barcelona. *Journal of the Knowledge Economy, 2*(1), 1–14.

Bollier, D. (2016). *The city as platform: How digital networks are changing urban life and governance*. Aspen Institute Communications and Society, from http://csreports.aspeninstitute.org/documents/CityAsPlatform.pdf.

Fernandes, G. (2017). *A framework for dashboarding city performance: An application to Cascais smart city*. Mestrado em Gestão de Informação, NOVA Information Management School, Universidade Nova de Lisboa.

FIWARE. (2016). *FIWARE core platform of the future Internet*. September 01, 2017, from https://www.fiware.org/.

Giffinger, R., Fertner, C., Kramar, H., Kalasek, R., Pichler-Milanovic, N., & Meijers, E. (2007). *Smart Cities: Ranking of European Medium-sized Cities*, Vienna: Centre of Regional Science.

Intergovernmental Panel on Climate Change Special Report on Global Warming of 1.5 °C approved by governments (2018).

International Organization for Standardization NP 37120:2017-pt.

ISO/TC 268 Technical Commission. (2014). *ISO 37120:2014—Sustainable development of communities, Indicators for city services and quality of life*.

Khatoun, R., & Zeadally, S. (2016). Smart cities: Concepts, architectures, research opportunities. *Communications of the ACM, 59*(8), 46–57. https://doi.org/10.1145/2858789.

Manville, C., Cochrane, G., Cave, J., Millard, J., Pederson, J., Thaarup, R., & Kotterink, B. (2014). *Mapping smart cities in the EU.* Retrieved from http://www.europarl.europa.eu/RegData/etudes/etudes/join/2014/507480/IPOL-ITRE_ET(2014)507480_EN.pdf.

Marsal-Llacuna, M.L., Colomer-Llinàs, J. & Meléndez-Frigola, J. (2015). Lessons in urban monitoring taken from sustainable and livable cities to better address the Smart Cities initiative. *Technological Forecasting and Social Change, 90*(PB), 611–622.

OECD. (2015). *Data-driven innovation: Big data for growth and well-being.*

Ojo, A., Curry, E., & Zeleti, F. A. (2015). A tale of open data innovations in five smart cities. In *Proceedings of the 48ᵃ conferência internacional do Hawaii em sistemas cientificos* (pp. 2326–2335).

Open Knowledge International. (2017). *Open knowledge definition.* Version 1.1, from http://opendefinition.org/od/1.1/.

Strategic Policy Forum on Digital Entrepreneurship. (2016). *Blueprint for cities and regions as launch pads for digital transformation.* Retrieved from http://ec.europa.eu/DocsRoom/documents/16762/attachments/1/translations/en/renditions/native.

Telefonica. (2016). *Smart cities—The city as a platform for digital transformation—policy paper.*

Telefónica IoT Team. (2016). *Challenges and opportunities for the digital transformation of smart cities,* from https://iot.telefonica.com/blog/challenges-and-opportunities-for-the-digital-transformation-of-smart-cities.

UNEP. (2017, March 09, 2017). *United nations environment programme,* September 01, 2017, from http://www.unep.org/.

Using Kahoot as a Learning Tool

Uso do kahoot como ferramenta de aprendizagem

Ernane Rosa Martins⊙, **Wendell Bento Geraldes**⊙,
Ulisses Rodrigues Afonseca⊙ **and Luís Manuel Borges Gouveia**⊙

Abstract The present work aims to investigate the use of kahoot as an educational resource in the teaching-learning process for high school students in the area of computer science. For this, an exploratory, descriptive and bibliographic approach was used. The research was carried out with 34 students of the technical course in computer science for internet of the Federal Institute of Goiás (FIG). The students performed the proposed activities and then answered a questionnaire using a GoogleDocs form. According to the results of the use of the platform, there was an improvement in students' learning by reviewing and reinforcing the concepts learned in a fun, engaging, motivating and interesting way.

Resumo O presente trabalho tem como objetivo investigar o uso do "kahoot" como recurso educacional no processo de ensino-aprendizagem para estudantes do ensino médio da área de informática. Para isso, utilizou-se uma abordagem exploratória, descritiva e bibliográfica. A pesquisa foi realizada com 34 alunos do curso técnico em informática para internet do Instituto Federal de Goiás (IFG). Os alunos realizaram as atividades propostas e em seguida responderam a um questionário através de um formulário do GoogleDocs. De acordo com os resultados da utilização da plataforma, verificou-se uma melhora na aprendizagem dos alunos revisando e reforçando os conceitos aprendidos de maneira divertida, engajadora, motivadora e interessante.

E. R. Martins (✉) · W. B. Geraldes · U. R. Afonseca
Federal Institute of Education, Science and Technology of Goiás (IFG), Luziânia, Brazil
e-mail: ernane.martins@ifg.edu.br

W. B. Geraldes
e-mail: wendell.geraldes@ifg.edu.br

U. R. Afonseca
e-mail: urafonseca@ifg.edu.br

L. M. B. Gouveia
University of Fernando Pessoa, Porto, Portugal
e-mail: lmbg@ufp.edu.pt

© Springer Nature Switzerland AG 2019
I. Ramos et al. (eds.), *Information Systems for Industry 4.0*,
Lecture Notes in Information Systems and Organisation 31,
https://doi.org/10.1007/978-3-030-14850-8_11

Keywords Kahoot · Gamification · Teaching · Educational technology · Mobile learning

Palavras-chave Kahoot · Gamificação · Ensino · Tecnologia educacional · Aprendizagem móvel

1 Introduction

Games are present in the lives of people of all ages. Children learn from an early age playing with games which is very important because it allows them to develop their skills. The use of games in school settings has become an excellent teaching strategy. de Macedo et al. (2000) argues that the use of games in teaching allows improving the ability to acquire abstract knowledge and content, develop skills, motivate learning, stimulate reasoning and understand rules. The same author also emphasizes that the choice of the game to use in a classroom is of great importance, mainly defining the objectives of the use, not to lose the focus of the content and the learning.

The game is a didactic strategy, and to get a positive result you need a set of strategies. Only the act of playing is not enough to achieve the educational goals expected by the teacher. Some factors should be taken into account when choosing a teaching technique, such as differences between students (age, cultural partner context, aptitudes, interests and needs of students); who employs it; what goals to achieve; what types of persons it is intended for; what content will be handled; at which point the technique will be applied. What has been demonstrated in the literature is that good results depend on the planning of the teacher and the conduction of the same in the classroom. Games should explore the possibility of combining entertainment with education, in this way knowledge and learning to become more motivating. (Covos et al. 2018).

Kahoot is interactive software that contains elements of the games and allows you to apply activity with specific content (Gazotti-Vallim 2017). The content is added by the teacher and applied in class, simply requiring a computer, internet and the students' own smartphones (Bottentuit Junior 2012).

The use of kahoot in the classroom aims to teach students to learn with more pleasure, to build their own knowledge and to promote better communication, so this study is important because it seeks to minimize the doubts of education professionals in using this tool educational, available, given the new digital profile of the students, allowing the teaching to be better transmitted, better absorbed by the students, less tiring and with greater concentration.

Thus, this work proposed to investigate the use of "kahoot" as an educational resource in the teaching-learning process for high school students in the area of computer science. Using an exploratory, descriptive and bibliographic approach.

This article is structured in five sections. In this section we present, besides the introduction, the definition of the research problem, the objective, the justification and importance of the study and the structure of the present research. Section 2 brings the theoretical framework, with the formation of a conceptual and theoretical basis, which provide support for the development of this study. Section 3 presents the method used and the techniques and methodological procedures used. Section 4 describes the results obtained in the research and discussion. Finally, Sect. 5 presents the conclusion and proposes the continuity of the research.

2 Theoretical Reference

Educators are challenged today to search for teaching tools that can be used within the classroom as interactive methodologies that make the educational environment increasingly digital (Prensky 2012). Gómez (2015, p. 29) emphasizes that "it is necessary to reinvent the school so that it can develop knowledge, skills, attitudes, values and emotions". Thus, Kahoot is a platform that can be used in the educational environment as a pedagogical proposal, which allows a class with different approaches and new possibilities of evaluation. Kahoot allows students to learn using a technological device (computer or smartphone) while having fun. Thus, students play as if they were participating in a game show, which allows them to learn in a fun, playful and interactive way, building their own knowledge (Kenski 2012).

Kahoot is a free, gaming-based learning platform with the institutional mission of "unlocking the deepest potential of every student of all ages and in all contexts" through fun, magical, inclusive and engaging learning (Kahoot 2018). This platform allows you to create questionnaires, discussions or surveys that can be answered by users who are connected to the internet through smartphones or computers. For its use, it is necessary to make a registration on the virtual teaching platform (https://kahoot.com/).

Kahoot's proposal is to engage students through questionnaires, discussions, and pre-elaborated game-like surveys with punctuation, interaction, and rankings (Dellos 2015). The teacher can use the content of a discipline as well as evaluate the student's performance. According to its creators, its goal is to be a game-based platform making learning fun (Izeki et al. 2016). Amico et al. 2017, emphasizes that this is an important tool in aiding educational technology.

No Kahoot students access with a nickname that appears on the screen, allowing identification of the groups that are playing. In this way, students are not exposed to the rest of the class. The teacher also sets the time to answer each question, and may have questions with different response times, depending on the difficulty of the question. Because it is similar to a game, the time should not be too long, otherwise the activity may lose its playability. But it also can not be very long because it would not allow the student to apply his knowledge to the resolution.

Students do not need to have an account to use the Kahoot to enter, they must enter a pin and the nickname. At startup, questions along with answers are displayed on the big screen, and students press the same color and symbol with the answer they believe to be correct on the screen of the cell. A timer is displayed, decreasing to zero, as well as the number of students who are answering the questions. At the same time, students receive individual feedback on how they responded to their devices. Student responses provide the teacher with feedback on students' understanding of the issue, and creates an opportunity for discussion about the question and answers. The score of the top five, with the dots and nicknames, is shown among the questions. Each student can also follow their own score and ranking on the mobile device itself. To get a high score, students need to answer questions correctly and quickly. Music and sound effects are used in the Kahoot to create suspense and atmosphere of a game show (Wang 2015). Figure 1 illustrates how students provide their answers through mobile devices in Kahoot.

The main idea of Kahoot is to be a platform where the teacher and the students can interact in the classroom simulating a game of competitive knowledge. The motivation is to engage students by transforming the classroom into a game show where the teacher would be the presenter and all students can compete by earning points through correct answers on various subject-related issues being taught in class (Wang 2015).

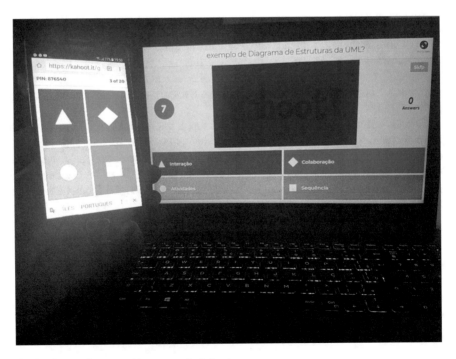

Fig. 1 How students provide answers in kahoot

3 Methodology of Research

The research is exploratory, descriptive and bibliographic. The bibliographical review allows to gather information about the subject, Fonseca (2002) says that a bibliographical research is carried out from the analysis of published theoretical sources, such as scientific articles and books. According to Silva and Menezes (2000, p. 21), the descriptive research aims at describing the characteristics of a given population or phenomenon or the establishment of relations between variables. It involves the use of standardized techniques of data collection: questionnaire and systematic observation. It assumes, in general, the form of survey." Triviños (1987) emphasizes that in the descriptive research the researcher seeks to describe the facts and phenomena of a reality. Exploratory research "tends to address new problems about which little or no previous research has been done" (Brown 2006). In addition, it should be noted that "Exploratory research is the initial research, which forms the basis of more conclusive research" (Singh 2007). Berverian (2007) argues that the exploratory nature of the research is related to the approach of the researcher to the field of analysis, since it is understood that he is unaware of the presented reality. This research was based on gamification in education with the Kahoot as an interactive activity in the classroom. This exploratory study was implemented in three stages: Creation, application and evaluation of the platform.

The first stage consisted of preparing the online quiz using the site https://kahoot.com/, before the lesson, by the teacher, to the Web Programming discipline of the technical course in computer science for the internet of the Federal Institute of Goiás (IFG) Luziânia Campus. At first the registration was done according to the information of the site. Then the Kahoot "quiz" mode was selected and the site filling instructions for the quiz were created.

The quiz was created with 25 questions of multiple choice, with questions of 3 incorrect alternatives and one correct, all approached the content taught in the discipline. In the creation was also defined the time of 30 s for the answer of each question.

On the day of the activity, the teacher opened the online quiz and made available the link and the access code for the students. These were familiar with the methodology, since another wanted to be had already been used by the students previously to present the tool and methodology. The class had thirty-three students who were divided into groups of three, the division of the groups was at the discretion of the students themselves. The quiz was played in a group, and they could discuss the best answer among them.

The platform takes place with the appearance of four screens for each question: first a screen with the question, the second screen with the question, the alternatives, and the time counting, the third screen with the marking of the right answer and the frequencies of hits and errors of that question and the fourth screen with the partial classification of the test until the present moment. After the last question, a podium appears with the classification of the first three places.

After the activity, students were invited to respond to a questionnaire online built using a form from GoogleDocs. The link was shared with students through a group of the WhatsApp class, which was created by the teacher, for the discipline, for the purpose of facilitating interaction between students and teacher, sharing information and study materials. They answered the form in room, individually. The form had five questions: What are the limitations of the use of mobile technology in the learning process? How did the use of the application during the activity contribute to your learning? What are the strengths of using mobile technologies in the learning process? What are the negative points in the use of mobile technologies in the learning process? What are your suggestions regarding the activity?

4   Results and Discussion

As main limitations of the use of mobile technology in the learning process, we had: an available by the institution, some of the pupils' screen, the ability to access other content that is unrelated to the lesson the proposed activity.

When asking how the use of the application during the activity contributed to your learning? They answered: the exchange of knowledge through the discussion left the class and the content more interest, increased student concentration and involvement, made learning more experiential, entertaining, and interactive, stimulated the student's insight, increased the speed of reasoning to respond in less time and correctly, and allowed group work.

When asked to point out the strengths in the use of learning process? They said: it encouraged everyone to participate in the activity in a more dynamic, modern, stimulated concentration, made learning more fun, competition among students, aroused students' interest in class, improved interaction between students and teacher and between students, and facilitated learning.

In the meantime, in relation to the negative points in the use of mobile technologies in the learning? They answered: possibility of being able to focus the learning and use the cell phone for other things, screen size and slow internet connections, device inequality among peers can create a certain disadvantage for some, or if a student does not have device or internet access.

When asked to provide suggestions regarding activity? Featured: more activities like this during the semester, new issues to repeat the topic, keep the application and if possible, adhere to others similar, use individually, more time to respond.

Much of the students' responses confirmed Dellos (2015), who states that Kahoot is a platform that allows for greater interaction among students, involving and encouraging them not to give up easily from the difficulties encountered in the subjects. The request by most students to continue to use Kahoot in class confirms Sandy and Sandy (2018) in saying that learning is a different process between each student, being essential, the use of different strategies, so that as many students as possible understand the contents covered.

It was observed by the teacher that the music and punctuation presented to each question makes the platform become more stimulating. Confirming the study by Wang (2015), who assessed the concentration, achievement, engagement and fun of students playing Kahoot using or not using audio and punctuation, and when they did not use audio and punctuation, students did not keep focus and concentration in the same way. The presentation of the score in each question made the students stay more focused and engaged, thus increasing their competitiveness. Showing that music and points can significantly influence learning.

The students' responses confirmed the work of Santos and Santos (2017), which also resulted in the perception that the students became more attentive and more interested in the classes when applying Kahoot Segundo Costa et al. (2017), students' participation in a virtual quiz type of activity such as kahoot favored student learning. Agreeing with Alves et al. (2015), that the platform also contributed to the construction of knowledge, by arousing the student's interest in answering each one of the questions and always wanting to surpass those who are in the best positions.

The kahoot as well as the work by Sandy and Sandy (2018) entitled "Use of kahoot as an evaluation and teaching-learning tool in the teaching of industrial microbiology", can also be used as an evaluation tool, proving to be very effective as a substitute for in the students' perception. According to most of them (60%) the tool allows an evaluation with different levels of complexity and allows a greater memorization and understanding of the contents than the traditional proof. The majority of the students (80%) concluded that this tool allows to evaluate all the theoretical content of the discipline in a more attractive and competitive way, creating a great stimulus. All students concluded that the tool has a fair punctuation system and allows notes to be obtained fairly. From the observation of the behavior of the students it was possible to perceive that besides the punctuation referring to the test it is convenient to have a prize involved with the application of the activity, as a bonus note for the first place or prize, because this way there is greater competition and encouragement to the correct ones. It was noticed that the technique presents some limitations of use, however, the game caused a stimulus in the students leaving the evaluation process more attractive and the learning more enduring. In this way, the students' perception and interest was positive in the face of experience, which places it at a level of valid strategy for teaching and assessment of the disciplines.

As in the work of Gazotti-Vallim (2017) titled "Experiencing English with Kahoot", this present work allowed the development of meaningful learning, since the students felt involved with the content. In addition, the fact that they used the digital educational game to do so increased their motivation, because the sensation of discovery, the curiosity, the fantasy, the challenge were not only related to the content addressed, but also related to the process to carry out the activity in a reflexive and strategic way. The existence of the competition, because there is an individual score visible on the scoreboard, and the music, elements present in the games, also engaged the students to participate in the game. In this way, we can observe another characteristic element of meaningful learning, self-initiation. It was also possible to note that the activities contributed to the active participation of the students in their respective teaching-learning processes since the immediate feedback provided in a playful way through the automatic responses of the game, with their correct scores, encouraged us to redo the activities in the search for more and more correct answers, which probably would not have occurred if the multiple-choice questions had been presented as quiz in printed material. Thus, it is also possible to conclude that this type of activity not only created an opportunity for the development of meaningful learning, but also stimulated the construction of new knowledge mediated by gamma present in Kahoot.

5 Conclusion

Through this work, it was possible to observe that the use of the kahoot platform in the classroom provided a greater and better interaction between student/teacher and student/student, transforming the teacher into a mediator of learning. With this, in addition to assisting in the teaching-learning process, it is noticed that the platform, when well used by the teacher, contributes to the social and moral formation of the individual, especially when worked in a group, arousing in individuals the respect among colleagues. The use of kahoot made it possible to obtain significant results in teaching, provoking in the students a feeling of challenge, generating more interest and pleasure in learning. For the continuity of the research it is intended to increase the number of classes and students in order to improve the sample and confirm the results obtained.

References

Alves, R. M. M., Geglio, P. C., Moita, F. M. G. S. C., Souza, C. N. S., & Araújo, M. S. M. (2015). The quiz as a pedagogical resource in the educational process: Presentation of a learning object. In: *Proceedings of the XIII International Congress on Technology in Education*.

Amico, M. R., De, A., Pra, R., & Moraes, J. P. (2017). The applications of kahoot! as educational technology. In: 22nd Seminar on Education, Technology and Society, Taquara, RS. Electronic Proceedings of the Interdisciplinary Educational Journal (REDIN).

Berverian, P. A. (2007). *Scientific methodology* (6th ed.). São Paulo: Atlas.

Bottentuit Junior, J. B. (2012). From computer to tablets: Pedagogical advantages in the use of mobile devices in education. *Revista Educa Online, 6*(1), 125–149.

Brown, R. B. (2006). *Doing your dissertation in business and management: The reality of researching and writing*. London: SAGE.

Costa, C. H. C., Dantas Filho, F. F., & Gonçalves, S. M. M. M. F. M. (2017). Marvinsketch E kahoot as tools in teaching isomerism. *Holos (Natal, Online), 1*, 31–43.

Covos, J. S., Covos, J. F., Rodrigues, F. R., & Ouchi, J. D. (2018). The new profile of students in higher education, and the use of play games to facilitate teaching learning. *Education in Focus (Amparo), 1*, 62–74.

de Macedo, L., Petty, A. L. S., & Passos, N. C. (2000) *Learn from games and problem situations*. Artmed, Porto Alegre.

Dellos, R. (2015). Kahoot! A digital game resource for learning. *International Journal of Instructional Technology and Distance Learning, 12*(4), 49–52.

Fonseca, J. J. S. (2002). *Scientific research methodology.* Fortaleza: UEC, Handout.

Gazotti-Vallim, M. A. (2017). Experiencing english with kahoot. *The ESPecialist: Description, Teaching and Learning, 38*(1), 1–18.

Gómez, A. (2015). *Education in the digital age—The educational school.* Porto Alegre: I Think.

Izeki, C. A., Walter, A., & Dias, R. M. C. (2016). Experience in using gamified online tools in introduction to computer programming. In: *Proceedings of the XXII Workshop on Informatics in the School (WIE 2016)* (pp. 301–310).

Kenski, V. M. (2012). *Education and technologies: The new rhythm of information* (8th ed.). Campinas, SP: Papirus.

Prensky, M. (2012). *Learning based on digital games.* São Paulo: Senac.

Sandy, D., & Sandy, D. (2018). Use of kahoot as an evaluation and teaching-learning tool in the teaching of industrial microbiology. *Holos (Natal, Online), 1,* 170–179.

Santos, D. S., & Santos, D. S. (2017). THE QUIZ DO BIS: Use of kahoot as a learning tool. In: *III Congress of Innovation and Methodologies in Higher Education, Belo Horizonte.* CIM. v. 3.

Silva, E. L., & Menezes, E. M. (2000). Methodology of the research and elaboration of dissertation. In *Graduate Program in Production Engineering, Federal University of Santa Catarina, Florianópolis* (118p).

Singh, K. (2007). *Quantitative social research methods.* New Delhi: SAGE Publications.

Triviños, A. N. S. (1987). *Introduction to research in social sciences: Qualitative research in education.* São Paulo: Atlas.

Wang, A. I. (2015). The wear out effect of a game-based student response system. *Computers and Education, 82.*

Author Index

© Springer Nature Switzerland AG 2019
I. Ramos et al. (eds.), *Information Systems for Industry 4.0*,
Lecture Notes in Information Systems and Organisation 31,
https://doi.org/10.1007/978-3-030-14850-8

Printed in the United States
By Bookmasters